WILDERNESS OF FORTUNE

for my All-Canadian Sister,
October 1983

love, Patti

Scots on the Glasgow docks, about to board the CP
liner *Montrose*.

The Story of Western Canada

WILDERNESS OF FORTUNE

JAMES K. SMITH

DOUGLAS & McINTYRE • VANCOUVER / TORONTO

Douglas & McIntyre
1615 Venables Street
Vancouver, B.C.

Canadian Cataloguing in Publication Data

Smith, James K., 1926-
    Wilderness of fortune

    Includes index.
    ISBN 0-88894-365-2

    1.   Northwest, Canadian — History. I.   Title.
    BC3206.S65   971.2   C82-091337-5
    F1060.S65

Design: Robert Bringhurst and Barbara Hodgson
Maps by Weller Cartographic Services Ltd.
Typeset, printed and bound in Canada
    by D. W. Friesen & Sons Ltd.

To Carol Waldock,
long-time editorial colleague
and friend

Contents

The Inuit igloo builder used snow packed hard by the wind and even in consistency, otherwise the blocks tended to split into layers.

1 The First Immigrants

Ever since Europeans set out to find a sea route to the spices and jewels of the East, it has been assumed that they were tho first people to discover North America. But did they? The most recent theory suggests that they were not the first; the real discoverers of this continent may have come from the opposite direction. The archaeological evidence is still circumstantial, but it points strongly to the probability of human migration from Asia to North America via Alaska. And these immigrants may have been followed by a strange assortment of visitors including Phoenician traders, Roman sailors, a Buddhist priest from China, Irish monks, Norse merchants, and a Welsh prince and his followers.

Christopher Columbus, who is credited with the European discovery of North America, deceived himself into thinking that he had found the fabled commercial paradise of the East Indies. He therefore called the brown skinned, black-haired people he met "Indians." Thanks to his eager error, the first known inhabitants of the Americas continue to be misnamed.

*

During the most recent ice age some thousands of years ago, the people of northeastern Asia were nomads who stayed alive by trailing roving herds of caribou, musk ox, bison and woolly mammoths, and hamstringing or killing stragglers and pregnant females. At that time, the monstrous accumulations of ice that covered large areas of the northern and southern hemispheres contained so much of the world's water that the level of the oceans had dropped considerably. Consequently, the short gap that separates the continents of Asia and North America — a gap now covered by the shallow waters of Bering Strait — was probably a grassy plain. Some herds and their hungry hangers-on could have wandered across this land bridge and into Alaska, which was free of ice.

The giant ice sheet that covered much of North America gradually melted. It left behind millions of square kilometres of living space for the first immigrants. Much of this land had been scraped bare of soil and vegetation. Northern Canada is still little more than a wilderness of lichen-covered rock, and the tundra is almost treeless. But the long valley of the Mackenzie River, where the land had been less severely gouged by ice, slowly sprouted a green cover of grass, bushes and trees, which sustained many species of animals.

Once in Alaska, the immigrants could ascend the Yukon River and one of its tributaries, the Porcupine, to reach the delta of the Mackenzie River, which is particularly rich in fish and wildlife. The People of the Small Knife, so called by ethnologists because the group made small cutting tools out of flint and other hard stone, fished and hunted in the long valley of the Mackenzie. The Long Spear People preyed on the Wood buffalo, a species of bison which had gravitated north from the Great Plains to the parklands and muskeg around Great Slave Lake. The Long Spears also corralled some of the caribou that journeyed to and from the tundra each summer and fall. A second group of buffalo hunters, the People of the Arrowhead, moved in around Lake Athabasca. Among the last to arrive in North America were the Denbigh People, better known as the Eskimo, or Inuit.

The different groups of native people in the north have at least one common denominator: the term that they use to describe themselves. The names now used to identify tribes of Athapaskan-speaking Indians — Chipewyan, Slave, Beaver, Yellowknife, Dogrib, Loucheux, Hare, Slave, Nahanni — are all names given by outsiders. They call themselves Dene, which

Plains Cree Indian camp alongside the Saskatchewan
River.

simply means "people." Similarly, the Eskimo call themselves Inuit, which also means "people." The name Eskimo originated with Indian tribes that came into contact with these Arctic nomads and means "eater of raw flesh."

The Inuit settled in hunting territories on the Arctic coast and on outlying islands as far east as Greenland. The Dene occupied what is now the Yukon Territory, the Northwest Territories, northern parts of the prairies, and northern and central British Columbia.

Dene and Inuit alike developed superb skills in hunting, trapping and fishing, using weapons and tools they fashioned from the materials at hand: stone, bone, antler, ivory, wood or shell. Home was a lean-to of branches or animal skins, a domed snowhouse, or the insulation of furred garments. The canoes and toboggans of the Dene and the kayaks and sledges of the Inuit reflected the harsh land and climate in which they lived. However, they found ways to bring beauty into their lives by tattooing their bodies and painting their clothing with red ochre and black graphite. Treasured possessions were decorated by carving and dyeing, and soapstone was carved into human or animal images.

*

The Great Plains stretch all the way from the tropical waters of the Gulf of Mexico to the lake and forest country of northern Manitoba, Saskatchewan and Alberta. Once, their rich grasses fed millions of buffalo, elk and deer; today, the land produces massive crops of grain and vegetables. The prairies, as Canadians call their section of the Great Plains, have a particularly generous covering of fertile soil. At least three times in North America's history, a mighty ice sheet, as much as three kilometres thick in places, built up in Arctic regions and flowed south at the rate of a few centimetres a year,

ultimately burying much of the northern half of the continent. Grinding and gouging southward, the ice absorbed billions of bits and pieces of the earth's surface. Blending these materials together, each awesome bulldozer in turn spread its mix as it melted and retreated northward in response to world climate changes. In this titanic fashion, nature kneaded and spread the soil-making components — mineral-rich pulverized rock, vegetation, clay, lime, sand, silt — that surface the prairies. Various hardy grasses rapidly took root in the rich soil.

Just as canoes and toboggans, kayaks and sledges reflected the landscape in which the Dene and Inuit lived, buffalo-hide backpacks and dog travois identified the environment of the prairie tribes — Plains Cree, Blackfoot, Assiniboine, Blood, Peigan, Sarcee, Gros Ventre and the Sioux. Unlike the Dene and Inuit, the best hunters on the prairies were not the cleverest stalkers or the most patient fishermen, but those agile enough to stampede a herd of buffalo over bluffs. On other occasions, after cunningly manoeuvring a herd into a well-disguised corral, they had to be bold enough to finish off their quarry with a stone club or knife. The buffalo, a mobile mountain of flesh that averaged 810 kilograms if a male and 540 if a female, supplied nearly all their food and materials for tools, clothing and shelter.

Except in winter, an abundant supply of game was available on the prairies — if a man was skillful with a bow and arrow. Each spring and fall, ducks and geese appeared in such numbers that they blackened the skies and blanketed ponds and marshes. In summer, mosquitoes drove moose out of the northern forest and onto the plains. There were elk and deer by the thousand and buffalo by the million, and the unpredictability of their migrations could be offset by storing a supply of pemmican. Strips of their flesh, dried in the sun or over a fire, were pounded into a fibrous state and then mixed with melted fat and sometimes flavoured with berries. As fur traders later found out, nine kilograms of this concentrated dried food was the equivalent of thirty-six kilograms of fresh meat or fish. And nearly every lake, river and valley was inhabited by a small, plump furry animal: the beaver.

When winter's bone-chilling winds howled across the gelid grasslands, prairie tribes passed the time by holding public feasts in a lodge built to seat from fifty to one hundred guests. Over wooden dishes of pemmican, they retold the exploits of their ancestors or argued the merits of the best hunter or warrior. Later, there was dancing, singing and gambling. Bets had to be paid promptly, or the picked warriors who acted as camp police would break up the game.

At any season, the women and girls were rarely without work to do. They sewed deerskin clothing, tanned buffalo robes, and decorated moccasins with dyed porcupine quills and feathers. They cooked meals, made pemmican, and gathered herbs to season soups and stews. Children loved to tag along behind a mother or grandmother gathering wild berries and beg for handouts of sun-warmed fruit.

The great male occupation, of boys and men alike, was practising the twin skills of the hunt: tracking and archery. Cunning in the chase and marksmanship had both practical and prestigious results. The successful hunter had a well-fed, well-clothed family, but also gained respect as the supplier of meat and skins to a family that had lost its provider due to accident, illness or war.

In the summer months, when movement was easy and game plentiful, it was not unusual for one tribe to raid another. These encounters were basically a form of game and a means of winning the respect of peers. Like any game, it had a scoring system, in this case by counting *coup* (the French word for "blow"). This is an apt term because prairie tribes considered it more honourable to tumble an enemy than to shoot him with an arrow or stick him with a spear. The finest coup was to succeed in laying a hand on a foe, and the next best was to manage to touch him with a coup stick carried for that purpose. A warrior with many coups won the right to wear certain kinds of feathers in a headdress or to paint certain patterns on his face. The enterprising could paint their deeds on a teepee or on a buffalo robe.

On a lone raid deep into enemy territory, a warrior might bring back a scalp as proof of superiority, though a man's word that he had counted coup was usually enough. Scalping was probably not a general Indian practice: it was almost unknown in South America and was common, on the prairies, among only the Sioux and Plains Cree. Many historians still question whether scalping was an Indian custom or behaviour learned from groups of rival Europeans, who were quick to pay bounties on scalps as proof of killing.

*

The Western Cordillera, the mountain backbone of North America, is a region of contrasts: deep, dark, winding canyons; high valleys as dry and grassy as the prairies; low-lying valleys veined by rivers, dotted with lakes, ponds and aspen groves, and inhabited by grazing deer and the ubiquitous, ever-industrious beaver.

In the Cordillera, trees cover the mountains like gigantic fur coats. The warm, westerly winds that sweep in off the Pacific bring abundant rains which help the Douglas fir, Sitka spruce, red cedar, hemlock and pine grow to giant proportions. Cedars are from three to ele-

This Thompson Indian belonged to a group of tribes famed for their basket weaving, carvings, and the jade they dredged from the Fraser River.

ven metres in girth; and pines, five to thirteen metres around, rise sixty metres without a branch and are topped by luxuriant heads. This wilderness is the home of two huge animals: the smooth-skinned elk, only slightly smaller and lighter than the buffalo, and the shaggy-haired grizzly bear, up to 675 kilograms in mass and 3.5 metres in height. The elk was as eagerly hunted by Indians as the "bear that walks like a man" was avoided.

An outstanding feature of the Cordilleran region is the Rocky Mountain Trench, one of the largest, continuous valleys on the face of the earth. An immense trough varying from three to sixteen kilometres in width, it separates the Canadian Rockies from the other western mountain ranges and is a natural spillway for many waters, notably those of the Finlay, Parsnip, Fraser, Columbia and Kootenay rivers. The Rocky Mountain Trench may well have been the route to the south used by those nomads who immigrated to North America. The Trench was certainly part of a dense network of later Indian trails and trade routes. Here lived the Kootenay, a plains people who had been gradually pushed west of the Rocky Mountains by their belligerent Blackfoot neighbours. Not surprisingly, these refugees used to sneak back over the passes to hunt buffalo and, if undetected by Blackfoot scouts, return with horseloads of choice meat and hides.

West of the Trench were wandering bands of Salish-speaking tribes called the Lillooet, Thompson, Okanagan and Shuswap Indians. Their equally nomadic neighbours to the north were Athapaskan-speaking tribes called the Chilcotin and the Carrier, the latter so called from their curious custom of compelling widows to carry on their backs for some years the charred bones of their dead husbands.

These interior tribes can be described as the

A Haida village in the Queen Charlotte Islands, B.C. Totem poles displayed their owners' family crests and depicted stories of famous ancestors. *See previous page.*

Among coastal tribes, the medicine man or shaman was usually a member of a family that specialized in treating illnesses and had knowledge of magic.

Salmon People, for this fish, sun-dried or smoked, was the food reserve that guaranteed their survival each winter. In late summer and early fall, Pacific salmon migrate by the millions to the headwaters of British Columbia's rivers to spawn and die. Fighting their way upstream in frenzied masses, many are gashed and badly bruised, but nothing defeats the instictive struggle to return to the very stream or rivulet in which they were born. In some rivers, the current brings salmon right alongside a flat stretch of ground where an Indian could spear several hundred fish a day, some weighing as much as twenty-two kilograms. His family promptly gutted them, sliced the flesh into thin strips, and hung these to dry in the open air or in a smokehouse. These fishing spots were used by the same family for generation after generation, and those who could not claim such a fishing right had to work for those who had one in order to earn a share of the salmon.

Every August and September, the valleys of the coastal mountains were hazy with the smoke from campfires of the tribes assembled to harvest wild fruit as well as fish. Just before the salmon run, the women went on berrypicking expeditions. Pressed into cakes and then laid out in the sun on drying racks, raspberries, blueberries and saskatoons were another valuable winter preserve. Dried berries and salmon were often mixed together in grease to make a form of pemmican. This was also a time for reunions with relatives and friends, some of whom had not seen each other since the previous summer, so there was much feasting, dancing, playing of games and story telling. And there was always that special joy — and a special feast — when the cry went up that the salmon had arrived.

*

British Columbia is shut off from the rest of Canada by wall after wall of mountains. Between the Rocky Mountains and the shores of the Pacific Ocean is a 960-kilometre stretch of peaks, ridges and broad, U-shaped valleys sculpted by ancient flows of glacial ice. There are some fairly level stretches of land, but the province's interior is mainly a region of towering crags and tumbling glaciers, rivers savagely foaming through deep canyons, and placid, finger-shaped lakes hemmed in by mountain masses. On the seaward side, a multitude of reefs and sandbars block river mouths, and confusingly look-alike inlets and fiords slice deeply into the land. Forests of giant firs and thick stands of cedar inhibit easy travel. Nonetheless, those people who located along this coast found a good living.

The Nootka of Vancouver Island's west coast and the Haida of the Queen Charlotte Islands built large dugout canoes and were expert deep-sea fishermen, as well as harpooners of seals, sea otters and sea lions. The Nootka even hunted the mighty humpbacked whale. The waters surrounding their densely forested island homes teemed with salmon, halibut, herring and cod; in the shallows was an abundant supply of oysters, clams and mussels.

The mainland beaches, bays, inlets and river valleys were inhabited by five major groups of fishermen-hunters. The villages of the Coast Salish were scattered all the way from the mouth of the Columbia River to a little north of the delta of the Fraser River, as well as on the southern half of Vancouver Island. Their northern neighbours, on the island and on the mainland, were the Kwakiutl, talented makers of masks and other wood sculptures. Into the mainland territory of the Kwakiutl jutted that of the Bella Coola, who prospered as middlemen by exchanging the various furs and hides produced by the interior tribes for fish and the seashells that were both ornaments and a form of money. Farther north

Indians Playing a Ball Game by an anonymous artist.

Two Indians Paddling Through Bulrushes by Frederick A. Verner.

still were the Tsimshian and the Tlingit. The Tsimshian, famed for their painting and carving skills, inhabited the valleys of the Skeena and Nass rivers; they depended on the salmon and oily oolichan (candlefish) for most of their food. The Tlingit, according to legend, were inland dwellers who had drifted to the coast, where they adjusted to a way of life that combined fishing with trading: they bartered copper, goat-wool blankets and sea shells for the furs of tribes in the interior.

The Indians of the North Pacific coast enjoyed a superabundance of food. Different species of salmon return from the ocean at different times of the year, so tribes could count on five, six or seven major spawning runs during the summer and fall. As for other foodstuffs, shorelines "grew" seaweed, and forest clearings could be harvested for shrubs with edible roots and wild berries. Preserved by smoking and drying, surpluses of food supported large groups of people. Since survival was not a struggle, they had leisure time to devote to art and evolved a complex social organization preoccupied with possessions and prestige. Families were fiercely proud of the degree of status given them by the ownership of a family crest, a particular name or a guardian spirit, or the rights to perform special songs and dances. Individuals accumulated material wealth in the form of beautiful goat-wool blankets, finely woven baskets, handsomely carved cedar chests and boxes, and strikingly decorated canoes. Men who had acquired considerable property and prestige were often made chiefs, and their families became a sort of nobility. Every tribal member had a definite status, mainly based on a relationship, no matter how distant, to the chief and his family. At the bottom of the social pyramid were slaves, people captured during raids on other tribes.

The most important ceremony in coast Indian life was the potlatch, a gift-giving ritual. Chiefs and nobles gave potlatches to announce important events such as a marriage; the raising of a new totem pole; and the bestowal of rights to fishing and hunting territories, or the "copyright" to a song, dance or drama. As many as five hundred guests might be invited to the feast, and the host gave gifts to each person, thereby confirming his status as a person rich enough to give away possessions.

*

Just how long it took the first immigrants to spread across the northern wilderness, discover the sunny prairies, and explore the misty islands and inlets of the Pacific coast and the wood-and-water wilderness of the Cordillera is not known. But Indian myth and legend suggest that they have lived in these particular regions for thousands of years.

2 Trappers and Traders

The way of life of the Indians of North America was revolutionized by contact with Europeans. French and English settlers arrived on the North Atlantic coast, and Spaniards and Russians explored the North Pacific coast.

The horse was introduced to North America by Spain, the first European nation to make its presence felt in the New World. The Spanish concentrated on looting and enslaving Indian civilizations in South America and Mexico, but a few gold-hungry conquistadors probed the southern edges of what is now the United States. And so it was in the summer of 1541 that plains Indians saw horses for the first time. Somewhere in the sun-baked, tall-grass country of northwestern Texas, a band of Apache tracking buffalo stopped to stare at a peculiar sight. Approaching them was a long, clanking column of bearded, pale-skinned men in dusty armour, some of whom were sitting astride large beasts.

Using sign language, the two groups talked together for several hours, in the course of which the annalist of the expedition (led by Francisco Vásquez de Coronado) recorded with amazement the simplicity of plains life based on the buffalo.

They neither grow nor harvest maize. With the [buffalo] skins they build their houses; with the skins they clothe and shoe themselves; from the skins they make ropes and also obtain wool. With the sinews they make thread, with which they sew their clothes and also their tents. From the bones they shape awls. The dung they use for firewood, since there is no other fuel in that land. The bladders they use as jugs and drinking containers.

And as Coronado's weary horsemen and wearier infantry plodded on across an awesome ocean of grass, they met other hunting parties using large, wolflike dogs as beasts of burden. Hitched to a travois or loaded like a pack mule, each of these animals was able to haul or carry anything up to twenty-two kilograms in weight – and howled with misery when a travois tipped over or a pack slipped under their bellies.

Spanish law prohibited the sale of horses to Indians, but, in later years, some of the animals escaped to range the plains and the foothills of the Rocky Mountains. (The Spanish called them *mesteños*, "wild ones", from which the word mustang is derived.) The Apache of Texas and New Mexico were among the first to capture these escapees – and promptly began raiding Spanish settlements to obtain more mounts. In time, a horse-trading system spread northwards to tribes on the Canadian prairies.

The horse brought radical change to life on the Great Plains. For instance, the Shoshone (Snake), who had been forced into the mountains of Wyoming by their traditional enemy, the Blackfoot, used the horse to reverse the balance of power. Swooping down onto the prairies on horseback, they helped themselves to a bonanza in bison. For years, the Blackfoot were frustrated by Shoshone raiders who rode through their encampments on these *mistutim* ("big dogs"), counting coup with ridiculous ease. Scouts on horseback could now reconnoitre hundreds of square kilometres of territory in search of a buffalo herd, and mounted hunters were far more deadly marksmen. A horse was stronger than a dog and could pull a travois loaded with several hundred kilograms, making it feasible to construct taller, roomier tepees. And the taking of horses from another tribe became an honourable pursuit among plains Indians, since it called for both skill and bravery. The greatest coup of all became the capture of a prized mount tethered next a tepee, a much riskier exploit than cutting one out from the herd hobbled in the camp's corral.

Sweeping as these changes were, they were

Indians Buffalo Hunting by Paul Kane.

On this buffalo skin, a Sarcee painted his lifetime deeds as a hunter and warrior: horses captured, weapons owned, combats and coups counted.

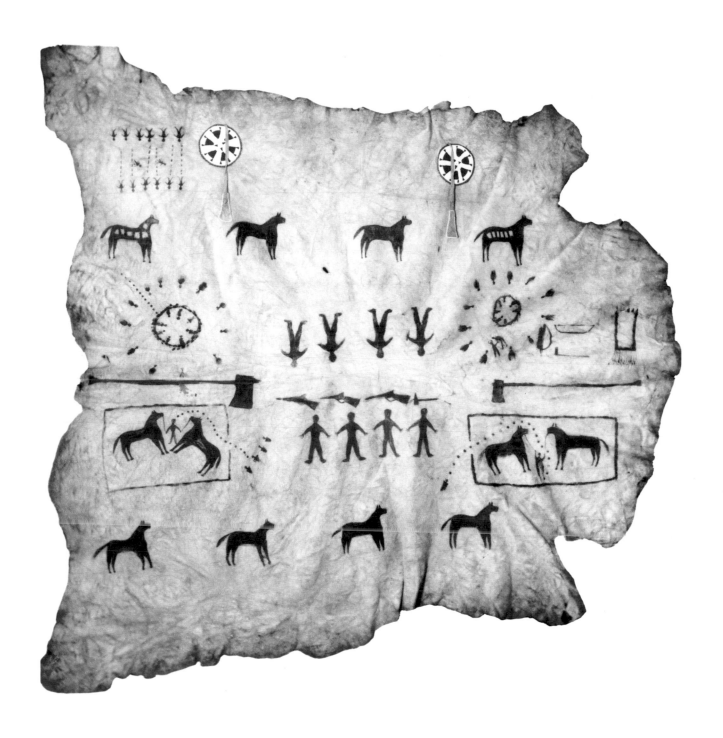

15

nothing compared to the impact of the fur trade on Indian life.

*

While Spain was exploring the southern edges of the continent, two other European nations were examining the east coast of North America. In 1497, John Cabot, sailing under the flag of England, discovered that a "New Found Lande" blocked the sea route he was trying to find to the spices and jewels of the East. Jacques Cartier, a French mariner with the same motivation, confirmed in 1534 that even more land lay beyond Newfoundland. He also discovered that local Indians would barter frantically for any item made of metal. They made "divers signs of joy and of wanting our friendship" and were willing to sell the very clothes off their backs — furs, of course. Obviously, Indians had come in contact with Europeans before, most likely enterprising but close-mouthed fishermen from England, France and Portugal who were quietly harvesting waters that, as Cabot had reported, were so thick with fish they could be hauled out by the bucketful.

The fur trade developed late in the sixteenth century when the beaver hat became fashionable among wealthy Europeans. The demand increased steadily over the next 250 years until it became a mania. The man of fashion rarely appeared in public without wearing a smooth, glossy, beaver hat. It might be tall or short, large or small, broad-brimmed or tricorne, and might be plumed, jewelled, braided or embroidered — for it was a highly visible indication of wealth and social status. And, by chance, just about the time that the beaver was becoming extinct in Europe, unlimited numbers of that animal were discovered in the New World. By 1608, when Samuel de Champlain arrived to found the colony of New France, a casual but complex system of collecting pelts and distributing European goods was beginning to develop in the valley of the St. Lawrence River.

The impact of European goods on the Indian was summed up in a simple statement made by a Fox chief to Nicholas Perrot, an early French trader-explorer in the Great Lakes region. The old man told Perrot "You gave birth to us for you brought us the first iron."

A knife blade of the poorest steel, an axehead of worked iron, a needle, a file, a pair of scissors, any piece of steel or iron meant comfort, ease, and power not possible to an Indian without it. Fell a tree with a sharpened stone or hollow out a log with fire, then with an axe; sew a dress with a bone awl and thread made of split animal sinew, then with a needle and silk or linen thread. A garment made of skins required the labor of hunting, skinning, curing, and tanning as well as tailoring, and it was in some weathers ineffective or unhealthy. Woolen cloth was immensely more versatile, comfortable, effective, and easier to work. . . . Steel and brass and copper wires were not only stronger than sinews or buckskin thongs but infinitely versatile. An iron or copper kettle required no labor, could hardly be broken, and made cooking less arduous. It could be hung over a fire; earthenware pots could not. . . . That the pigments, paints, glass and porcelain beads, tin and brass ornaments, mirrors, burning glasses, and functionless novelties which formed so large a part of the trade had an equally revolutionary importance is not always obvious to modern students, but it always was to Indians. Finally there was alcohol . . . it opened to the Indian experiences that, quite literally, were beyond all price.

*

Ironically, it was England, not France, that benefited first from the initiative of French trader-explorers probing westward. The Hudson's Bay Company (HBC) owes its origins to a couple of sharp-witted *coureurs de bois*. (The term meant "runners of the woods" and was used to describe

The royal charter of 2 May 1670 that granted various rights and privileges – and about one-third of North America – to what became the Hudson's Bay Company.

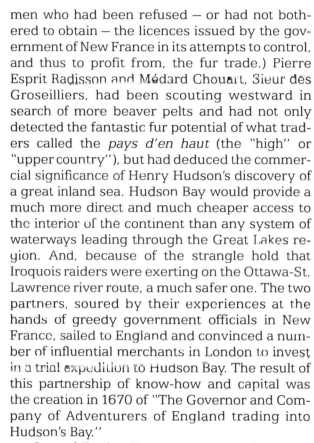

On the Move by Gerald Tailfeathers.

men who had been refused — or had not bothered to obtain — the licences issued by the government of New France in its attempts to control, and thus to profit from, the fur trade.) Pierre Esprit Radisson and Médard Chouart, Sieur des Groseilliers, had been scouting westward in search of more beaver pelts and had not only detected the fantastic fur potential of what traders called the *pays d'en haut* (the "high" or "upper country"), but had deduced the commercial significance of Henry Hudson's discovery of a great inland sea. Hudson Bay would provide a much more direct and much cheaper access to the interior of the continent than any system of waterways leading through the Great Lakes region. And, because of the strangle hold that Iroquois raiders were exerting on the Ottawa-St. Lawrence river route, a much safer one. The two partners, soured by their experiences at the hands of greedy government officials in New France, sailed to England and convinced a number of influential merchants in London to invest in a trial expedition to Hudson Bay. The result of this partnership of know-how and capital was the creation in 1670 of "The Governor and Company of Adventurers of England trading into Hudson's Bay."

One of England's many mercantile enterprises, the Company was given special privileges by its royal sponsor, King Charles II. The charter granted to these Adventurers empowered them to establish their own army and navy, administer both civil and criminal justice, and even wage war "on any prince or people not Christians." The charter also ordered all officers of the British navy, army and government to give the Adventurers every assistance in their endeavours to trade in Rupert's Land, meaning all those lands in North America whose rivers emptied into Hudson Bay. Named after the king's cousin and the first governor of the HBC,

19

Rupert's Land was an unwitting gift of approximately one-third of modern Canada.

The establishment of the Hudson's Bay Company increased the demand for pelts, beaver in particular, and induced many Cree to migrate westward in search of furs. Having become dependent upon HBC traders for weapons and warm woollen clothing, the Cree established themselves as the mercenary middlemen of the northwestern fur trade. If any Dene dared to challenge their business monopoly with the HBC, he found himself looking down the barrel of a flintlock musket. The Cree harassed and drove the Chipewyan farther away from Hudson Bay, forced the Slave to retreat down the long Mackenzie River valley, and so intimidated the Sekani and Beaver that some bands sought safety in the Rocky Mountain section of the Peace River. Some Cree even moved out onto the prairies, acquired horses, and enjoyed the double role of buffalo hunters and traders.

In time, Cree and Ojibwa gradually prodded the Sioux (the Dakota, as they called themselves) out of their hunting grounds in the Sault Ste. Marie district and out onto the plains. And it is with this branch of the Siouan-speaking Dakota that the story of the fur trade in western Canada begins to come into focus.

Various bands of Dakota lived in the wilderness region between Lake Superior and Lake Winnipeg, most of them in the Lake of the Woods-Rainy Lake district, where wild rice was a valuable food resource. They harvested enormous quantities of this rice, which they cooked in skin or bark pots by dropping in heated stones. This explains why the neighbouring Ojibwa called them the Assiniboine ("people who cook with stones"), and why many a fur trader referred to them as the Stone or Stoney Indians.

The Assiniboine, like the Cree, were quick to act as middlemen for Great Lakes neighbours shortly after the Company of Adventurers established factories (trading posts) on the subarctic shores of Hudson Bay. Drawn westward in search of new, naive customers, they also became both buffalo hunters and traders. In summer, the Assiniboine went the rounds of their customers in the Lake Winnipeg drainage basin and then congregated near the mouth of the Saskatchewan River. Leaving their families there for several months, they made the laborious canoe and portage journey to salt water to barter for the marvellously convenient, wondrously satisfying articles the HBC had to offer.

*

Hudson's Bay Company executives in London ordered the governor at York Factory to expand trade with whatever tribes lived in the far interior of the continent, and he reported in 1690 that he had "sent up Henry Kelsey . . . into the country of the Assinae Poets [Assiniboines], with the captain of that nation, to call, encourage and invite the remoter Indians to a trade with us." The nineteen-year-old Henry Kelsey was a distinctly unusual "servant," as the HBC termed its rank-and-file labourers, carpenters, gunsmiths and storekeepers. Fascinated by Indians, he sought their company on every possible pretext. Curious about the country west of Hudson Bay, during his five years with the Company he had shown a natural aptitude for wilderness travel.

Kelsey and a band of Assiniboines endured many miles of paddling and portaging, plus the itchy attentions of insects, until they reached that great prairie highway, the Saskatchewan River. At a place where its tawny-coloured, swift-flowing waters made a sharp curve round a prominent point of land, they established a base camp. At this spot (which may have been the site of The Pas, Manitoba), canoes could be

In 1672, in Garraway's Coffee House in London, England, the first HBC furs — beaver, plus some otter and moose hides — were auctioned for £3860.

Kelsey on the Plains by Rex Woods.

easily repaired and stored, and the fishing was dependable. From this location, under the guidance of Assiniboine and Cree friends, Kelsey twice set out on long marches into what he described in his journals as an "Inland Country of Good Report" — with neither surveying instruments nor maps to aid him.

Kelsey reached this inland country by breaking out of the thick evergreen forest that blankets much of northern Canada, passing through a parkland region of aspen groves and innumerable clumps of saskatoons and chokecherries, and finally emerging onto the plains somewhere in Saskatchewan. He must have questioned his companions closely about the lie of the land because he worked out a remarkably accurate picture of the prairies. A large river, he noted, went "much to ye Soothward and runneth through a great part of the Country": the South Saskatchewan River. He stayed well clear of its twin, the North Saskatchewan, where, he was warned, buffalo were seldom found in summer. He even seems to have sorted out the rough geography of the lake strewn valleys of the Qu'Appelle and Assiniboine rivers and their tributary relationship to the Red River.

Kelsey found, however, that the South Saskatchewan River led to a region where pelts were both few and poor. On a hot August day in 1691 he made a diary entry that the party's tents were pitched where "This plain affords Nothing but short Round sticky grass and Buffilo." The ground was "more Barron," meaning treeless, covered with the sharp-pointed brittle bunch grass typical of the drier sections of the Great Plains, and the occasional pool or pond held harsh, alkaline water. Around him, stretching away until they were lost in the summer haze, lay the prairies, where the bison browsed in such myriads that they seemed like dark cloud shadows drifting lazily across the earth's surface.

Turning in a northwest direction, his friends led him to a very different landscape: wooded hills, meadows of waist-high grass waving in the cool September breeze, and numerous brooks and streams of sweet water. The region was a favourite camping ground of both Assiniboine and Cree. Here, they trapped beaver, hunted buffalo and moose, and even tried to pick off eagles which nested in high bluffs that dotted the area. Just how far west Kelsey had travelled is uncertain, but he may have been in the Eagle Hills of Alberta.

In Kelsey's writings there is one very puzzling omission. They contain descriptions of the dominant Canadian landscapes: the burnt brown tundra lands immediately west of Hudson Bay; the dark green forest belt that spreads across the country from Labrador to the Yukon; the gold-and-green foliage of the park belt; and the yellow-blue of the prairies. But he records nothing about the massive, saw-toothed barrier of the Rocky Mountains, though it seems unlikely that he lived with the Assiniboine for so long without hearing about mountains to the west. If, on his return to the Bay in 1692, he said anything about mountains to his superiors, none of them passed on the information to head office. But then, Kelsey's great feat of discovery was itself ignored. The Company saw no reason to follow it up with further exploration or the establishment of advance posts on the prairies. Customers had, so far, come to the Bay. They would continue to come.

*

The luxurious sheen and hard-wearing quality of the beaver pelt dominated the trade from the start, but other furs were utilized. Hats of lesser quality, as well as trimmings and ladies' muffs, were made from otter, muskrat, ermine, fox, lynx, mink, fisher and marten skins. So the money to be made in the fur trade, despite competition from the Hudson's Bay Company, interested French merchants in underwriting expeditions to what they called *le pays sauvage*, "the Indian country" north and west of Montreal.

By going to the most distant customers, French traders managed to intercept them on their way to HBC posts, all of which were situated alongside salt water. And the man largely responsible for this development was Pierre Gaultier de Varennes, Sieur de La Vérendrye, the last of the line of great French trader-explorers that begins with Champlain.

La Vérendrye spent the early part of his life as a soldier: a cadet before he had even reached his teens, by the age of twenty-four he had battled the English in the New England colonies, Newfoundland and Europe. When he finally returned to his birthplace of Trois Rivières, his body bore the scars of nine wounds received in the service of his king. He married and seemed content to manage his farms, run a small, local fur business, and raise a family of four sons and two daughters. But, at heart, he must have been restless. When, in 1728, the governor general of New France offered him the trade monopoly of the *postes du nord* territory, La Vérendrye accepted without hesitation.

The *postes du nord* was an undefined region between Hudson Bay and Lake Superior. To this day, it is a wilderness dotted by a bewildering number of lakes and streaked by an equally confusing number of rivers. Portages are frequent obstacles, and head winds often sweep the larger lakes, bringing an end to canoeing. When this happens, there is nothing to do but pull ashore and stoically endure attack by hungry squadrons of mosquitoes and black flies. Winter conditions were well described by an early French visitor, who wrote of the region: "to withstand the cold, one ought to have his Blood compos'd of Brandy, his Body of Brass, and his Eyes of Glass."

The *postes du nord* was also a powderkeg of jealousies and vengefulness that any random spark could ignite. Its Sioux inhabitants were enemies of the Cree and Ojibwa with whom canadien traders had long been business allies. Sioux ambushes and raids (and retaliatory raids by Cree and Ojibwa) disrupted trapping and trading, and forced La Vérendrye to make many a journey to negotiate peace — or at least a truce. Indeed, one explosion of Sioux wrath wiped out twenty of La Vérendrye's men, including his eldest son. On this occasion, the Sioux decapitated their victims; this was a grim pun because, in sign language, the gesture for decapitation also meant "Sioux." So they wrapped each head carefully in a beaver skin, a derisive reminder to the canadiens of their passion for that article of trade.

La Vérendrye's basic difficulty was one that would always cripple and ultimately defeat every western Canadian fur-trade operation based in Montreal: distance. His source of money, men and materials lay 1600 kilometres to the east across the same rock-strewn, heavily timbered wilderness in which he travelled and traded. He could do business only after bringing from Montreal, at considerable cost, relatively small quantities of trade goods. His rival, the Hudson's Bay Company, enjoyed the advantage of a salt-water route all the way into the heart of the continent and could bring in trade goods cheaply by the shipload. In addition, the HBC could feed its employees with imported provisions, whereas La Vérendrye and his men were dependent on the hunt, their own or that of friendly local Indians. On several occasions, his operations were interrupted by mutinies of canoe crews who feared death by starvation if they went north of Lake Superior. And, of course, the farther north and west La Vérendrye expanded his trading, the deeper he went into debt: some years the costs of supply and transportation made it impossible to earn a profit.

In the end, sheer persistence paid off. La Vérendrye managed to placate rival Indian groups and to revive the confidence of disillusioned Montreal backers; he also organized a stable supply of food based on the cultivation of corn at his posts and the mass cultivation of wild rice by local Assiniboine and Ojibwa. He recruited reliable canoemen and, aided by his three remaining sons, pioneered a new, shorter route through the maze of muskeg, lakes and rivers between Lake Superior and Lake Winnipeg.

The French breakout onto the prairies began in 1734. La Vérendrye, who had a superb sense of geography, built posts at the mouth of the Winnipeg River, at the forks of the Red and Assiniboine rivers, farther west on the Assiniboine itself, alongside Lake Manitoba, and at the mouth of the Saskatchewan River — three of these being the sites of the future Manitoba centres of Winnipeg, Portage la Prairie and Dauphin. At these posts he and his employees talked, ate, drank and danced with customers, persuading them to barter their lightest, silkiest pelts for guns and axes, blankets and beads — and good French brandy. Some of the rich flow of furs to HBC posts was siphoned off to distant Montreal.

The London governors of the Hudson's Bay Company should have been curious about the activities of their canadien competitors. As early as 1732, the annual total of beaver pelts shipped from York Fort, the Company's westernmost depot, dropped from 57 000 to 37 000. Had the Company bothered to investigate this circumstance, it would have found out that the La Vérendryes were establishing a chain of fur posts as they worked their way closer and closer to Lake Winnipeg. And, ahead of the La Vérendryes were the advance scouts of the trade, the coureurs de bois. A handful of them were working the Lake Winnipeg region several years before the La Vérendryes built their first prairie post in the valley of the Red River.

The great flaw in the way that the HBC conducted its business was its policy of insisting that its customers travel hundreds of kilometres to trade, thus exposing Indians to contact with French brandy long before they reached Hudson Bay. The man who proved this policy foolish was Anthony Henday. In typical HBC fashion, he was sent inland in 1754 on the basis that "presents to the Indians" would be a means of "drawing down many of the Natives to Trade." At least the factor (manager) of York Fort showed good sense in choosing Henday to do the job. Although employed as a labourer and netmaker, Henday had shown some ability as an amateur surveyor. Factor James Isham also knew that Henday had once been a smuggler, an occupation that demanded a clear head and cool nerves.

Henday travelled to the interior with a number of homeward-bound Cree who guided him onto the Saskatchewan River. Like Kelsey before him, he had to abandon canoe travel and journey overland in the company of various groups of Cree and Assiniboine. Ranging even farther west than his predecessor, Henday received the first of a number of shocks. In the neighbourhood of modern Red Deer, Alberta, he met some members of the Blackfoot nation. One of them was a "Great Leader" who treated him in a very friendly, very hospitable manner, though Henday's request that some young warriors come with him to the fort, "where they would be kindly received and could get Guns" was pleasantly refused. His host explained that

it was far off, & they could not live without Buffalo flesh; and that they could not leave their horses; and many other obstacles, though all might be got over if they were acquainted with a Canoe, and could eat fish, which they never do. . . . The Chief further said . . . he was informed the Natives that frequented the [HBC] Settlements, were oftentimes starved on their journey. Such remarks I thought exceedingly true.

That winter, Henday wondered why his Assiniboine guides were unwilling to trap for him. Their camp was in a well-watered, wooded section of foothills country, but the Assiniboine killed only enough beaver so that their women could make cold-weather clothing. When he asked them where they would get furs to take to the HBC, their only answer was to laugh among themselves. In the spring, on the return journey, he found out why. Waiting at several points along the North Saskatchewan River were bands of Blackfoot men and women, who eagerly bartered wolf, beaver and fox pelts for the well-worn guns and hatchets, knives and kettles of his guides. To add to Henday's frustration, each group of Blackfoot refused invitations to accompany him to Hudson Bay; and when he tried to get the Assiniboine to persuade them, his guides remained silent. As he wrote, "if they [the Blackfoot] could be brought down to trade, the others would be obliged to trap their own Furs; which at present two thirds of them do not."

More revelations awaited Henday. A few days of paddling brought his party to the main stream of the Saskatchewan River, where there was a "French Trading House." Here, his companions "received from the Master ten Gallons of Brandy half adulterated with water" and promptly traded "nothing but what were prime Winter furs. . . . It is surprising to observe what

an influence the French have over the Natives; I am certain he hath got above 1000 of the richest Skins." About a week later, much the same trading pattern was repeated at another post farther downstream. This time, Henday noted, "the French talk several [Indian] Languages to perfection; they have the advantage of us in every shape; and if they had Brazile tobacco, which they have not, would entirely cut off our trade." As he sadly reported, the French ignored the least desirable pelts, which were all the HBC was going to get in return for the baubles, blankets, guns, ammunition and tobacco advanced to the Assiniboine the year before at York Fort.

The Hudson's Bay Company paid scant attention to Henday's revealing report, though he had observed and pointed out the elements of successful trading. Save the customer time and trouble by going to his home territory, soften him up with friendly talk and liquor, then bargain for the best furs.

*

A few years after Henday returned from the prairies, Wolfe defeated Montcalm on the Plains of Abraham, and France lost its North American possessions to Britain. A number of Scots and English merchant-adventurers took over the Montreal fur trade in its entirety — language, transport methods and routes, and the trading practices that Henday had noted. At first as enterprising individuals and later as competing companies, they caused the HBC tremendous losses for the better part of fifty years by expanding the trade all the way to the Arctic and Pacific oceans — and turning *le pays sauvage* into a battleground for furs.

*

The Pedlars from Montreal, as the HBC men contemptuously called their new rivals, were

The HBC's Fort Prince of Wales on Hudson Bay, unoccupied from the day in August 1782 when French
warships forced its surrender and spiked its cannon.

An engraving of HBC and NWC clerks dickering for furs in an Indian encampment, circa 1800.

motivated by the prospect of making a good deal of money. Some were French Canadian, some were from the American colonies (notably a handsome huckster named Alexander Henry), a few hailed from Europe, more from England, and even more from the Highlands of Scotland.

Alexander Henry and two fellow Pedlars were trading on the Churchill River when they intercepted some Chipewyans who were on their way to Hudson Bay. These Indians were attempting to act as middlemen between the HBC and tribes living where winters were, they said, "eight to nine moons long," and animal furs were correspondingly thick and glossy. Henry and his companions were amazed by the magnificent quality of these furs from Athabasca which they purchased from the Chipewyan. The news of their good fortune gradually became known, and some traders decided to exploit this new untapped source of pelts by pooling their resources of goods and pemmican in order to send Peter Pond into the Athabasca country.

Pond was a born wanderer from Connecticut. He seems to have been a loner, and a quick-tempered one at that, though he is reported to have always got on well with Indians. He was one of a tough breed in a tough business, a business that thrived on cutthroat competition and price wars because the great demand in Europe for beaver hats showed no signs of diminishing. The only concern of the Pedlars was to collect as many pelts as possible, even if, in the process, they cheated or robbed Indian trappers outright. These traders used liquor, guile, even threats, so that they could send canoeloads of pelts to their sponsors in Montreal. Peter Pond was a leading member of this unholy fraternity.

Pond headed for the Athabasca region, which was said to be somewhere northwest of the headwaters of the Churchill River. Once as far west on the Churchill as Lac Ile-à-la-Crosse,

he then trekked across the punishing nineteen-kilometre Methy Portage. And found himself in a completely different landscape: the taiga, a sub-arctic region of muskeg and stunted forest that is more water than land. As one historian aptly remarks of Athabasca, "the country is four-fifths drowned and when not frozen is half-hidden by mosquitoes and black flies." Pond was 4800 kilometres from Montreal, but, as his canoes glided past greenish-black stands of slender spruce, birch, fir and jackpine, he was looking at what would prove to be the richest fur resource in North America.

In the 1780s, Pond became preoccupied with charting the rivers, mountains and ultimate boundaries of the lands beyond his remote Athabasca post. He was particularly curious about the Pacific Ocean. How did one reach it overland? Was there a canoe route to salt water? If so, could furs be taken out and trade goods brought in via Pacific transshipment, which would be cheaper than the difficult canoe routes to and from Montreal? By piecing together the jumbled mixture of facts that he knew, and the vague, contradictory information he gathered from Indians, voyageurs and fellow traders, Pond managed to work out one vital fact. The Athabasca River, which flowed lazily past his post, together with the more powerful Peace River, formed the forked tail of a mighty water system that flowed far to the north.

Unfortunately for Pond (and for Alexander Mackenzie, who later served under him) he deceived himself into thinking that this water system flowed north and then turned west to empty into the Pacific. He also theorized — correctly this time — that the Peace River actually pierced the Rocky Mountains and led to the Pacific Ocean.

As the Montreal fur trade reached farther into the north and west, more and more money was needed to pay for the transport of goods into the interior and to bring out furs. However, longer supply lines to and from the *pays d'en haut* and rising costs were not the only problems. Competition had become more intense with the emergence about 1779 of a combination of certain Montreal fur merchants and their traders. Known as the North West Company (NWC), it threatened to take over the entire *pays d'en haut*.

The North West Company was, in fact, a loose association of a number of fur companies. Motivated by the money-making possibilities of the superb pelts that came from Athabasca, the corporate members of the NWC made a prolonged effort to make the region their exclusive sales territory by establishing copartnerships with each other and also with a number of wintering partners, each of their senior traders in the *pays d'en haut*. No one has described these winterers – Nor'Westers as they pridefully called themselves – better than Canadian historian W. Stewart Wallace:

The story of the Nor'Westers, though not without its darker pages, is a brilliant chapter in the history of Canada. No braver or more picturesque band of adventurers ever put it to the touch, to gain or lose it all. Some of them were French-Canadian traders and voyageurs, the sons of those who had followed La Vérendrye to the rivers and prairies of the West in the dying days of the French régime. Others were American frontiersmen who had served their apprenticeship in the fur-trade in the valleys of the Ohio and the Mississippi. Most of them were Scottish Highlanders. . . . The names of the North West Company partners sound like a roll-call of the clans at Culloden. These men were hardy, courageous, shrewd, and proud. They spent a good part of their lives travelling incredible distances in birchbark canoes, shooting rapids, or navigating inland seas. They were wrecked and drowned. They suffered hunger and starvation. They were robbed and murdered by the Indians, and sometimes by one another. They fell victims of smallpox, syphilis, and rum. Yet they conquered half a continent . . .

With few exceptions, Nor'Westers displayed unrelenting opposition to anyone who was not of their number. Whether competing with winterers who worked for other Montreal merchants or with the men from the Bay, Nor'Westers often used tactics similar to those of the Mafia: threats of violence, hijacking of supplies and bribery. If these tactics did not work, their colleagues in Montreal neutralized competition by bringing rivals into the company as partners – which is what happened to Alexander Mackenzie and his employers – and giving them a share of the profits. The Montreal members were always careful to give British officials the impression that their wintering partners were an unselfish group of trader-explorers busy extending the limits of British influence and territory in North America. Ruthless, powerful, but outwardly respectable, the North West Company was the earliest example of big business in North America.

The North West Company made life hard for everybody else in the fur business, because it had a simple but successful structure based on the principle of profit sharing. The Montreal partners, the merchants, put up the money to finance operations; their wintering partners in the *pays d'en haut* formed the sales force – but all partners received payment in the form of one or more shares in the NWC. Even the lowly clerks (apprentice traders) knew that, in time, they would become wintering partners and share in the profits. Clerks were paid a salary that varied with length of service (£100 to £400 a year), as well as food and clothing. The merchants and wintering partners received their money when the year's profit was calculated and

Bateau Running the Chute by John Innes. The painting illustrates why the bowsman and the steersman were paid special wages by their fur-trade employers.

divided by the total number of shares. Even as late as 1802, when many of the best regions had been nearly trapped out, a North West Company share was worth over £3000 – in an age when an annual income of £1500 was a very comfortable living.

An equally important factor was the actual labour force. All the members of the Montreal fur trade, NWC or otherwise, were utterly dependent on their tough, tireless French-Canadian voyageurs. These canoemen had the strength and stamina to take hundreds of tonnes of goods thousands of kilometres into the continental interior and bring out precious cargoes of furs. They were either *mangeurs du lard* ("pork eaters") manning *canots de maître* (freight canoes) between Montreal and Lake Superior, or *hommes du nord* ("northmen"), the elite canoemen who travelled the *pays d'en haut* in the smaller, lighter *canots du nord*. Voyageurs had the skill to take a fragile, heavily laden birchbark canoe safely through the seething waters of a *sault* or, more laboriously, to "line" or haul the craft all the way through it. Their endurance was legendary. They kept up a killing pace, paddling forty strokes a minute for fifteen hours a day, with time off for only two meal breaks and a few pipe-smoking spells of ten or fifteen minutes each. They travelled at an average speed of six to ten kilometres an hour for weeks on end.

The pay of the *engagé*, the salaried voyageur of the fur companies, ranged from £15 to £50 a year; he was also issued a blanket, a shirt, a pair of trousers and a few pounds of tobacco a year. He lived on the plainest of rations — a mush of corn, peas and pork fat — on the two-month run between Montreal and Lake Superior; or, in the *pays d'en haut*, pemmican in raw chunks or boiled with flour to make a gooey but nourishing mess called rubaboo. The monetary rewards were out of all proportion to the rigours and dangers of the job, for death was always around the next bend of the river or somewhere out on the waters of the lake ahead, but the type of man who chose to become a voyageur regarded the presence of death as an added spice to life. His job was an escape from the dull routine of rural Quebec and offered him the chance to see and experience a different world.

The voyageur has been romanticized as a happy-go-lucky, colourfully dressed character who was much given to drinking and wenching (which he was). However, the canadien canoeman was the indispensable workhorse of the trade. Without him, there would have been no fortunes in furs.

3   West of the Mountains

Europeans were first attracted to the North Pacific coast of the continent by the beaver's cousin, the sea otter, whose pelt is the finest and hardest-wearing of all furs. From Alaska in the north to California in the south, herds of these sleek, handsome animals inhabited thick beds of kelp, a submarine jungle in which they were safe from their natural enemies — sea lions, sharks and killer whales. In the late eighteenth century, when rumours began circulating in Britain and the United States that a single sea-otter pelt had been sold in the Chinese port of Canton for several hundred dollars, the hunt began. The sea otter suddenly acquired a new enemy: the fur trader. And the North Pacific coast gradually became a region of conflicting claims to ownership.

*

Spaniards had taken over much of Central and South America, and the French had reached the prairies, before the first Russians landed in North America — by accident. In 1741, a storm-battered ship was hurled onto one of the long arc of Aleutian Islands that curves from the Alaskan coast towards the Asian mainland. Aboard the doomed *St. Peter* was Vitus Bering, the navigator and leader of a Russian expedition charting the unknown waters that lay beyond the easternmost tip of Asia. Bering died on that sand-and-rock island of exhaustion and scurvy, but the few survivors of his crew who managed to return to Asiatic Russia brought back with them sea-otter pelts obtained as souvenirs from the local native people. Sea beaver was what they called the reddish brown fur with enough underlying streaks of silver to give it a singular sheen.

These shipwrecked sailors accidentally initiated the maritime fur trade in North America. News spread rapidly that caravan merchants travelling the borders of Russia and China had paid top prices for these pelts. High-quality furs had long been coveted by Chinese mandarins and their women for trimming silk gowns or as ornaments on caps and mittens. Then, a former Russian army sergeant named Basov brought back from Alaska a shipload of sea-otter furs worth close to a million dollars, and Russian traders stampeded to the Aleutians, hazarding the blizzards and ice floes of the Bering Sea in makeshift rafts and barges.

Russian soldiers, officials, and merchants poured into Alaska. The advance scouts of this extraordinary expansion were the *promyshelenniki*, ostensibly fur traders though bandits would be a more accurate description. Determined to acquire as many furs as possible, as cheaply as possible, they operated on the terror principle. Each tribe was given a fur quota; if the quota was not met, the chief and his headmen were tortured. Resistance to the quota system was broken by executing every tenth person in a village or tribe, and a number of settlements were wiped out in this way. As soon as the fur-bearing animals in one region were exterminated, the *promyshelenniki* greedily hurried on to the next unexploited area.

Meanwhile, several thousand kilometres to the south, officials in Mexico City resented this Russian intrusion into territory that Spain had long considered its private preserve. This resentment coincided with a new policy from Madrid of northward expansion and exploration. Juan Pérez, a veteran navigator of Pacific waters, was sent north in 1774 to chart the coast and got as far as the Queen Charlotte Islands before consistently bad weather forced him to turn back. On the return leg of the voyage, Pérez stopped off for a while in a mountain-enclosed inlet (which later visitors named Nootka Sound) and invited some local Indians aboard. One of them stole two silver spoons from Esteban Martínez, the ship's pilot, an incident that acquired political significance some years on. This voyage was but the beginning of a much more intensive coastal survey, and the next year Pérez was sent out under the command of naval lieutenant Bruno Hezeta; an accompanying vessel was commanded by another lieutenant, the noble-born Juan Francisco de la Bodega y Quadra.

Of all the various Spanish explorations north from Mexico, this one was probably the most gallant. Despite the age-old problem of scurvy, which sickened or killed many crewmen, despite treacherous mists and horrendous gales, Hezeta and Bodega gave Spain a clear claim to owner-ship of the northwest coast of North America. Hezeta got as far as Nootka Sound before scurvy took the life of Pérez and threatened to rob the ship of manpower. But Bodega navigated stormy seas all the way to 58°N, landed, and claimed Alaska for Spain before scurvy, too, reduced his crew to the point where hardly any able-bodied men were left to work the ship.

Bodega returned to Alaskan waters four years later to reinforce his country's claim. On this occasion, he got as far north and west as the Aleutian Islands. That seemed to make the northwest coast of the continent an exclusively Spanish possession. At least to officials in Mex-ico City, Bodega's achievement prevented any trespassing by other nations. But trumpeting ownership was no good if the Spanish were not right there on the land itself to back up their claim — and the Russians were. Bodega had not encountered them, but groups of *promyshelenniki* were working out of their main Aleutian base of Kodiak Island and also pushing their trading operations as far south as the Queen Charlotte Islands. Worse still from the Spanish point of view, the world's greatest naval power was just about to enter the race for em-pire that was developing in North Pacific waters.

*

In the year 1778, two weather-worn ships entered Nootka Sound to make repairs and refill their water casks. They were neither Russian nor Spanish: at their foremasts flew the Red Ensign.

Commanded by the Royal Navy's finest navi-gator, Capt. James Cook, this tiny task force was about to take a close look at the no man's land that lay between Russian-held and Spanish-held territories in the North Pacific. Cook's orders were to locate, somewhere along this unknown coast, the elusive Northwest Passage that British merchants hoped ran through North America to join the Atlantic and the Pacific oceans because they wanted a direct seaway to and from the silks and spices, tea and chinaware of China. As it happened, Cook proved that there was no "river or inlet . . . pointing towards Hudson's or Baffin's Bays . . . or even a probability of a water passage into the aforementioned bays." He fought foul weather all the way to Bering Strait to do so and was turned back only by arctic ice nearly four metres thick and "compact as a wall." But, if Cook killed one hope, he created another with his description of an estuary at 60°N, into whose waters emptied a powerful river that was filled with "large trees and all manner of dirt and rubbish." (Actually, the "es-tuary" was a complex of minor waterways close to the modern city of Anchorage, Alaska.) When this information appeared in the published ac-count of his voyage in 1784, it mesmerized at least two members of the North West Company. A large, westward-flowing river emptying into the Pacific at roughly the same latitude as the fur-rich Athabasca country? "Cook's River" just *had* to be the short, cheap route that would take the place of the long, expensive haul from Montreal to Athabasca and back again. Hence

A map of Spanish explorations on the coast of North America, published in 1795.

View of Nootka Sound from the shore of the Spanish settlement by Gabriel Gil. *See next page.*

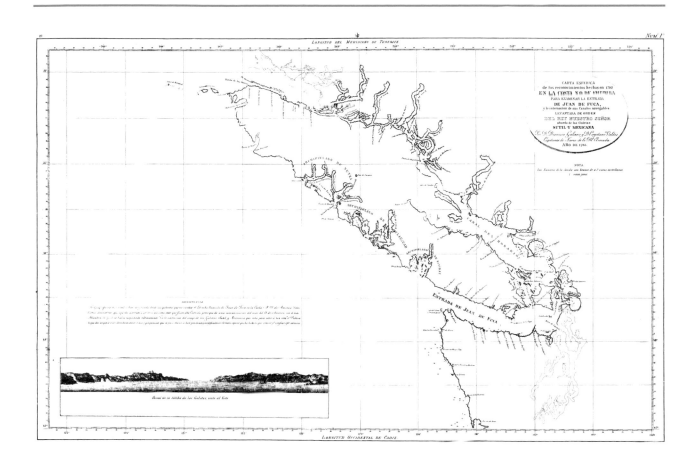

A painting by John Webber, an artist who sailed with
Cook. As can be seen, this Nootka home made great
use of cedar-bark furnishings.

An engraving from Vancouver's published account of his mapmaking travels. It shows the village of the "Friendly Indians" at the entrance to "Bute's Canal."

the optimistic cartography of Peter Pond and the courageous ventures of Alexander Mackenzie.

Cook also made a surprising discovery during the month he spent refitting his ships in Nootka Sound at a place he called Friendly Cove. From the moment the anchors went down, the Nootka in the nearby village of Yuquot swarmed out to His Britannic Majesty's ships *Resolution* and *Discovery* to bargain for any object made of metal. And Cook's seamen responded with equal enthusiasm, asking for "the skins of various animals . . . in particular, that of the sea-otter." Watching an exceptionally magnificent pelt being exchanged for a couple of rusty nails, Cook realized that the Nootka already knew the usefulness of metal. He guessed that metal objects these Indians already owned might have come from Spanish settlements in Mexico, or possibly via merchants in Montreal. His second guess was right: he was seeing trade goods that had been passed from hand to hand across the continent.

A little over a year later, Cook was dead, killed on a Pacific island in the course of an argument with natives, but his admiring remarks about the sea otter's fur were fully substantiated. When the *Discovery* and the *Resolution* put in at Canton, China, on their way back to Britain, some of the prime pelts, which had been acquired at Nootka for a length of pretty ribbon or a bent, battered fork, sold for so much money that both ships' crews demanded an immediate return to the northwest coast. One of Cook's officers later reported that the seamen were close to mutiny in their desire to return to the Pacific coast and "buy another cargo of furs to make their fortune at one time."

Several British traders in the Orient soon learned of the stupendous prices — a minimum of $120 a pelt — that Cook's sailors had received from Cantonese merchants and made a beeline for Nootka Sound. First to arrive was James Hanna, who did not scruple to kill a few Indians while rounding up pelts worth about $20,000. Another, John Meares, bartered two pistols for a plot of ground, built a fortified trading post, and constructed a small schooner for coastal trade operations. Close on the heels of these hustlers came Yankee merchant ships from Boston, notably the *Columbia Rediviva* commanded by Robert Gray and the *Lady Washington* captained by John Kendrick.

The Nootka fur trade almost led to war. The trouble started in 1789, when the twenty-six-gun Spanish warship *Princesa* and its commander, Esteban Martínez (the same Martínez whose silver spoons had been stolen fifteen years earlier) entered Nootka Sound. He found Britons and Americans busy packing their holds with furs that he considered had been taken from Spanish territory. Martínez's superiors in Mexico City were again anxious to forestall any Russian expansion towards California, the more so since there had been rumours of Russian naval vessels ranging the northwest coast to chase away British traders. An actual occupation of Nootka Sound seemed a good way of warning off Russian, British and American traders.

Discerning that the Americans respected Spain's ownership of the entire coast and that the British did not, Martínez took over Meares's post. Then he erected a fort and placed a battery of guns at the entrance to Nootka Sound. In an elaborate ceremony, he proclaimed Spain's ownership of the sound and the rest of the North Pacific coast. To show that he meant what he said, he seized three vessels, two British and one American, and sent them and their crews to captivity in Mexico.

When news of these actions reached Europe, the British and Spanish foreign offices immediately exchanged stiff notes of protest which

The Spanish Insult to the British Flag at Nootka Sound is pure propaganda. In 1789, Martínez simply arrested the captain of a British merchantman for trading in Spanish territory.

Capt. George Vancouver, whose charting and mapping of the jagged British Columbia coastline involved some 16 000 kilometres of rowing in ships' boats.

became steadily angrier and more accusing. Spain could claim to be first there, thanks to Martínez's stolen spoons, which had been offered to Cook in trade by the Nootka. On the other hand, Britain's Royal Society had encouraged the publication of Cook's accounts of his worldwide explorations, whereas Spain had been particularly secretive about its surveying activities in the Pacific. So who had the stronger claim?

In the end, compromise prevailed, and a settlement was negotiated. Spain prudently backed away from war with a much stronger foe, and Britain grudgingly agreed to recognize Spain's claims to those parts of North America actually occupied by its settlers. Spain also decided to abandon any ownership claims made at Nootka. The question of the northern limit of Spanish territory was left open — though this would soon be settled by yet another member of the Royal Navy.

George Vancouver had served under the great James Cook on voyages to Antarctica and to the Pacific. By 1791, Vancouver had experience and reputation enough to be picked to command a two-ship expedition to oversee the transfer back to Britain of land and property seized by Martínez at Nootka. Vancouver's orders included instructions to look for a water link from the Pacific to the prairies, the more so since Cook had proved that there was no Northwest Passage through the continent.

Vancouver arrived at Nootka with little to do: detailed orders regarding the handover were aboard a supply ship that had still to catch up with him. So, in amicable company with two Spanish vessels, he sailed into what he named the Gulf of Georgia (now the Strait of Georgia) in honour of King George III. Here, Vancouver spent a couple of busy months trying to untangle the puzzling geography of a maze of off-

shore islands and a mountainous shoreline deeply indented by winding fiords. At one point, he saw but paid little attention to the wide, muddy mouth of a river called the Blancho (Fraser) by its original Spanish explorers. However, his orders were to look for a river large enough for an ocean-going vessel to enter, and the shallows of the Fraser delta forced him to stay offshore. Vancouver probed steadily northward through the Strait of Georgia's rock-strewn channels. At different times, each of his ships ran onto a reef but, luckily, avoided capsizing and floated free on the next high tide. Eventually, the four British and Spanish vessels separately reached the open sea again in Queen Charlotte Sound, thus discovering that Nootka Sound was part of island, not mainland, territory.

Vancouver's opposite number at Nootka was the same Bodega y Quadra who had carried the Spanish flag into Alaskan waters. A naval officer by training and a gentleman by nature, he so won the respect of his visitors that Vancouver commemorated their association by naming his recent discovery Quadra and Vancouver's Island (later shortened to Vancouver Island). The two commanders even exchanged copies of British and Spanish coastal survey charts, an unheard of degree of international co-operation in those days. Negotiations about the handover, however, were much less successful. Each man was hampered by instructions from a government that took a different view of how much property was involved in the transfer of authority. Thus, they agreed that, for the time being, Nootka would remain a Spanish port.

Vancouver left to continue his work of surveying the northwest coast (and, contrary to orders from the Admiralty in London, claimed it for king and country). Tracing the shoreline in ships' boats was a tedious task because of the numerous fiords that cut deeply into the coastal

43

---

mountain ranges, but it was necessary to examine each one to prove or disprove the existence of a waterway through the mountains to the interior plains. On one typical survey, the ships' boats spent twenty-three days laboriously mapping about 1120 kilometres in order to advance a mere 96 kilometres. The Vancouver expedition spent much of 1792 to 1794 in the coastal channels of British Columbia and southern Alaska, mapping and naming important geographical features, but did not find a navigable waterway leading into the continental interior, for the simple reason that there wasn't one.

History is full of fascinating coincidences and near coincidences. In Vancouver's case, it was one of the latter. On 3 June 1793, his men were making soundings in an inlet that he christened Dean's Canal (now Dean Channel). They were just six weeks too early to witness an arrival that would have astounded them. On July 20, in a borrowed Indian canoe, a wintering partner of the North West Company and his voyageurs came down one of the branches of the Bella Coola River and out onto the salt waters of Dean Channel.

*

Like many heroes, Alexander Mackenzie could be a charmer. As a trader-explorer, he appreciated the value of good relationships and unlike many of his colleagues in the fur trade, he treated his Indian customers firmly but fairly. When dealing with his voyageurs, he used a skillful blend of sternness and kindness, to which they responded with a magnificent loyalty. He was a highly acceptable member of Montreal and, later, London society; in strictly male gatherings he was a droll drinking companion. His early success in life and his early retirement, however, were due to his dour determination to succeed in any enterprise he attempted, whatever the cost and regardless of opposition. Later in his life, as a business executive, his self-assurance and self-righteousness were such that he alienated many of his peers.

Mackenzie's career began in 1770 at the age of fifteen, as a bookkeeper in the counting house of Finlay, Gregory & Company, a firm of Montreal fur merchants. While still in his teens, he worked as a trader in the *pays d'en haut* and in 1787, when he became a Nor'Wester, was sent to Athabasca to take over the region from Peter Pond. Presumably Pond told Mackenzie about two rivers (now called the Mackenzie and the Peace) that might lead to the Pacific Ocean. At any rate, in the summer of 1789 Mackenzie set off down the great river that now bears his name and was bitterly disappointed to reach the "frozen" or Arctic Ocean. In the course of his return to Athabasca, he first heard echoes of a European presence on the Pacific when he met a band of Indians who recounted an Inuit report of meeting white men "in large canoes" far to the westward and exchanging leather for iron. (This contact could have been with Cook, but was more likely with Russian traders.) Some days later, Mackenzie's Chipewyan interpreters talked with a Dogrib, who repeated a Hare Indian story about a mighty river, on the other side of the western mountains, that fell into the "White Man's Lake" far to the northwest. The Dogrib said that the Indians who lived at the river mouth made "canoes larger than ours" and "killed a kind of large beaver, the skin of which is almost red" — an unmistakable description of the sea otter.

Long after returning to his Athabasca depot of Fort Chipewyan, Mackenzie decided that the Pacific could be reached by the "Great River which falls into the Sea to the Westward of the river in which I voyaged." The problem was that the more he questioned Indian customers, the

Coat of arms of the North West Company.

In NWC and, later, HBC days, the Athabasca depot of Fort Chipewyan was called "the Athens of the North" because it housed rare commodities: British books and magazines.

FORT CHIPPEWAYAN

more it seemed that there were *two* great rivers beyond the Rocky Mountains. They were variously described as the "Great River of the West" and the "river that runs towards the midday sun"; evidently both led to the "White Man's Lake," but did so far to the south of Athabasca. (Mackenzie must have been getting bits and pieces of information about the Fraser and Columbia rivers, but at this time no European suspected that there were two mighty water systems west of the mountains.) However, the reports were so confusing that Mackenzie decided he was really hearing about only one large waterway. Logically, he had a chance of reaching the Pacific by exploring westward on Pond's second choice of a canoe route to the Pacific: the Peace River.

Early in May 1793, Mackenzie headed up the Peace, taking with him clerk Alexander McKay, six voyageurs – two of whom, Joseph Landry and Charles Ducette, had accompanied him to the Arctic – and two Indian guides. They all travelled in a canoe built to Mackenzie's specifications. The craft was large enough to carry the ten men (and a dog) and 1350 kilograms of provisions, trade goods, ammunition and baggage, yet on an easy portage two men could carry it for four kilometres without resting.

By the end of an unusually cold May, they had passed through the Rocky Mountains and come to where the Finlay River, racing down the Rocky Mountain Trench from the northwest, joined the Parsnip River from the southeast to form the Peace River. Directly ahead of them was a chain of mountains "running south and north as far as the eye could reach." Which waterway should he follow? The Finlay led north and looked easier, and the men made it quite clear that it was their choice. Mackenzie, however, recalled the advice of an aged Beaver warrior

not, on any account, to follow it, as it was soon lost in various branches among the mountains, and that there was no great river that ran in any direction near it; but by following the latter [the Parsnip], . . . we should arrive at a carrying-place to another larger river, that did not exceed a day's march, where the inhabitants build houses and live upon islands.

He ordered the steersman to proceed up the narrower Parsnip and had to endure days of bitter complaint from his men, as they battled its swollen, savage waters, and growing personal doubts as to the wisdom of his choice. The decision, however, was crucial, for the Finlay would have led them to where the headwaters of the Liard, Skeena and Stikine rivers interlock in a maze of streams and where, in all likelihood, they would have lost their bearings.

Some days later, guided by a local Sekani, they left the Parsnip and traversed a three-kilometre-long body of water (Arctic Lake). A brief entry for June 12 in Mackenzie's journal notes: "We landed and unloaded, where we found a beaten path leading over a low ridge of land of eight hundred and seventeen paces in length to another small lake [Portage Lake]." In portaging these 817 paces, Mackenzie and his followers had crossed the continental divide. For the first time they were, in his words, "going with the stream": they were on water that would find its way to the Pacific Ocean.

Towards the end of June, somewhere just below the junction of what are now called the Quesnel and the Fraser rivers, Mackenzie landed to question some Salish families about the best route to the Pacific. The next day he did the same thing with other Indians and was intrigued enough by their friendly reception to stay for a whole day of questions and answers. After a restless night, he made the second major decision of the voyage.

Mackenzie had to consider several matters.

He had provisions for only thirty days, and the sole food reserve was a 40.5-kilogram bag of pemmican he had cached three days before. Supplementing this with game would be difficult because they had lost much of their stock of musket balls in a canoe upset. Unless he could barter for food, or his Indian guides proved unduly skillful with bow and arrow, the party would have to go on short rations. An equally strong factor was his growing conviction that the river flowing past his encampment was not "Cook's River." He was sure he should have come across it about 56°N, yet his calculations indicated that he was somewhere about 52°N on a waterway that apparently ran far to the south. The river he was on was probably the "Great River of the West." (In later years he decided that it was the Columbia; it was, as another Nor'Wester would discover, the Fraser.) Thus, he would have to backtrack and find the waterway he named the West Road River (Blackwater River) that, as local Indians said, led to the "lake whose water is nauseous."

Having made his decision, Mackenzie spoke to his men. He commended their "fortitude, patience, and perseverance," but stressed that he intended to reach the sea, either by an overland journey with an Indian guide or by returning to where they now were and going downriver to its mouth — whatever the distance. The self-control of the men had been slowly giving way to the fear and panic that, in the wilderness, means death. But Mackenzie's continuing confidence and dogged determination were, to his voyageurs, the only certain things in an uncertain world. They unanimously agreed to follow wherever he might lead.

Mackenzie found his guide, and the remainder of his westward journey is yet another example of his unshakable will: the return some distance upriver in their "crazy vessel," which finally proved unrepairable and had to be replaced by building another from scratch and caching it for their return; the winding ascent into the cold, cloudy, blue-and-white world of the coastal mountains and a slogging march for almost two weeks through uplands sodden with rain and meltwater. Finally, they reached the lush, sheltered valley of the Bella Coola, who worshipped and ate the salmon. Borrowing a canoe, the adventurers arrived at Pacific waters on July 20.

Mackenzie twisted truth when he later wrote that he had proved "the practicability of a commercial communication through the continent of North America between the Atlantic and Pacific Oceans." He certainly proved that communications could be effected, but in commercial terms, in fur-trade terms, he had proved exactly the opposite. No birchbark craft could survive the raging mountain waters he had travelled, least of all one heavily laden with trade goods or bales of fur. Mackenzie had failed to find a navigable route to the Pacific through the jumbled geography of the Cordillera. But, of course, his characteristically stubborn refusal to accept defeat and his heroic odyssey made failure seem a triumph.

*

The history of the fur trade in North America is the story of a slow movement from one overtrapped region to the next untouched one westward. Thus it was fellow Nor'Westers who followed Mackenzie up the Peace River, one of whom was the pioneer of permanent settlement in British Columbia.

Simon Fraser, the eighth and youngest member of a Loyalist family settled near Montreal, joined the North West Company at the age of sixteen in 1792. Some years later, he was serving as a clerk in the Athabasca Department and

at the age of twenty-six was promoted to partnership. His journals and letters indicate that he was an energetic, robust man, prematurely toughened by the hardships of wilderness life; an exacting, but remarkably even-tempered, disciplinarian; brave without being foolhardy; and just a bit snide in his journal references to Alexander Mackenzie.

In 1805, Fraser was deputed to establish a chain of trading posts west of the Rocky Mountains and, in addition, to trace the mysterious Columbia River to its mouth. The Nor'Westers still wanted to find a canoe route to the Pacific.

The Columbia River was a great puzzle at this time. Little was known except the location of its mouth at 46°N latitude. The first European to sight its strong current flowing into the Pacific was Bruno Hezeta of Spain in 1775. Robert Gray of the United States had sailed into its enormous mouth in 1792 and named the waterway after his ship, the *Columbia Rediviva*. George Vancouver of the British navy had sent one of his officers about 160 kilometres inland on its broad waters. Alexander Mackenzie thought he had been on its upper waters in 1793, though he had actually been travelling along part of the Fraser River, but his commercial instinct was right when he wrote that the Columbia was "the line of communication from the Pacific Ocean . . . as it is the only navigable river in the whole of Vancouver's minute survey." Thus, Simon Fraser was ordered to trace the Columbia's course as soon as possible.

Sometimes following trails blazed by his famous predecessor, Fraser and his men made their way through the rain-lashed, moss-carpeted forests west of the Rocky Mountains. Each day was an exhausting routine of part-paddling, part-hauling canoes up waterways surging with spring runoff. In a confusing land of big and little lakes and massive mountain ranges, they built several trading posts: Fort McLeod alongside the lake of the same name; Fort St. James next to Stuart Lake; and Fort Fraser at Fraser Lake. The savagely beautiful region was so reminiscent of the Scotland that Fraser's mother had often told him about as a boy that he named it New Caledonia.

Over the next two years, Fraser took time out from fur trading to make many local explorations. But he was forced again and again to the same conclusion. There was no route to the Pacific through his sales territory except by way of the fierce, fast-flowing river that had forced Mackenzie to backtrack and march overland to salt water. Logically, that river had to be the Columbia, the waterway described by Indians as the "Great River of the West." And so, late in May 1808, the phlegmatic Fraser led a party of twenty-four men down that same fierce, fast-flowing river.

Sheer rock walls hemmed in its waters and multiplied the violence of their flow. Indeed, one day early in the journey, Fraser estimated that melting snow in the mountains had raised the river at least 2.5 metres. Some stretches were so violent that he would not risk the lives of his canoemen, so considerable distances had to be covered on foot. And some of these Indian trails were hard on the nerves, particularly with a 90-pound pièce (40-kg pack) on the back to hamper movement. Fraser felt he and his men "had to pass where no human being should venture" and notes

there was a kind of beaten path used by the natives, and made passable by means of scaffolds, bridges, and ladders so peculiarly constructed, that it required no small degree of necessity, dexterity, and courage in strangers. . . . For instance we had to ascend precipices by means of ladders composed of two long poles placed upright and parallel with sticks crossways tied with twigs. . . . Add to this that the ladders were often so slack that the slightest breeze put them in motion – swinging them against the rocks – while the steps were so narrow and irregular, that they could scarcely be traced by the feet without the greatest care and circumspection; but the most perilous was, when another rock projected over the one you were leaving. The Indians deserve our thanks for their able assistance through these alarming situations.

By July 1, Fraser knew the sea was not far off, for the river's banks were low and covered with trees, and the current was slackening. (Like Mackenzie's crew at the seaward end of their journey, Fraser and his men were travelling in borrowed Indian canoes.) A day later, he and his men were gazing at a "bay of the sea" in which there were "several high and Rocky Islands [Vancouver Island] whose summits are covered with snow." Thirty-six days and 800 kilometres from their starting point, they had arrived at Vancouver's Gulf of Georgia.

Nothing is more eloquent of Fraser's character than his journal entry that day. He made no attempt to evade or rationalize failure. There is just the honest admission that "The latitude is 49° nearly, while that of the entrance of the Columbia is 46°20'. This River, therefore, is not the Columbia."

*

The first European to travel and to chart the complex 1920-kilometre ramble of the Columbia River to the Pacific Ocean was David Thompson. No portrait of him is known to exist, but contemporaries described him as of short but sturdy stature, black-haired and snub-nosed, with strong, homely feature. They stress that he was a quiet and observant man; his speech revealed Welsh parentage.

Although David Thompson earned his living as a fur trader, first with the Hudson's Bay Company, then the North West Company, in the course of twenty-eight years in western Canada he managed to survey, plot and map about five million square kilometres of territory. (Ironically, the Thompson River named after him was one of the few waterways he did not survey; Simon Fraser named that tributary of the Fraser as a mark of respect and admiration for his colleague.) In addition, he found time to record a considerable body of information on natural history and anthropology. For descriptive power and sheer readability, *David Thompson's Narrative of his Explorations in Western America 1784-1812*, based on years of daily notetaking, has few equals in the literature of exploration.

Towards the close of his long career of trade, travel and exploration, Thompson made a westward journey that fulfilled Mackenzie's dream of finding a navigable canoe route to and from the Pacific Ocean. It was a fitting climax to the life of a man who has been described by one of his biographers as "the greatest land geographer who ever lived."

From 1807 to 1810, Thompson was the partner in charge of what the North West Company called its Columbia Department — all the lands west and south of the Rocky Mountains; in effect, parts of present-day southern British Columbia and much of northern Oregon, Idaho and Montana. During these years, he crossed and recrossed the Rocky Mountains via a pass (Howse Pass) roughly halfway between the modern resort towns of Banff and Jasper. However, in the late fall of 1810, he and his voyageurs found their way barred by angry Peigan warriors who described themselves as the "frontier tribe of the Blackfoot nation." They halted Thompson because he was selling goods and guns directly to

A Portage by John Innes.

the Kootenay and several other tribes west of the mountains, thereby ruining a very profitable trade that the Blackfoot had been engaged in for some years as middlemen.

Luckily for Thompson, he learned from a fellow trader that there was another crossing place near the headwaters of the Athabasca River. So he and his men set off northward, hacking a trail through heavily timbered foothills country. Although they loaded all their goods and belongings on pack horses, it took them nearly a month to cover the 320 kilometres to the Athabasca River. Guided by a man known as Thomas the Iroquois, seven weeks of trudging upriver in minus-zero temperatures brought them to today's Jasper National Park.

By this time, most of the horses were so exhausted that the bulk of their loads had to be transported on hastily constructed dog sleds. The party plodded on through ever-deepening snow in which the dogs floundered and the sleds kept getting stuck. Thompson had no option but to lighten their loads by caching some of his goods. He also turned loose the horses that had not been slaughtered for food, so some of his voyageurs had to shoulder the packs that these animals had carried.

Thirteen men and eight dog sleds laboured on up the wide, wooded valley of the Athabasca until Thomas the Iroquois stopped and stared at a particular snow-capped peak on the west side of the river. Satisfied that he recognized the "Mountain of the Grand Crossing" (Mount Edith Cavell), he pointed to a frozen waterway (the Whirlpool River) that came from the southwest out of a mist-shrouded valley. At a word from Thompson, the little party entered it and trekked painfully but steadily up to the 1200-metre level.

On 10 January 1811, they were almost clear of the timber line, and Thompson sensed that they were very close to the continental divide. That night, a clear and brilliant one, he walked a little way from the campfire and found that he was in an immense gap in the mountains. Far below, he saw a ribbon of ice that wound towards him and then swung around a big, hairpin bend and moved away towards the southwest. Thompson did not know it at the time, but he had sighted the Columbia, the navigable waterway to the Pacific that Alexander Mackenzie and Simon Fraser had sought in vain.

As Thompson and his men stumbled and plunged through the deep snows and tall timber of the western slopes of the Rocky Mountains, they were unaware that they were blazing a trail many would follow. Because of the continued hostility of the Peigan, the crossing Thompson had just made became a regular route of the Nor'Westers and, later, the men of the HBC. Traders and supplies poured over the Athabasca Pass and down to the big bend of the Columbia River that became known as Canoe Encampment. From here, they journeyed into the "Inland Empire" (southern British Columbia and the state of Washington), which would yield tens of thousands of valuable pelts.

Until spring came, Thompson patiently passed the weeks hunting game and writing up his notes in a hut. He examined the white birch all around for rind or bark, but it was too thin, so he had a canoe made out of split cedar.

Thompson did not realize that the river to which he and his men carried their cedar canoe was the Columbia. He was fairly certain that it was what he called the Kootenae and decided to ascend it, go down McGillivray's River (the modern Kootenay) to the Salish country, and pick up reinforcements and supplies. He feared that his party was too small, too poorly armed and without enough provisions or trade goods to venture down a river that passed through districts inhabited by many Indian groups, some of whom might be unfriendly.

In the middle of June, Thompson paused at the NWC post of Spokane House to borrow supplies and horses before going across country on an old Indian trail to Ilthkoyape Falls (Kettle Falls). While his men made yet another cedar canoe, he calculated that he was not far from the mouth of the Columbia and was now fairly certain that he was on the river itself.

Thompson set out downstream, writing in his journal that "We set off on a voyage down the Columbia River to explore this river in order to open out a passage for the interior trade with the Pacific Ocean." The voyage was unhurried and broken by several halts to talk with natives encamped along the banks. Through interpreters, he carefully explained the advantages of trapping and trading with the North West Company.

On July 14 the presence of seals playing in the river confirmed that he was very near salt water. The next day, Thompson at last caught sight of the Pacific,

which to me was a great pleasure, but my men seemed disappointed. They had been accustomed to the boundless horizon of the great lakes of Canada and their high rolling waves. From the ocean they expected a more boundless view, a something beyond the power of their senses which they could not describe; and my informing them that directly opposite to us, at the distance of five thousand miles, was the empire of Japan added nothing to their ideas . . .

At the same time, on the south bank of the Columbia estuary, he spotted Fort Astoria, the newly built trading post of the Pacific Fur Company.

*

The story of Pacific Fur Company and how it got to the mouth of the Columbia ahead of the Nor'Westers begins with an extraordinary man called John Jacob Astor.

Astor was born near Heidelberg, Germany, and emigrated at the age of sixteen to New York City. He found employment with a fur merchant and became so intrigued by the steady demand for beaver hats that he studied the British and European fur markets and then went into business for himself. By 1800, he was shipping thousands of furs annually to London, England.

A short, stocky, stolid-looking man with a marked Teutonic accent, Astor was often patronized or ignored by his fellow fur merchants, American and Canadian alike. They would have done well to follow where he led, for he was a master of that trade and could think in continental terms as astutely as Alexander Mackenzie. Astor sought not only to outsell the North West Company but every other Montreal fur mer-chant into the bargain. He planned to establish fur posts along the westward trail to the Pacific blazed by Lewis and Clark in 1804-1806 but, above all, wanted to secure its strategic western end: the mouth of the Columbia River With this in mind, he organized the American Fur Company and its offshoot, the Pacific Fur Company, based at Fort Astoria on the south bank of the Columbia estuary.

Astor nearly succeeded in monopolizing the fur trade of the entire Pacific Northwest, as well as the highly profitable trade in sea-otter pelts with China. Had it not been for the war of 1812, which the Nor'Westers used as an excuse to seize Astoria, he probably would have accomplished what he planned. However, Astor did achieve for the United States what Mackenzie had tried to do for Britain. In building Fort Astoria, Astor gave the United States an undeniable territorial claim on the North Pacific coast.

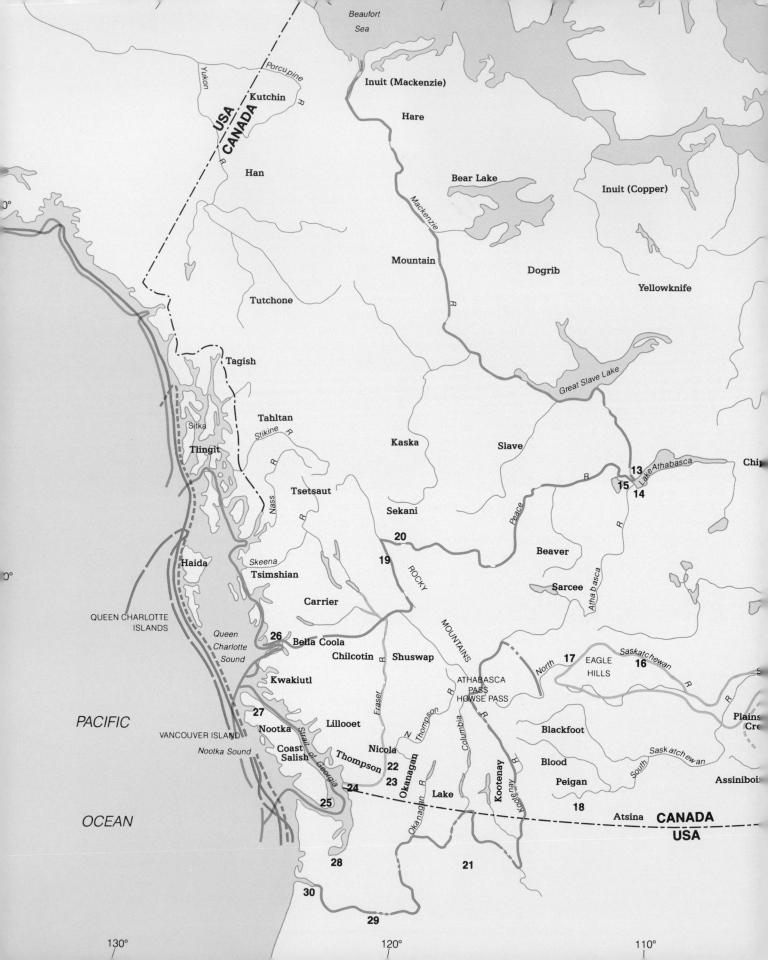

Beaufort
Sea

Inuit (Mackenzie)

Hare

Bear Lake

Inuit (Copper)

Yukon

Kutchin

Porcupine

USA
CANADA

Han

Mackenzie

Mountain

Dogrib

Yellowknife

Tutchone

R

Tagish

Great Slave Lake

Tahltan

Sitka

Tlingit

Stikine
R

Kaska

Slave

Tsetsaut

Nass
R

Sekani

Peace
R

R

Lake Athabasca
13
15 14

Chip

Beaver

20

19

Sarcee

ROCKY

Athabasca

Haida

Skeena

Tsimshian

Carrier

QUEEN CHARLOTTE
ISLANDS

MOUNTAINS

Saskatchewan

26 Bella Coola

Chilcotin   Shuswap

*Queen
Charlotte
Sound*

North

17   EAGLE
      HILLS   16

Kwakiutl

ATHABASCA
PASS
HOWSE PASS

Blackfoot

Plains
Cre

27

Fraser

Lillooet

Nootka

Thompson

Nicola

Columbia

Saskatchewan

Blood

South

Assiniboi

VANCOUVER ISLAND

Nootka Sound

Coast
Salish

Strait of Georgia

Thompson
22

Okanagan

Lake

Kootenay

Peigan

PACIFIC

24

23

R

18

Atsina   CANADA

25

Okanagan
R

Kootenay

OCEAN

USA

28

21

30

29

130°   120°   110°

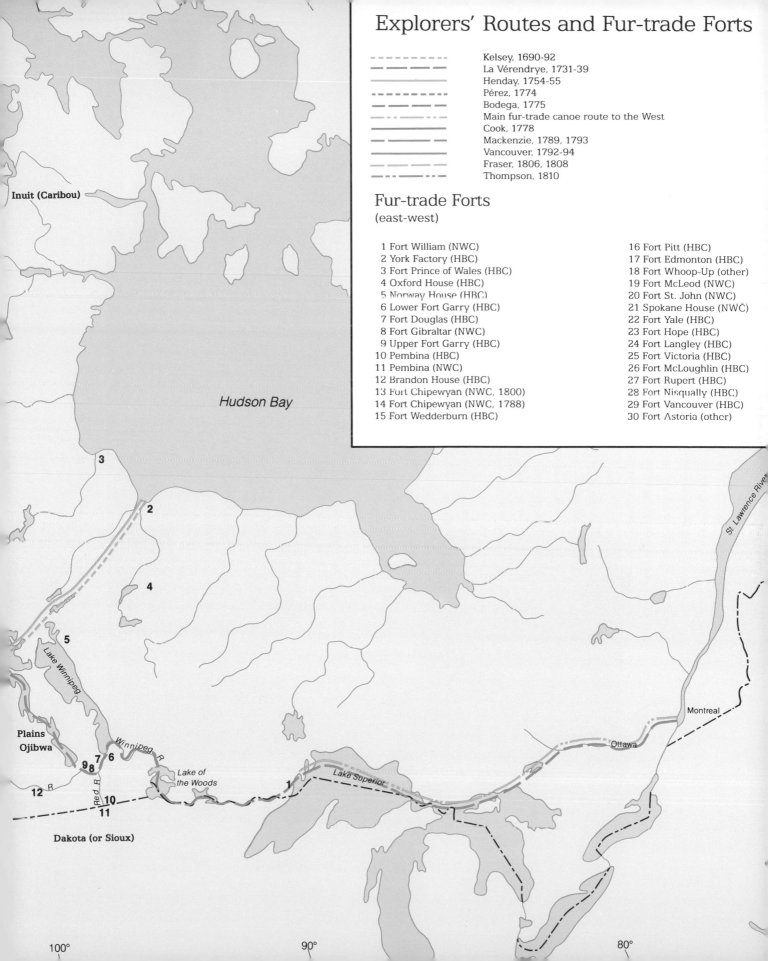

Explorers' Routes and Fur-trade Forts

Kelsey, 1690-92
La Vérendrye, 1731-39
Henday, 1754-55
Pérez, 1774
Bodega, 1775
Main fur-trade canoe route to the West
Cook, 1778
Mackenzie, 1789, 1793
Vancouver, 1792-94
Fraser, 1806, 1808
Thompson, 1810

Fur-trade Forts
(east-west)

1 Fort William (NWC)
2 York Factory (HBC)
3 Fort Prince of Wales (HBC)
4 Oxford House (HBC)
5 Norway House (HBC)
6 Lower Fort Garry (HBC)
7 Fort Douglas (HBC)
8 Fort Gibraltar (NWC)
9 Upper Fort Garry (HBC)
10 Pembina (HBC)
11 Pembina (NWC)
12 Brandon House (HBC)
13 Fort Chipewyan (NWC, 1800)
14 Fort Chipewyan (NWC, 1788)
15 Fort Wedderburn (HBC)

16 Fort Pitt (HBC)
17 Fort Edmonton (HBC)
18 Fort Whoop-Up (other)
19 Fort McLeod (NWC)
20 Fort St. John (NWC)
21 Spokane House (NWC)
22 Fort Yale (HBC)
23 Fort Hope (HBC)
24 Fort Langley (HBC)
25 Fort Victoria (HBC)
26 Fort McLoughlin (HBC)
27 Fort Rupert (HBC)
28 Fort Nisqually (HBC)
29 Fort Vancouver (HBC)
30 Fort Astoria (other)

Inuit (Caribou)

Hudson Bay

Lake Winnipeg

Plains
Ojibwa

Winnipeg R.

Lake of
the Woods

Red R.

R.

Lake Superior

Dakota (or Sioux)

Montreal

Ottawa

St. Lawrence River

100°   90°   80°

Selkirk's greatest strength was his own indomitable will; perhaps his greatest weakness a habit of picking men of lesser spirit to be his deputies at Red River.

4   A Battleground for Furs

The North West Company was a superbly manned, superbly managed business organization, but it could not match the Hudson's Bay Company's enormous financial advantage of easy access to the heart of the *pays d'en haut*. HBC ships took a mere four weeks to return with cargoes of furs to England, whereas NWC canoes took four months to make the haul from Athabasca to Montreal, from which there was a six- or seven-week ship voyage to London. Nonetheless, the Nor'Westers' aggressive tactics did bring the Hudson's Bay Company close to financial collapse; after years of yielding a ten per cent return, HBC dividends dropped to eight per cent and then sank to four per cent.

The bitter struggle between the two companies for the fur trade was fought in the Athabasca country and in the Red River country. Two of the leading participants were Alexander Mackenzie of the North West Company, and Thomas Douglas, fifth Earl of Selkirk, a philanthropist who bought his way into the Hudson's Bay Company.

In 1799, ten years after his voyage to the Arctic and six after his journey to the Pacific, Alexander Mackenzie was working as an executive in Montreal. "Nor'West" Mackenzie was one of that city's better-known figures, a hero to many of the younger wintering partners in the North West Company, and financially secure. Yet he was happy with neither his position nor his prospects in the firm of McTavish, Frobisher & Company, which had become the virtual directorate of the NWC. Being the fifth of five copartners, he had little say in determining corporate policy. His long-cherished plan to expand, regulate and control the fur trade — including the operations of American rivals — had not been advanced one whit.

Mackenzie's plan was simplicity itself. The Nor'Westers, he insisted, had only to persuade the British government to lease them Hudson Bay transit rights and their heavy transportation costs would be reduced and profits thereby increased. Each time he tried, he failed to overcome their obsession with a Montreal base, for it gave them a solid, historic claim — inherited from the French — to the *pays d'en haut*. Montreal also represented an enormous investment in offices and warehouses, as well as providing the necessary pool of voyageurs. (Years afterwards, NWC partners reluctantly admitted the truth of Mackenzie's arguments and wished, too late, that they had taken his advice.) Finally, Mackenzie decided to quit the trade and try his logic on the British government.

In 1801, his book, *Voyages from Montreal, on the River St. Laurence, through the Continent of North America to the Frozen and Pacific Oceans in the Years 1789 and 1793*, was published in London and Edinburgh. A large volume of 550 pages illustrated by maps, it became a best seller. Mackenzie published the book not only to draw attention to himself but to prod the British government into acquiring territory in western North America before the newly established United States of America did so. In addition to providing the general reader with a travel account in the form of an explorer's logbook, he offered officialdom an economic treatise on the fur trade and policies for a mighty expansion of it under the British flag.

Mackenzie ended his book with a clever economic argument and also a strangely prophetic vision of a Canada extending from sea to sea:

the Columbia is the line of communication from the Pacific Ocean . . . its banks . . . suitable to the residence of a civilized people. By opening this intercourse between the Atlantic and Pacific Oceans and forming regular establishments through the interior, and at both extremes, as well as along the coasts and islands, the entire command of the fur trade of North America might be obtained. . . . To this may be added the fishing in both seas, and the markets of the four quarters of the globe. Such would be the field for commercial enterprise, and incalculable would be the produce of it, when supported by the operations of that credit and capital which Great Britain so pre-eminently possesses.

(The route of the Columbia River was not known at this time. Mackenzie was mistakenly writing about the great river he had been on – the Fraser – which he thought was the Columbia.)

Barely a month after the publication of the *Voyages*, the pragmatic Mackenzie submitted to the British government a detailed plan of fur-trade consolidation and expansion which, despite his various influential contacts in cabinet and court, was ignored by a government busy fighting Napoleonic forces in different parts of the world. All he got out of his time in London was a knighthood, so he returned to Montreal to join a newly formed fur company that was going to compete for the Athabasca trade. Like the North West Company, it was an association of several companies of merchants. Officially registered as Sir Alexander Mackenzie and Company, it was more commonly referred to as the XY Company.

Even with Mackenzie's expertise, the contest was hardly waged on equal terms because the Nor'Westers had a decided edge in veteran personnel who knew how to cajole or bully Indians into bringing them furs pledged to rival traders. The NWC wintering partners were also ordered to keep close watch on XY traders during the time Indians made their final hunt of the winter.

Naturally, XY wintering partners received the same instructions. They were urged not to rely solely on barter at their posts but to send out their clerks among Indian groups, check on the activities of the opposition, and shadow them wherever they went. All this cloak-and-dagger activity meant increased costs because more men, goods and trading posts were required. The competition also led to violence: scuffles and fist fights were common, canoes were seized and their cargoes destroyed, and there was even a killing.

A major feature of the rivalry was the way each company lavished liquor on its customers. At the height of the struggle, the XY Company was using an average of 22 500 litres of spirits a year, but the Nor'Westers, with the advantage of freight boats on the Great Lakes, were handing out at least 67 500 litres annually. Traders' journals casually record many commonplace incidents of mayhem and murder caused by a highly concentrated form of alcohol known in the trade as high wine, composed of two parts of wine to one of rum or brandy. The wintering partners of each company cynically plied their customers with straight liquor or high wine

to get them to come to the post, to welcome them on arrival, to buy their loyalty, to keep it, to induce them to default on the credit they had had from the opposition, to put them in a mood for trade, to inflate the price of goods, to reward them for virtue, to express your everlasting admiration of their brave deeds, or because they drove you crazy begging for it.

*

The loyalty one Highlander expects of another runs deep, and Mackenzie's defection from the NWC had been neither forgotten nor forgiven. When the problem of punishing costs forced Nor'Westers and XY men to merge and form a stronger North West Company in 1804, Mackenzie was allowed the status of a partner but denied any role in management. So he returned to England to become a fur-trade spokesman, requesting a charter that would give the NWC the

The Company Canoe by John Innes. These HBC voyageurs have just entered today's Jasper National Park on their way upstream to the Athabasca Pass.

same monopoly on the Pacific coast that the Hudson's Bay Company enjoyed in Rupert's Land. For various reasons, notably his stiff-necked ways, nothing came of this or later efforts at lobbying.

The tenacious Mackenzie then began to buy Hudson's Bay Company stock — which had sunk from £100 to £60 a share, thanks to the rival activities of the "Wolves of the North." His aim was to acquire control of the HBC and arrange at least Hudson Bay transit rights for the Nor'Westers, if not also exclusive trading rights in Athabasca. He was helped in this endeavour by a wealthy Scot, Thomas Douglas, Earl of Selkirk — until Mackenzie discovered Selkirk's real reason for seeking policy-making power and ended their co-operation.

Lord Selkirk's interest was, in his words, "at the western extremity of Canada, upon the Waters which fall into Lake Winnipeck," where "with a moderate exertion of industry" colonists could be sure of "a comfortable subsistence." He dreamed of founding a settlement at Red River, and was interested in the Hudson's Bay Company because it had a solid legal claim to ownership of the area. Mackenzie realized if farming spread all over the Red River region where buffalo, the source of huge Nor'Wester supplies of pemmican, were accustomed to roam freely, the great herds would abandon the area. This could create immense difficulties, if not hardship or death, for men serving in the *pays d'en haut*. By 1811 however, Selkirk had persuaded the governor and committee of the HBC to accept his colonization scheme, and Mackenzie could do little but harass Selkirk's lieutenants in various minor ways as they organized the dispatch of the first group of settlers to Red River.

Hereafter, Alexander Mackenzie fades from history, to become a country squire and succumb nine years later to Bright's disease.

However, before he died peacefully in his native Scotland, other men had died violently in the *pays d'en haut*.

*

One biographer of Lord Selkirk describes the founder of the Red River settlement as a "tall, handsome youth with his ready smile, auburn hair, and searching blue eyes." The seventh son of a rich Scots nobleman, there seemed little chance that Thomas Douglas would succeed to the family title. He lazed his way through university, studied some law, toured his native Scotland and made leisurely visits to various parts of Europe before deciding to work on one of his father's farms. To the astonishment of his family and employees on the Selkirk estates, Thomas, whose health had never been robust, laboured in the fields as hard as any tenant farmer, even at the backbreaking work of scything wheat, oats, and barley.

Quite unexpectedly, the premature deaths of all his brothers, and then that of his father, elevated him in 1799 to the privileged status of Earl of Selkirk. The new nobleman, however, became neither a part-time politician nor a gentleman of leisure. What came to dominate Selkirk's attention above all else was the tragedy of the Highland Clearances.

Seven years earlier, he had seen for himself the uprooting of Highland society as family after family was forced off the small holdings where their forebears had lived for generations. Many chieftains had decided that their lands would be, in Margaret Laurence's words, "cleared of unprofitable people to make room for profitable sheep."

The Highland clan system was similar to tribal systems anywhere. The chief was believed in, not so much as an individual as a symbol, a father, a king figure who possessed almost mystical powers of pro-

64

tection and strength. To be betrayed by one of these must have been like knowing, really knowing, that one's own father intended, if he could, to murder you. The outcast Highlanders must have arrived in Canada as a people bereft, a people who had been wounded psychically in ways they could not possibly have comprehended. . .

. . . What appeared to be their greatest trouble in a new land — the grappling with an unyielding environment — was in fact probably their salvation. I believe they survived not in spite of the physical hardships but *because* of them, for all their attention and thought *had* to be focused outward. They could not brood. If they had been able to do so, it might have killed them.

The Clearances bred a deep compassion in the young nobleman as he gradually became aware that hundreds of clansmen, their wives and their children were emigrating from the Highlands to bleak fishing ports and city slums. But it was when he learned that Highlanders were emigrating to the newly established United States of America in ever-increasing numbers that he seems to have discovered an aim in life. Why not help these families to resettle in Canada? If they could be persuaded to do so, thus strengthening Britain's hold on North America, would not their loss be converted into a gain? With his money and the family's political connections in London, who was in a better position to aid these penniless people than the fifth Earl of Selkirk?

The location he favoured for a settlement was the prairie region surrounding the junction of the Red and Assiniboine rivers, perhaps after reading a description of it in Mackenzie's *Voyages from Montreal*. The choice was a good one. The valley of the Red River, the major waterway of the region, contains thousands of hectares of fertile, black soil and has a growing season of almost 170 days a year. Selkirk reasoned further that cattle would have little diffi-

culty surviving on the lush grasslands that nourished innumerable buffalo. The one vital matter he underestimated was the essential part that the Red River country played in Nor'Wester operations.

For some years, Selkirk was far too absorbed in organizing the settlement of Highlanders in Prince Edward Island and in Upper Canada to carry out his Red River colonization scheme, his "favourite project." He and his partner and brother-in-law, Andrew Wedderburn Colvile, were too busy reviving an ailing HBC. They fought off proposals by a dispirited directorate to leave fur trading to the Nor'Westers and engage, instead, in whaling and fishing operations. Colvile introduced more efficient rules and regulations, which included a profit-sharing plan for the Company's servants. Selkirk and Colvile also worked out a scheme to establish an agricultural colony in Red River that would supply the HBC with foodstuffs and future employees. Selkirk was quite prepared to finance the colony himself — provided he was given the land grant of his choice: an immense territory of about 300 000 square kilometres comparable in size to Great Britain. He was intent on finding new homes for thousands of Highlanders.

Selkirk's colonization plan alarmed not only the NWC but HBC employees. His critics raised all sorts of objections. It was a departure from "traditional policy." Farming and fur trading were "opposing pursuits" because buffalo, the source of pemmican, would be scared away from the region; and settlers would not only have difficulty farming in a "howling wilderness" that was prone alternately to drought and flooding but would probably engage in trapping on the side. Even Lady Selkirk was alarmed by her husband's obsession with the project and often teased him, lovingly but anxiously, about his "Kingdom on Red River." Selkirk, however, had a strong streak of stubbornness and was backed by Colvile, a powerful voice in the deliberations of the HBC governing committee. Although far from convinced of the wisdom of the plan, committee members agreed to the colonization venture and in 1811 — for the nominal sum of ten shillings — authorized the grant of Assiniboia to the fifth Earl of Selkirk and his heirs.

*

The Hudson's Bay Company had long regarded the fur trade of North America as an exclusive possession, yet had lagged far behind its rivals in establishing trade outlets in the *pays d'en haut*. One hundred and forty years after its founding, it still had no permanent footing in the Athabasca country and contented itself with setting up posts to compete with those of Nor'Westers on the Saskatchewan and North Saskatchewan rivers. Now that Lord Selkirk as good as owned the HBC, he was determined to force recognition from the North West Company of HBC fur-trading and settlement privileges in the *pays d'en haut*, in order to ensure the welfare of his Red River settlement. To that end, Selkirk arranged the despatch of an expedition to Athabasca.

In the winter of 1812-13, a rumour raced along the Peace River from one Nor'Wester post to the next that the Hudson's Bay Company was going to invade the region. Nothing happened until the fall of 1815, when John Clarke of the HBC led a force of almost a hundred men into the Athabasca country. Clarke was a former Nor'Wester and, as such, was typically courageous, ambitious and not a little vainglorious.

The proud Highlanders who ran the North West Company were enraged. The HBC could perhaps lay legal claim to all lands and territories draining into Hudson Bay, but it was Nor'Westers who had explored much of these same lands and territories, and then pushed even farther west and north into an entirely different watershed. At Selkirks' dictate, the region that produced the finest furs on the entire continent — and which was certainly no part of King Charles II's grant of Rupert's Land to the "Company of Adventurers trading into Hudson's Bay" — was to be taken over from its rightful owners! They had, at considerable personal and corporate cost, earned the right to trade there. So they ensured the failure of Clarke's expedition by ordering Indians not to hunt for him or to sell him food. Some HBC men died of starvation, and the remainder, including Clarke, surrendered their trade goods to the Nor'Westers to save themselves.

Undaunted by the defeat of his first attempt to establish the HBC in Athabasca, Clarke returned the next year with new men and supplies. However, he decided to contest matters at Fort Wedderburn, directly opposite the Nor'Wester depot of Fort Chipewyan on the northwest shore of Lake Athabasca, in order to draw away customers from the opposition. Here, thanks to excellent fishing grounds, at least he and his men would not starve.

Clarke had little chance to win over customers. For one thing, his men were greatly outnumbered. For another, his opponent, a veteran wintering partner named Archibald Norman McLeod, regularly humiliated his competitors and showed everybody who was master of the situation. He had a blockhouse constructed right next door to Fort Wedderburn so that his men could remonstrate with any Indians bringing furs to "the English." Abusing his authority as a justice of the peace, McLeod would, from time to time, force his way into the HBC post on some legal pretext, arrest personnel, and then free them on their guarantee to keep the peace — all this in front of Indian trappers. On one occasion,

This 1817 sketch of part of the Red River settlement is believed to have been drawn by Lord Selkirk himself.

McLeod even impounded fishing gear and the men using it to obtain the only steady source of nourishment available. Finally, A. N. McLeod, J.P., seized Fort Wedderburn itself.

Clarke, forced to hand over trade goods to the value of £3000, was sent as a prisoner to a Nor'Wester post on the Peace River. Thus ended the HBC campaign of 1816-17.

The gang warfare between the two companies went on for four more years, disrupting the Athabasca fur trade, wasting huge sums of money, and costing further lives. The whole thing developed into a sort of crazy contest of tit for tat: one side would capture and imprison a rival wintering partner, and then the other side quickly retaliated. The struggle for domination of the trade eventually spread beyond Athabasca. And, like his rivals, Lord Selkirk obtained warrants for the arrests of this, that, and the next Nor'Wester. In the end, the tangled affairs and conflicting lawsuits of each company took years to sort out in the law courts of Upper and Lower Canada.

*

In Rupert's Land, the spring of 1812 was long and cold: lake and river ice that usually broke up in April or May stayed rigid until the middle of June. It was early July before Miles Macdonell, appointed governor of Assiniboia by Selkirk, could journey inland from the HBC depot of York Factory with a group of Scots and Irish labourers. They paused at the Company post of Oxford House to hire an Indian guide, purchase a bull and a cow (promptly christened Adam and Eve), and rest their tired bodies. By the end of August, having travelled 1120 kilometres from Hudson Bay, the advance party reached the junction of the Red and Assiniboine rivers.

Just south of the junction of these waterways stood the Nor'Westers' Fort Gibraltar, a collec-tion of well-built log buildings within a stockade nearly six metres high. Here, Macdonell and his men were able to buy some food to eke out their limited catches of fish. Across the Red from Fort Gibraltar, they pitched their tents. A day or two later, they had a strange experience.

From over the plain there suddenly rushed toward them a wild-looking band of horsemen, accoutred in war paint and feathers, and brandishing tomahawks. The first fear of the settlers was that they were being attacked by Indians; but when the riders came within close range, yelling and gesticulating, it was evident that they were not Indians . . .

The attackers were Metis, dressed in Indian costumes for the sake of effect. Their hostile greeting had been instigated by the Nor'Westers in charge of Fort Gibraltar, and they

had come to inform Macdonell, which they did in no uncertain terms, that the Red River Valley was a fur-trade domain, that farmers were not wanted, and that the settlers must go elsewhere. In equally plain language the Governor retorted that the Red River Valley belonged to Lord Selkirk, and that if anyone was forced to go elsewhere, it would be the fur trader and not the settler. Thereupon the dusky riders withdrew.

The term Metis is derived from the French verb *métisser*, "to cross" or "mix breeds." This mingling of peoples began when the first coureurs de bois from Quebec, Trois Rivières or Montreal married Indian women *à la façon du pays*, "after the fashion of the country," a formality that required the approval of a woman's parents and was substantiated by their acceptance of various gifts. The children of these marriages inherited the language and religion of their fathers, and the wilderness knowledge and skills of their mothers. Many a guide or trader for the La Vérendryes was a Metis. Many an *homme du nord* manning a Nor'Wester canoe or crewman on an HBC York boat was a Metis. At first

The Fur Trader (portrait of John Budden, Esq.) by an
anonymous artist, circa 1855.

A Peter Rindisbacher watercolour showing the departure from the HBC depot of York Factory on Hudson Bay of immigrants to Red River.

the term had a distinct cultural meaning: it was applied to Roman Catholics of French and Indian ancestry. In particular, it meant the mounted hunter who disputed the Sioux claim to hunt the buffalo of Assiniboia and the adjoining plains of Minnesota and Montana. Later, it was also applied to those with British and Indian ancestry. The Metis were known to the French as *bois brûlés*, "scorched wood," because of their skin colour, and to the English as half-breeds.

Macdonell's response to the Metis attempt at intimidation was to make Assiniboia an official fact by holding a carefully rehearsed ceremony at his encampment. Attended by men carrying firearms and flags, he read aloud in English and in French the deed that transferred the land from the HBC to Lord Selkirk. Having declared his master's legal claim, Macdonell proceeded to demonstrate the reality of it by picking a location for the settlement. About three kilometres north of Fort Gibraltar, on the same side of the Red River, he named a stretch of land Point Douglas. There, his men cleared ground to plant winter wheat and construct a storehouse in readiness for the first group of settlers. It was fortunate that they did so, the first group of families sent out by Selkirk in 1813 were equipped with farm implements that were no match for the tough prairie sod and had to endure a winter of near starvation. As the days were already growing chilly and provisions were getting low, Governor Macdonell took most of his followers south to an HBC post that was near the wintering grounds of several buffalo herds.

The Nor'Westers in charge of Fort Gibraltar — Duncan Cameron and Alexander Macdonell (a cousin and brother-in-law of Governor Miles Macdonell) — incited the already uneasy Metis. The two Nor'Westers were quick to point out that the Red River settlement was founded on two dubious claims: Selkirk's personal owner-

Cuthbert Grant was arrested for the murder of Governor Semple. Jumping bail in Montreal, he returned west and, in later years, joined the Metis in shielding the Red River colonists from the Sioux.

ship of Red River soil, and the HBC's arbitrary right to govern all who lived in Rupert's Land. Yet, as the two kept repeating, were not the Metis, through their Indian mothers, the real owners of the land? Like the prairie tribes, were they not a free people? Indeed, were they not the "new nation" of the north? Sensing that the long-time trade alliance between Metis and Nor'Westers could be shaped into a semimilitary one by choosing as leader a forceful personality, Cameron shrewdly appointed Cuthbert Grant a "captain" of the Metis.

Cuthbert Grant came into the stark spotlight of history at the height of the struggle between the North West and Hudson's Bay companies for control of the fur trade. Named after his father, a wintering partner in the North West Company, he was Cree, French and Scots by descent, but a Nor'Wester in outlook. After a "gentleman's" education in Scotland and some time at NWC headquarters in Montreal, he gladly returned as a clerk to the company's Red River Department in 1812. Home was his mother's country of the buffalo prairies of the upper Assiniboine. An expert horseman and marksman, Grant's skills were unusual in a Nor'Wester but essential to his duties. Assiniboia was a greater source of meat and fat than of furs. It was for its buffalo, not its beaver, that the region was vitally important to the rival fur companies: in the *pays d'en haut*, pemmican was often the difference between survival and starvation.

And, like any other Nor'Wester, Grant was suspicious of the settlement at the junction of the two waterways that led to NWC pemmican posts at Lake Winnipeg, the more so as the arrival of every new group of Selkirk's people increased the numerical odds.

In 1814, learning that a second group of settlers was coming to join the colony, Governor Macdonell forbade the export of pemmican from Assiniboia — except with a licence from him to do so. (Selkirk overestimated the abilities of Miles Macdonell, who proved to be a hot-headed deputy.) This was a direct threat to the NWC, many of whose men working in the *pays d'en haut* were utterly dependent upon Assiniboia's supply of pemmican to make it through the winter. The pemmican embargo was, according to NWC chief William McGillivray, "the first time the North West Company has ever been insulted," and he was coldly determined to repay the insult. Macdonell also outlawed the Metis custom of "running the buffalo," as this drove the herds far out onto the plains. This arbitrary decision was fatal because it alienated the Metis. The buffalo hunt was the institution around which their communal way of life revolved and from which they derived food, clothing and income.

In accordance with McGillivray's instructions, Cameron and Macdonell exploited Grant and his influence over the Metis by encouraging them to run the buffalo and harass the settlement. Thus, with the self-confidence born of his upbringing and the loyalty inspired by his blood ties with the Metis, Grant led some of his people to the settlement to drive off cattle and fire warning shots. (This was done not just to dishearten the colonists but to divert their attention from canoe loads of pemmican going downriver to the Lake Winnipeg posts.) Duncan Cameron further terrified the settlers with random cannon fire.

Fearing that the destruction of the colony was possible, Governor Macdonell gave himself up to ensure the safety of his people and was sent to Fort William, the NWC stronghold on Lake Superior. With the "the damned robber," as the Nor'Westers called their opponent, in captivity, the "Rascally Republic" of Selkirk's settlement was theirs to dispose of. Some families

were induced to go to Upper Canada and were taken away in NWC canoes; others were allowed to sail off to the protection of the HBC depot of Norway House at the head of Lake Winnipeg. Then Nor'Wester clerks, including Grant, led a few Metis into the abandoned settlement to burn houses, trample crops and kill or drive off the cattle and sheep.

Elated that the insult of 1814 had been avenged, Macdonell and Cameron celebrated success by drinking and feasting with their employees and Metis allies — unaware that a spark of resistance remained on the east bank of the Red River. A Hudson's Bay Company clerk, John McLeod, and three labourers had decided to stay and look after their employer's goods and property as best they could.

Those families that had sought refuge at Norway House were contacted by Colin Robertson, another of Selkirk's deputies, and led back to Red River in the spring of 1815. Here, a welcome surprise awaited them. McLeod and his companions had rounded up stray cattle and raised crops of wheat, barley, oats, peas and potatoes. A few weeks later, the settlement was strengthened by the arrival of a fresh group of settlers under the command of Robert Semple, the newly appointed governor of HBC territories in North America.

Like Macdonell before him, Semple badly underrated the Nor'Westers. He was contemptuous of what he called in a letter to Selkirk "miserable opponents . . . Half-breeds and Old worn out [French] Canadians." Worse still, with the sublime confidence born of total ignorance, he refused to believe that his opponents were again plotting the destruction of the settlement. When his second-in-command, Colin Robertson, intercepted the North West Company's famed Northern Express, a winter mail service by sled, and read letters confirmng the Nor'Westers' in-

tention, Semple simply refused to believe it. (As an ex-NWC clerk, Robertson knew just how ruthless his former colleaues could be.) Oddly enough, with much reluctance, Semple did allow Robertson to seize and tear down Fort Gibraltar, and to arrest Duncan Cameron and send him to England to stand trial for his misdeeds. Robertson also captured the NWC pemmican post at Pembina.

Nothing daunted by the loss of Fort Gibraltar, the Nor'Westers were rounding up bands of Metis for the coming assault on the settlement. However, a group that could not be incited was the local Saulteaux tribe, whom Alexander Macdonell tried to persuade that the "English . . . are spoiling the Lands that belong to you, and to your Relations the Metifs only." But the Saulteaux had never resented Selkirk's people and had befriended them every winter with gifts of food and clothing. Chief Peguis refused the Nor'Wester's plea that some of the young men be allowed to join him.

If Metis and Nor'Westers needed further proof of the need to oust "the English," they now observed signs of what they took to be hostile preparations. Colin Robertson converted the buildings on Point Douglas into Fort Douglas by enclosing them within a palisade topped by a watchtower; most ominous of all, a small schooner, the *Cuchillon*, was being armed with captured Nor'Wester artillery. Moored at the junction of the Red and the Assinboine or at the mouth of the Red, the mini-warship could effectively blockade NWC canoe traffic.

Uneasiness filled the Red River country in the first few months of 1816. Everyone could sense the gradual buildup of tension. Even within the settlement all was not well. Semple and Robertson argued long and angrily on what action to take against their opponents, and the colony began to split into factions. Eventually,

Robertson left in a huff for York Factory. Then, in May, Cuthbert Grant started a chain of events by seizing pemmican-laden boats coming down from an HBC post on the Qu'Appelle (a tributary of the Assiniboine) to supply the settlement.

At the Grand Rapids of the Assiniboine, Grant had organized an ambush. Under the levelled muskets of his men, boatload after boatload of pemmican was taken over — except one, which was allowed to go on downriver to the settlement as a token gesture of mercy. Now manned by crews of Metis, the convoy carried on down the Assiniboine, guarded by outriders on the banks. At the junction of the Souris and Assiniboine, Grant and his followers captured the HBC post of Brandon House. He then pushed on, determined to supply the NWC canoe brigades that would be expecting to pick up their lifesaving supplies of pemmican at the Lake Winnipeg posts.

Since Fort Douglas threatened movement by water, Grant decided to take his party overland with some of the pemmican. Unfortunately, at one point on the journey he had to veer closer to the settlement to prevent the carts from becoming bogged down in swampy ground; his Metis were spotted by the watchtower lookout. Semple was called to the tower and noticed that some settlers were working in fields through which the Metis would ride. He decided to protect them and also question the Metis as to why they were anywhere near the settlement.

Grant was passing around a tree-lined ravine known as the Seven Oaks when his scouts hurried up to tell him that "the English" were approaching. Ordering the cart and an escort to keep going, he led his men to meet Semple and his followers.

The two parties confronted one another, silent and motionless except for the snorting of a pony or the flash of a bayonet in the sunlight. In the west the sun was dropping quickly down the sky, and the shadows of man and horse lengthened darkly on the plain.

. . . Semple stood stiffly in front of his line but did nothing. Grant acted. Quietly he ordered the brûlé beside him, François Firmin Boucher, to "go to them, and tell them to ground their arms, and surrender, or we will fire upon them."

"What do you want?" asked Boucher in broken English as he came up on Semple's right. "What do you want?" retorted the Governor. . . . "We want our fort [Gibraltar]," returned Boucher curtly. "Well, go to your fort," snapped Semple, stung by the brûlé's tone. "Why you have destroyed our fort, you damned rascal!" shouted Boucher. Semple then lost his temper and, seizing Boucher's rein and grabbing at his gun-stock, said "Scoundrel, do you tell me so?"

. . . A shot rang out. It was fired by Semple's men at an Indian who had kept edging forward when they warned him back. A second shot came from the brûlés. It was fired by Grant and it hit Semple in the thigh. . . . Semple's men began to crowd up to their leader to see how he was hurt. The Metis discharged a volley in their midst. Many of Semple's men fell. The rest turned to fight and returned the fire as best they could. . . .

The fight itself . . . lasted only fifteen minutes. Semple and twenty of his officers and men were killed. One Indian of Grant's party had been killed, and one brûlé, young Trottier, wounded. The victory was as complete as the fight was sudden.

The defeat at Seven Oaks, and the details of the use of knives and tomahawks on Semple's wounded men as told by one of the survivors, John Pritchard, so terrified the settlers that all they wanted to do was flee Red River. Terms of surrender were promptly made with Grant, who promised the settlers safe conduct out of the area. Despite a later order from Alexander Macdonell to detain Selkirk's people, Grant stood by his word and let them sail away downriver. But again crops were trampled and buildings burned.

All merchandise — and every fur — was rated in terms of one Made Beaver, the pelt of an adult male in prime condition. This NWC token was worth some (fluctuating) purchasing equivalent of one MB. The HBC token (wrongly engraved ½NB) was worth ½MB in goods.

*

While the corpses of Governor Semple and his followers lay strewn about Seven Oaks, vengeance was already closing in on the Nor'Westers in the person of Lord Selkirk himself. He was on his way to Red River when he heard the grim news of Semple's death, but Selkirk had with him the means to overpower his opponents: 120 veterans of the War of 1812 from the de Meuron and de Watteville regiments. Having appealed in vain to officials in Britain, Upper Canada and Lower Canada to protect the colony, Selkirk had hired his own private army.

Canoeing along Lake Superior's north shore, Selkirk and his soldiers reached Fort William, the great transshipment point of the North West Company, and arrested William McGillivray and several of his partners (one of whom was trader-explorer Simon Fraser). Selkirk's red-coated mercenaries held their muskets at the ready while their commander searched the fort for incriminating evidence and stolen HBC goods and furs. Finding all three, Selkirk sent McGillivray and his colleagues to Montreal under armed guard to be tried for treason, conspiracy and as accessories to murder.

Eager to restore his beloved colony, the next point of attack was the Red River valley. Despite the onset of freezing weather and heavy snowfalls, Selkirk sent a party, dragging light cannon on sleds, to clear Assiniboia of his enemies. Fittingly, the leader of the expedition was Miles Macdonell, the first governor of Assiniboia, who had been released from captivity in Fort William. Macdonell took pleasure in threatening to pound the Nor'Wester post at Pembina to pieces with his cannon. His hunger for revenge was so great that on a frigid winter night he led Selkirk's soldiers up and over the palisaded walls of Fort Douglas; by daybreak, the HBC flag once

again whipped in the wind. Macdonell sent word to the fugitive settlers at Norway House that they could return in the summer to start again, this time under the protection of the muskets of Selkirk's mercenaries. When the ice broke up on lake and river, the settlers and their sponsor arrived at Red River at about the same time.

Selkirk's reorganization of the colony was done with, as one historian has said, "a wisdom and generosity which were still spoken of in the country a century later." His soldiers and their officers were given the choice of prime lots of land at Red River or free transportation back to Montreal: many decided to stay. To returning settlers who had lost everything, he made outright gifts of land; to others, he sold lots on easy terms. In addition, Selkirk donated two large lots as sites for a Protestant church and a school and constructed, at his expense, an experimental farm, bridges, mills and a road. On the east side of the Red River, he set aside 4000 hectares for the Roman Catholic church in anticipation that missionaries would settle there and minister to the Metis of the region.

Selkirk discovered soon after his arrival that Assiniboia did not belong to the Hudson's Bay Company. It never had. Historically, it was an age-old hunting ground of the Plains Cree and the Assiniboine, though its occupants were now the Saulteaux. In order to avoid the possibility of future quarrels with the North West Company or the Metis over land ownership, he made a treaty with the local Saulteaux and Cree with the help of Chief Peguis. In exchange for an annual payment of "one hundred pounds weight of good merchantable tobacco" to each tribe, Selkirk secured the right to certain strips of land alongside the Red and Assiniboine rivers.

As it turned out, neither the soldier-settlers nor a land treaty were necessary to safeguard the settlement. When Selkirk left Red River in

A watercolour by Peter Rindisbacher showing the face-to-face NWC and HBC pemmican posts at Pembina – which was technically on U.S. soil. *See previous page.*

the summer of 1817, the Nor'Westers were being worn down, slowly but surely, by the force of Canada's awkward geography. Their chief, William McGillivray, admitted that they could not compete forever "against a Chartered Company, who brought their goods to the Indian country at less than one half the Expence that ours cost us." The Red River settlement was not troubled again by its former oppressors. Its greatest problem was posed by nature in the form of grasshoppers; in 1818 and 1819 millions of them devoured grain and vegetable crops to the last stalk and leaf. Only by retreating to Pembina to live off the buffalo did the settlers survive. With financial help from the earl to purchase seed in the neighbouring Minnesota Territory, the settlement got back on its feet and was able to grow enough food each year thereafter.

This was the last aid Selkirk was able to give his colony; he had contracted tuberculosis during his time in North America. Advised by his doctors to seek a dry, warm climate to ease the ravages of his disease, he reluctantly agreed in 1819 to go to southern France. There, early in April 1820, his mind still clear and absorbed by ideas and plans for an experimental farm at Red River, Selkirk died.

Over the years, the founder of Manitoba has had many admirers, one of whom wrote what is perhaps his finest epitaph:

It seems unlikely that Selkirk had heard the Chinese proverb
    If you plant for a year plant rice
    If you plant for a decade plant trees
    If you plant for a century plant people
yet the same wisdom was in him. He had founded a city and staked out a province, the hinge on which Canada would one day swing open. This had not been mere chance, for he had always believed – when to others it was a foolish vision – that the prairies could provide food for millions. And he had seen his settle-

ment as the bastion against American encroachment which it later became – Canada's most tangible claim to the prairies it had long neglected.

*

By 1820, the North West Company was on the defensive, and the Hudson's Bay Company was establishing footholds in Athabasca and in the Peace River country. There, the men from the Bay were winning over customers by patience, firmness and a spirit of fair dealing, and had even managed to establish a post as far west as the modern site of Fort St. John, British Columbia. More importantly, the HBC had greater resources of money than the Nor'Westers, whose finances were becoming greatly hampered by debt charges. A few NWC wintering partners, angered and finally alienated by the uncompromising attitude taken by their Montreal agents in the struggle with Lord Selkirk, had already secretly contacted the HBC in England with suggestions of a merger.

Yet another Highland Scot arrived in the Athabasca country in 1820 to work for the Hudson's Bay Company. A distant relative of the great Alexander Mackenzie, he would make a reality of his kinsman's dream of a unified fur trade between the Atlantic and Pacific oceans.

*

Doubtless, the valued Scots virtues of diligence and fortitude were taught to the blue-eyed, red-haired, under-sized George Simpson by the family of his grandfather, the Rev. Thomas Simpson. Luckily for the lad, the illegitimate offspring of a ne'er-do-well son of the manse and an unknown woman, he was given a thorough education in reading, writing, grammar and a subject called commercial arithmetic. George's mastery of this last skill may have prompted one of his uncles to offer him a job as a counting-house clerk in the sugar-importing firm of Graham, Simpson, and Wedderburn in London.

Now, the Wedderburn in the firm's name was Andrew Wedderburn, the man whose sister had married Lord Selkirk and who sat on the governing committee of the Hudson's Bay Company. As canny a man as ever came out of Scotland, he had renamed himself Andrew Colvile and eventually become the dominant member on the HBC board of governors, overshadowing even Lord Selkirk. In fact, Colvile outlasted Selkirk by several decades.

Colvile proposed that George Simpson be sent to North America to take care of HBC affairs, for the Company needed a man to act as a backup to the overseas governor, William Williams. Colvile decided that his protégé's qualities of energy and efficiency, courage and coolness more than made up for his lack of practical knowledge of the fur trade and of North America. Thus began George Simpson's long, enormously successful career with the Hudson's Bay Company.

Simpson arrived in the *pays d'en haut* to find that William Williams had successfully eluded attempts by Nor'Westers to capture him. The new employee lost no time in following his orders to supervise the HBC's 1820-21 campaign in Athabasca.

When dealing with Nor'Wester bullies, Simpson adopted a courteous but no-nonsense attitude from the start.

The Nor'Westers at Fort Chipewyan tried various tactics to oust the HBC from Fort Wedderburn, but Simpson countered these by arming his traders and demonstrating every intention of meeting force with force. For a man who was never violent by nature or act, Simpson spent a lot of time that winter carrying a double-barrelled gun in his hand and a loaded pistol in his belt. Word spread through the Lake Athabasca area that the new man at Wedderburn was not going to be browbeaten.

Despite the war of nerves, Simpson's task was to run the business of the Company in Athabasca, which involved a considerable amount of daily correspondence with the other posts. The main problem was discipline, which was either poor or nonexistent. So Simpson wrote his post managers to inform them that those servants who were disobedient, neglectful, dishonest or impertinent would be punished by fines, imprisonment or reduced rations. He also sent polite but pointed letters to the effect that the trading system would soon be "improved." Instead of extravagance, which "seems hitherto to have been the motto," it would now be "oeconomy." Thus, "A sufficient quantity of fish should be taken in the fall for the maintenance of the people during the winter . . . they cannot expect meat except by the way of a treat on particular occasions." As for customers, "Every encouragement should be held out to them to renew their habits of industry; they should not be overloaded with Debt; short and frequent supplies [of trade goods] may answer better than giving them their full equipments in the Fall." He constantly reminded his subordinates that beaver was the sole object of the Company's mission and that it was by the number of packs of furs that the "Honourable Hudson's Bay Company can appreciate the Talents of their Traders."

No detail escaped Simpson's inquisitorial eye and ear. Even such a minor matter as sled dogs claimed his attention. Shocked to the depths of his thrifty Scots soul by their high price — mainly the result of their Indian owners' habit of eating those which had survived the winter in reasonable shape — he issued an order that the Company should keep only bitches. Under such an arrangement, "we shall always have a good

Sir George Simpson, governor-in-chief of all HBC territories from 1826 to 1860, was known to his fur-trade contemporaries as "The Little Emperor."

Dog Trains by John Innes. In winter, HBC traders routinely made round-trips of hundreds of kilometres just for the pleasure of visiting a compatriot or collecting mail. *See next page.*

stock of dogs, and can supply the people at fair prices."

He was the apostle of economy. To indulge in what Simpson called luxuries — and other men thought of as ordinary European household supplies — grated on his frugal sensibilities. "One would think, from the quantity you order that it is intended to be used in the Indian trade," was his outraged reply to a post manager's indent for mustard. He was a typical, nineteenth-century captain of industry — and the scene of his endeavours called for an administrator as hard as the environment itself.

After that first busy winter, Simpson came out of Athabasca to find that the bitter war for the fur trade was over. At Grand Rapids on the Saskatchewan River — the very place where the rival concerns had in turn ambushed each other — a Nor'Wester clerk informed him that a union of the two warring companies had taken place. Simpson's reaction was the small man at his battling best. "I must confess my own disappointment that instead of a junction our Opponents have not been beaten out of the Field, which with one or two years of good management I am certain might have been effected."

His disappointment was short lived. For Simpson, the merger of 1821 was the stepping-stone to power. That same year, he was put in charge of all HBC operations north and west of the Great Lakes. Five years later, he was governor-in-chief of Company operations in British North America. In due course, he was knighted by Queen Victoria.

*

Of the many problems posed by the parliamentary Act of Union of 1821 that merged the two companies under the name of the older one, the greatest one was psychological. How could the largely Highland-born wintering partners, whose entrepreneurial energies had spanned a continent and both created and sustained the North West Company, be persuaded to become members of the staid organization that they had long derided as "the English"? For that matter, how were the men from the Bay going to feel about receiving into their midst those who had mocked or injured many an HBC field officer in the course of fifty years of unremitting rivalry?

Simpson gently bullied or flatteringly manipulated this divergent group of men to build a bigger, better Hudson's Bay Company. He accomplished this by an efficient administration and a strict discipline. He was their boss, and in various ways he never let them forget it. But perhaps his greatest strength in their eyes was that he proved to be a money-making boss. Dishonest or inefficient traders and clerks were fired. Posts that did not pay their way were closed down and those not well positioned were relocated. Personnel surplus to Simpson's idea of requirements were, if possible, shifted from trading activities to maintenance and supply work. In four years, he reduced the total of employees from 1983 to 827 and cut the wages of some employees almost fifty per cent. Transportation systems and methods were overhauled.

When chief factors and chief traders noted that their shares were paying increasing dividends — the Company had sensibly adopted the Nor'Wester profit-sharing principle — they responded more readily to the stream of directives that flowed from Simpson's pen or mouth. Four years after he took over the reins of management, dividends were back up from four per cent to ten per cent — and also paid a bonus of a further ten per cent.

Governor Simpson bent every last member of the North West Company to his will, which he always thought of as an extension of the will of *the* governor, and his committee, in England.

5 "The Father of British Columbia"

James Douglas was born in 1803 on the "wrong side of the blanket," a major handicap in the status-conscious age in which he lived. Worse still for his prospects, he was part black. His mother was described as a Creole who lived in the West Indies, but HBC records politely refer to Douglas as a "Scotch West Indian" or, bluntly, as a "mulatto." Fortunately his father, a wealthy Scots merchant, did not abandon his swarthy skinned son. James was sent to school in Scotland and thoroughly drilled in the three Rs, in French and in bookkeeping.

At sixteen, he signed on as a clerk with the North West Company, then almost at the end of its long struggle with the Hudson's Bay Company. Some years later, after the merger of the two companies, he was still working in New Caledonia to the satisfaction of his HBC masters, except for one highly embarrassing fact. Douglas had personally executed an Indian who had killed two company employees. The popular version of this incident says that the young clerk trailed the murderer to an Indian village and "blew out his brains, in the centre of his tribe."

This deed, much resented by friends of the dead man, may have triggered Douglas's transfer to Fort Vancouver very shortly afterwards. Or the move may have been the result of George Simpson's shrewd appraisal of the young clerk in the course of a visit to Douglas's post. The HBC governor-in-chief rated Douglas highly in his "Character Book" — a private dossier he kept on all company personnel.

A stout powerful active Man . . . tolerably well Educated, expresses himself clearly on paper, understands our Counting House business and is an excellent Trader. Well qualified for any Service requiring bodily exertion, firmness of mind and the exercise of Sound judgement. . . . Has every reason to look forward to early promotion and is a likely man to fill a place at our Council board in course of time.

Whatever the reason, the twenty-seven-year-old clerk had been started on the path to promotion, both inside and outside the Company.

*

Douglas arrived at Fort Vancouver, the headquarters of the HBC's Columbia District, when it was enjoying its last years of prosperity. In addition to the New Caledonia posts established by Simon Fraser and his successors, the HBC had by 1840 built Fort Langley on the lower Fraser River, Fort Nisqually on a direct, overland line between Fort Langley and Fort Vancouver, Fort Simpson on the Nass River (the modern Port Simpson), Fort McLoughlin on Milbanke Sound, Fort Durham on the Tako River and Fort Stikine on the Stikine River. The wealth being funnelled from the trapping grounds of the North Pacific coast through Fort Vancouver was comparable to that which, many years later, poured from the gold fields of the Fraser River and its tributaries. More town than fort, it was the only significant British settlement west of the Rocky Mountains. Outside its walls grazed hundreds of cattle, sheep and oxen, and HBC servants raised huge crops of wheat, barley, oats, peas and potatoes.

Here, Douglas settled down to a clerk's duty to "keep accounts and copy letters," a daily chore little different from his previous one in the northern wilds of New Caledonia — with one important difference. There, his post had been a few huts in the middle of nowhere; at Fort Vancouver, located on the north bank of the Columbia River, he was in a frontier zone of vital concern to both Britain and the United States.

The persistent problem that troubled the Company about its Columbia District was the sovereignty of the region. For years, officials in London and Washington had been unable to resolve their claims to ownership and hammer out an agreement acceptable to each government.

In recognition of his many services to the Crown, Queen Victoria conferred a knighthood upon James Douglas. And, later, an annual pension of £500.

Britain could point to the work of Cook and Vancouver, but the United States, which had purchased Spain's rights to the North Pacific coast, could counter with the names of Pérez and Martínez. Mackenzie's exploration of the northern interior in 1793 strengthened the British case, but this was balanced by the Lewis and Clark overland expedition to the mouth of the Columbia. Added to which, Astor's Pacific Fur Company had operated a trading post on the Columbia ahead of the Nor' Westers.

In 1818, both nations finally agreed that, as far west as the summits of the Rocky Mountains, the 49th parallel of latitude would be the boundary between their territories. Beyond the mountains, however, was a no man's land where traders of any nation (including those of imperial Russia) could conduct their business in competition with each other. The British government and the HBC, anticipating that the Columbia itself might become the boundary line, had established Fort Vancouver on the north side of the river. But, with every passing year, it was becoming obvious that whoever occupied the disputed region and established permanent settlements would have the strongest claim to ownership.

This was exactly what troubled the HBC. It was not in the Company's interest to encourage settlers to farm or to set up lumbering and sawmilling operations: trapping and settlement had always been opposing occupations. Yet, across the river from where James Douglas sat six days a week adding up columns of figures and drafting business reports, American settlers were already moving into what was called the Oregon country. In the late 1830s, wagon train after wagon train lumbered westward along the Oregon Trail between Independence, Missouri, and the fertile valleys of the Williamette and lower Columbia rivers. Indeed, in the vicinity of

Fort Victoria by James Madison Alden.

Fort Vancouver, which was situated close to the junction of those rivers, the Company experienced a surprisingly profitable business selling seed and stock, tools and provisions to those who had survived the 3200-kilometre trek west. Douglas himself could clearly foresee what would happen. In a letter to Governor Simpson, he quoted the comment made in the Congress of the United States by one of its members: "Let us encourage emigration . . . fill Oregon with our citizens, and it will become ours as certainly as a ripe peach drops to the ground in autumn."

If the times had changed, so had the man. The hot-tempered young clerk was now the patient chief accountant and the trusted second-in-command at Fort Vancouver, "the grand mart and rendezvous for the Company's trade and servants on the Pacific." And, as Simpson had foreseen, a council member. On behalf of the HBC, he had negotiated business deals with the Russian American Company in Alaska and had even persuaded the Mexican governor of California – a very touchy nobleman – to allow the Company to establish a trading outfit in San Francisco. Douglas's only disappointment at this point in his career was what he frostily called the "foreign and independent interests" across the Columbia River in the lovely valley of the Williamette. As he wrote Simpson, "the Settlement of the Boundary Question is likely to drag on, from year to year, without being settled, as the Americans will soon leave nothing to settle."

In 1841, that whirlwind of energy, the governor-in-chief of all the Hudson's Bay Company territories in North America, made yet another tour of his far-flung fur empire. In due course Simpson arrived at Fort Vancouver, paused to make a brief inspection, and then bustled off on a tour of the Company's operations as far north as Russian-held Sitka, taking Chief Factor Douglas with him. While journeying in the Company's steam vessel *Beaver*, Simpson decided that the southern end of "Vancouver's Island" would be a good place to establish a substitute for Fort Vancouver. After all, if the 49th parallel should become the international border west of the Rocky Mountains, the Company would lose its great depot on the Columbia. In addition, Simpson saw advantages to this new location: it would give the HBC an indisputable claim to Vancouver Island; being close to the mainland, the island would make communication easier with Fort Yale on the Fraser and with the posts farther north in New Caledonia; and the posts on the northwest coast could be closed down, their work being handled by the *Beaver* operating out of this new depot.

Douglas was assigned to select the exact site for the new depot and settled for a place local Indians called Camosack. It had a good anchorage, land nearby suitable for farming, a natural supply of fresh water, and abundant timber for building material. Writing to a colleague and friend, Douglas rejoiced that the site "appears a perfect 'Eden' in the midst of the dreary wilderness of the Northwest coast and so different in its general aspect, from the wooded, rugged regions around, that one might be pardoned for supposing it had dropped from the clouds into its present position. . . . And not a musquitoe, that plague of plagues, did we feel!"

In the spring of 1843, he returned to his "Eden" with a party of men to build a large new depot, christened Victoria in honour of the young queen of Great Britain.

Fort Victoria became a vitally important location sooner than Douglas or Simpson – or the British government – expected. The summer it was constructed, American settlers in Oregon organized a government of their own, and that fall the "Great Immigration" brought almost a thousand new settlers along the Oregon Trail; in

An Indian paddles past New Westminster, the capital of British Columbia. This status was transferred to Victoria in 1868, when the island colony was annexed to B.C.

1844, 1400 arrived; the year after, 3000. Flooding into the Oregon country, the newcomers gave the United States government valid reason to press its claim to land as far north of the Columbia River as the 49th parallel. At the same time, Simpson's removal of the Company's main Pacific storage and shipping depot from Fort Vancouver to Fort Victoria gave the British government the impression that the Columbia River was no longer vital to HBC interests. And, as if an augury of things to come, a president of the United States had just been elected to office on the rallying cry of "Fifty-Four Forty or Fight!", meaning the extension of American territory all the way to 54°40'N, the southern boundary of Russia's Alaskan possessions.

Thus, in 1846, the Oregon Boundary Treaty limited British ownership west of the Rocky Mountains to the territory between the 49th parallel and 54°40' N, plus Vancouver Island. The United States promised that the HBC could retain its properties south of the new international boundary and use the Columbia River. But Douglas and Simpson recognized that this was just a temporary gain: sooner or later, American settlers and free traders would clean the Columbia region of furs.

*

In 1849, James Douglas was forty-six years of age and had served for three decades in the fur trade. He had greatly loved the work, for all its hardships and its almost total isolation from contact with civilization. However, in 1849, a succession of events began that changed his life and ultimately forced him to resign from the Hudson's Bay Company.

To avoid a repetition of the trouble that started when settlers began pouring into the Oregon country, the Company persuaded the Vancouver Island; in 1849, the governor and British government to give it legal ownership of committee of the HBC were made the "true and absolute lordes and proprietors" of the island. In return, they agreed to encourage settlement by selling land "at a reasonable price" and to use the money from the sale of mineral and timber rights to construct roads and schools and establish churches. However, the basic Company attitude to settlement did not change: it sold land at the then prohibitive price of £1 per acre (0.4 ha) and required every purchaser to bring out five labourers from Britain. Settlers also had to buy goods — with a three hundred per cent markup — at HBC stores, because private individuals were not allowed to set up retail outlets.

The whole arrangement was neat and tidy. On the one hand, the HBC would continue to enjoy its fur-trading monopoly with the official support of the British government; on the other, Britain would maintain a foothold on the Pacific coast at no cost to the British taxpayer. However, the first governor of the Crown Colony of Vancouver Island, Richard Blanshard, learned a bitter lesson. He was expected to start literally from scratch, and

without headquarters, without law officers, without an army, without police and without a gaol, Queen Victoria's representative was expected to introduce the pattern of government existing in all British colonies.

For Blanshard, there was an awkward complication:

In the Colony of Vancouver Island, all the real power was concentrated in the hands of James Douglas. In addition to his position as Chief Factor and as senior officer of the Board of Management, Douglas acted as the Company's Agent for the sale of lands, mineral, and timber. . . . By habit and by custom, everyone

Yates Street, Victoria by Sarah Crease, circa 1860.
See previous page.

respected the decisions of the Chief Factor. To super-impose the institutions of self-government on a society organized as a hierarchy would be a mighty task.

Before a year passed, Blanshard had had enough: lacking money to work with, an office to work in and a salary to live on, he resigned. Douglas was appointed governor in his place. With the aid of several members of a legislative council, most of whom were HBC members, he undertook his duties as leader of the infant colony. Given his personality, that meant a benevolent but businesslike despotism.

Douglas ruled a tiny domain centred on Fort Victoria, whose cedar stockade towered above a cluster of cabins and a few stone houses occupied by families raising crops, cattle and poultry. There was a church and several schools, but no streets, and everybody had to wear sea boots to get around in the ever-present muck and mire. Nearby was a busy sawmill, already sending shipments of lumber to San Francisco. The only other activities were fur trading and some coal mining at Fort Rupert and Nanaimo, to supply fuel to HBC vessels servicing the coastal forts on the mainland and the depot at Fort Langley. Elsewhere in the island colony lived several thousand Indians who, Douglas reported to his political masters in London, were left "in the possession of their village sites and enclosed fields . . . and . . . were at liberty to hunt over the unoccupied lands, and to carry on their fisheries with the same freedom as when they were the sole occupants of the country." The few new settlers who arrived from time to time and who needed land obtained it only after Douglas had negotiated a land-transfer treaty with its Indian owners.

The government of Vancouver Island soon acquired some money to operate with, because Douglas persuaded his council to levy a tax on the import and sale of liquor. He justified this action to the Colonial Office by deploring that "Drunkenness is now the crying and prevalent sin of this colony and will, I fear, continue to be so, until a better and more responsible class of people are sent to this country, or a great improvement takes place in the moral tone of the present population." The first thing the governor did with the money was to build a gaol and establish a police force of "four active men." The tax was used to build roads and bridges, but Douglas also had the great satisfaction of having storehouses constructed at nearby Esquimalt, which he hoped would become a regular Pacific base for British warships and thus a source of protection for the HBC.

Every day, the HBC officers and clerks at Fort Victoria dined in the mess hall in the comfort of a spacious room with a large open fireplace and at a table with snow-white linen and solid silver cutlery. According to his son-in-law, Dr. John S. Helmcken, "Mr. Douglas came primed with some intellectual or scientific subject, and thus he educated his clerks." One evening in 1857, however, the chief factor and governor casually produced a few grains of gold that had been brought to him from the North Thompson River, a tributary of the Fraser. Helmcken noted that his father-in-law attached great importance to the discovery and was convinced it indicated "a great change and a busy time."

When news of the finding of the precious metal north of the border filtered down to the California gold fields, the trickle of immigrants quickly became a steady stream — and then a flood. At Fort Victoria at midday on 25 April 1858, families walking out from the morning service at the church were astonished to see a shipload of would-be gold miners disembarking in the harbour. Of the several hundred men who invaded Victoria that day looking for provisions, tools and boats to take them to the mainland, only sixty were British subjects: the rest were mostly American with some Germans, Frenchmen and Italians. Every week thereafter, more men arrived on their way to the gold fields of the mainland. By May, Douglas was reporting an alarming situation to Her Majesty's government.

Boats, canoes, and every species of small craft are continually employed in pouring their cargoes into Fraser's River, and it is supposed that not less than one thousand whites are already at work, and on the way to the gold districts.

Many accidents have happened in the dangerous rapids of that river; a great number of canoes have been dashed to pieces, and their cargoes swept away by the impetuous streams, while of the ill-fated adventurers who accompanied them, many have been swept into eternity.

The others, nothing daunted by the spectacle of ruin, and buoyed up by the hope of amassing wealth, keep pressing onwards . . .

On upriver they went, past Fort Langley to Fort Hope and then Fort Yale, finding gold in the shifting sandbars of the Fraser.

Douglas was doubly alarmed, for he could never forget that the arrival of numbers of Americans in the Columbia District had enabled the United States to push the HBC back beyond the 49th parallel. The latest newcomers, he warned London, would always be "hankering in their minds after annexation to the United States . . . they will never cordially submit to English rule, nor possess the loyal feelings of British subjects." Yet it was impossible to halt the immigrants by using HBC vessels to keep them out of the Fraser River: travelling overland from California, they would simply "force a passage into the Gold District by way of the Columbia River" —as some were already doing. Victoria itself was being transformed by "foreigners" and their money from a peaceful agricultural village into a busy commercial town with its own newspaper, freight companies and stores, which competed with the HBC. Even outlying land at Saanich and Cowichan was being bought by American settlers, eager to cash in on the need of thousands of miners for fresh farm produce.

Four months and 9600 kilometres from advice and help, Douglas was very much "the man on the spot." Characteristically, he decided that it was better to do something, however incorrect in London's eyes, than do nothing. Delay, he knew, would be as fatal as inaction.

Douglas had already announced that all gold in the Fraser and Thompson river districts belonged to the British Crown and that miners must obtain $5.00 licences at Victoria "to dig or disturb the soil in search of gold." Now, His Excellency, the Governor and Commander-in-Chief of the Colony of Vancouver's Island and Dependencies, and Vice-Admiral of the same, issued a stern proclamation. He forbade foreign vessels to enter the Fraser River to trade and threatened seizure if their captains lacked a trading licence from the HBC, plus a certificate of clearance from the Customs Office in Victoria. To back his threat, he called on a visiting vessel of the Royal Navy for assistance, and HMS *Satellite* was stationed at the mouth of the Fraser to check all incoming shipping. Next, Douglas offered a franchise to an American steamship company to carry miners and supplies between Victoria and the rapids of the Fraser some two hundred kilometres upstream—provided that its ships carried none but HBC goods and none but persons licensed by the government of Vancouver Island to mine gold. Then His Excellency set off in the HBC vessel *Otter* on a tour of the gold diggings.

Douglas had promised a group of miners in Victoria that "the law of the land will do its work without fear and without favour," and he was as good as his word. He seized from some gold seekers a quantity of goods that they had smuggled in to avoid buying supplies from the HBC. Finding several miners without a licence, he promptly charged them $5.00 each before letting them go on their way. And he discovered that the diggings were indeed rich in gold: one group of men was panning $50 a day, and there were reliable reports of even richer deposits farther upriver. It gradually dawned on Douglas that the Fraser and its many tributaries were, as he later informed London, "one continued bed of gold of incalculable value and extent."

The trader-governor continued to act on his own initiative. Ignoring the fact that his responsibility for the mainland was only in his capacity as the chief factor in charge of HBC affairs, he began to set up the machinery of official government.

First, Douglas appointed a revenue officer at Fort Yale to check that all gold mining in the vicinity was being done under licence. Then, at various places, Douglas deputed justices of the peace to attend to any Indian complaints about sudden invasions of their tribal territories; he persuaded several Indians to act as magistrates "to bring forward, when required, any man of their several tribes who may be charged with offences against the laws of the country." Next, he appointed an assistant commissioner of crown lands to oversee the proper sale and transfer of ownership of tracts of territory. Finally, in the area of the main diggings, Douglas established a police force of "six men; namely, a serjeant at a dollar and a half, and the remainder at one dollar per diem each, with rations . . . and with clothing." Their duties included "taking especial care that drinking and gambling and other disorders are as much as possible put down."

Douglas even organized a temporary highways department. He persuaded five hundred miners to deposit $25.00 each with the HBC as a guarantee that they would construct — without pay — a road to avoid a particularly vicious section of Fraser River rapids. By the time the Harrison-Lillooet Trail had been built, albeit it was little more than a pathway for pack horses and mules, the men got back their deposit — not in money, but in HBC goods! Finished that same year, this rough-and-ready roadway was the first start on opening up the vast region that was soon to become another British colony.

London was not pleased by the proclamation of 1858, and the British colonial secretary disallowed it in no uncertain terms.

The Hudson's Bay Company have hitherto had an exclusive right to trade with Indians in the Fraser's River Territory, but they have had no other right whatever. They have no right to exclude strangers. They have had no rights of Government, or of occupation of the soil. They have had no right to prevent or interfere with any kind of trading, except with Indians alone. . . . Her Majesty's Government have determined on revoking the Company's licence (which would itself have expired next May) as regards British Columbia . . . whenever a new Colony is constituted . . .

The reprimand, however, was not really directed at Douglas: it was, at long last, official admission that he could no longer be expected to serve two employers. Shortly after the arrival of this rap on the knuckles, a confidential letter came from the colonial secretary stating that the new colony of "British Columbia" was to be established. If Douglas wanted, he would be appointed its first governor — provided he resigned from the Company. However, London well knew the worth of its "man on the spot" and his sense of duty to his Queen and country: his commission as governor was sent before his written acceptance had arrived at the Colonial Office.

Once again, a double burden was placed on

Matthew Baillie Begbie (1819-1894) was not, as reputed, severe in all his judgements. There are recorded instances of his compassion and understanding of the human condition.

the shoulders of James Douglas. In 1851, he had been entrusted with the governorship of Vancouver Island in addition to his HBC duties as the senior official west of the Rocky Mountains. Now, in 1858, after resigning from the HBC, he was governor of both Vancouver Island and the new mainland colony of British Columbia.

*

Douglas soon had to handle the complications of a *second* stampede for gold. And the extent of this one took everybody by surprise.

By the summer of 1859, all of the soft, heavy, yellow metal seemed to have been taken from the Fraser. The higher up the river miners went, the poorer their findings. The sudden inflow of adventurers to Langley, Yale and Hope gradually became a steady outflow, and Victoria merchants found themselves idling in the doorways of their stores and gazing at near-empty streets. Or they sold their businesses and joined the crowds heading back to San Francisco. But in the fall of 1859, four determined prospectors began exploring the Quesnel River country east of the Fraser. (The first great river Simon Fraser had noted flowing in from his left he had named for his trusted Nor'Wester associate, Jules Quesnel.) They reached Quesnel Lake, investigated the creeks emptying into it — and hit pay dirt. Sometimes they panned as much as $200 worth of gold a day.

This news raced down the Fraser, and hundreds of men struggled up to Quesnel Lake before winter set in. As on the lower Fraser, the streams were quickly cleaned out, but, the very next spring, at nearby Cariboo Lake, another group of prospectors found nuggets of gold by the panful. The first of the famous "big pay streams" of the Cariboo had been located. By the summer of 1861, $2,500,000 worth of gold had been found in the Cariboo country. To add to the

Sluicing for pay dirt. The sluice box was lined with corduroy or some such ridged material, to which gold stuck as water drained through the box.

A cattle drive through downtown Barkerville, B.C. In 1868 the town was destroyed by fire, supposedly started by a drunken miner upsetting a stove while chasing a dance-hall girl.

excitement, gold was soon found on the Kootenay River in the southwest corner of the mainland colony.

Word of these incredible riches brought the adventurous from as far away as Europe and China. Once again, Victoria was crowded by thousands of would-be millionaires in search of provisions, and long lines of men and animals backpacked north along the Harrison-Lillooet Trail alongside the Fraser or eastward over the Dewdney Trail into the Kootenay country. The gold rush magically stimulated the economy. Imports of flour dropped as local supplies of wheat increased. Coal production was stepped up to meet the demands of merchant shipping. Towns like Yale and Kamloops sprang up along interior transportation routes.

This time, Governor Douglas realized he had much more than a gold rush on his hands. This time, he knew he was witnessing the start of settlement, which needed, above all, law and order. By chance, the Colonial Office in London had appointed two exceptional men to help Douglas achieve such a task.

British Columbia's chief law official, the large-framed and fierce-eyed Matthew Baillie Begbie, was accurately characterized by a miner as "the biggest man, the smartest man, the best-looking man, and the damnest man that ever came over the Cariboo Road." A failed London lawyer, Begbie welcomed the opportunity to become a wilderness jurist. Like Douglas, he had a stern sense of duty and a deep desire to build a second Britain on the shores of the Pacific.

He shared with the Governor a passionate love for the new country, for the mountains and the sombre forests, the undulating grasslands of the Interior, and the gentle uplands, the oak thickets and the rocky headlands of southern Vancouver Island. For the welfare of the native Indian, each had a sensitive regard; for the American character and the American political tradition, neither had great respect.

Begbie's guiding principle, as someone once described it, was that "in the Queen's dominions, an infringement of the law was really a serious matter, and not a sort of half joke as in California." He never held court without wearing his judicial wig and robes, whether he was in a formal courtroom, or a makeshift one held in a saloon, a barn, a miner's cabin or in the open air — sometimes astride his horse. He made many a long circuit of the mining camps, handing out justice to the unlawful and, at times, stern advice to prisoner and jury alike. On one occasion, after a not guilty verdict with which he disagreed, Begbie told the accused, "Go, and sin no more." Begbie was a believer in law and order off duty, too. He once knocked out a saloon rowdy with a single punch.

Begbie has been dubbed the "Hanging Judge" and described as single-handedly upholding the law among thousands of desperadoes. Neither description is accurate. He did condemn men to death, but, in several such instances, sent Douglas a letter recommending that the sentence of death be amended to a prison term. And, of course, Begbie was but the vivid personification of the law at work in British Columbia.

Chartres Brew, a gold commissioner and the colony's first chief inspector of police, arrived from Britain to organize a small force of constables in the mining areas. These men, some the adventurous younger sons of well-to-do English or Irish families, served bravely and well; for £25 a month, they often risked a broken head or limb to maintain order among hordes of men bent on making a fortune any way they could.

Begbie also had the support of county court magistrates and the gold commissioners. The

The Cariboo Road – 1862 by Rex Woods. Col. Richard
Moody's Royal Engineers constructing the Cariboo
Road through the Fraser Canyon.

latter were particularly hardworked: not only did they settle disputes over mining claims but each acted as a justice of the peace, a commissioner of land, a collector of revenue, an Indian agent and a coroner. One of them is said to have kept his area peaceful by announcing, on the very day of his arrival there, "Now, boys, there must be no shootin', for if there is shootin' there will surely be hangin'!"

Douglas's other senior official was Col. Richard Clement Moody. Commander of a small force of Royal Engineers, he was also chief commissioner of lands and works and lieutenant-governor of British Columbia. Moody had a very good opinion of himself, but he also had guts.

Shortly after arriving in Victoria, Moody set off with Begbie on a tour of inspection of the mainland colony. On their way up the Fraser, Douglas sent word that an American roughneck, Ned McGowan, had taken over the community of Hill's Bar, near Fort Yale. Moody headed straight for Hill's Bar, to be met at the dock by a short-tempered group of miners wielding revolvers. Ordering his engineers and the judge to stay aboard ship, the colonel disembarked and walked – unarmed – towards the miners. In Moody's words, these "manly, energetic fellows" responded with "a salute, firing off their loaded revolvers over my head. If it was to try my nerves, they must have forgotten my profession." He promptly took off his hat and "thanked them in the Queen's name for their loyal reception." Baffled by Moody's coolness, McGowan surrendered, was tried by Begbie, and received a severe lecture on the difference between right and wrong – and a heavy fine.

Moody and his Royal Engineers made several vital contributions to the growth of the new colony. They surveyed and laid out the townsites of New Westminster (the capital), Lytton, Lillooet, Clinton, Quesnel and Richfield, built or improved several wagon roads, and constructed many bridges. Their finest achievement, however, was the creation of a road that ran the 640 kilometres between Yale, the head of navigation on the Fraser, and Barkerville, the unofficial capital of the Cariboo gold fields.

The Great North Road or Cariboo Trail was a magnificent feat of engineering. (As usual, Governor Douglas lacked both authority and money. So he borrowed the necessary funds from banks in Victoria and informed a stunned Colonial Office at a later date.) Constructed partly by civilian contractors and partly by Moody's Royal Engineers, this "golden road to Cariboo" hung from the face of sheer precipices and soared over deep chasms. In some places, the roadbed had to be blasted out of solid rock: in others, it reared up from the river's edge in monstrous structures of timber packed with rock ballast. Once beyond the worst canyons of the Fraser, still other obstacles had to be overcome. As one of Moody's officers reported, "It is difficult to find language to express in adequate terms the utter vileness of the trails of Cariboo — slippery, precipitous ascents and descents, fallen logs, over-hanging branches, roots, rocks, swamps, turbid pools and miles of deep mud."

When the gold of the Cariboo was finally gone, the highway served Douglas's ultimate purpose: the means by which families could enter the farming and grazing lands of the interior plateaus and give the colony a solid backbone of settlement.

*

One year before the completion of the Cariboo Trail in 1865, Douglas retired from public life. The citizens of Victoria and New Westminster held banquets in honour of Sir James and Lady Douglas (he had just been knighted by a grateful Queen Victoria). Now that Douglas was about to

This scene looks like a still from a western movie but was photographed on a stretch of the Cariboo Road in the semiarid central interior of B.C.

F. J. Barnard started his business by backpacking mail
to and from Barkerville. By 1862, he controlled most
of the Cariboo freight and passenger service.

give up the responsibility of ruling two colonies, people were prepared to admit that "he was not a bad governor after all." There was, in fact, a sudden reappraisal of "Old Squaretoes," as a number of young civil servants in Victoria called him behind his back.

The nickname was not entirely undeserved and explains a great deal about the man. Having spent his adolescent and early adult years in an occupation that condemned any display of indecision or weakness, he had learned to be cool and calm at all times, in all situations, even social ones. Married to a woman of Indian ancestry, he had steeled himself to endure slights and sneers directed at his beloved wife. Then, quite unexpectedly, he found himself ordered to act both as an HBC executive and his nation's representative, to perform the delicate balancing act of loyalty to the Company and loyalty to the Queen. In addition, he had had to cope with a rising tide of democratic feeling, for which he had neither liking nor sympathy. It was his belief that "people do not naturally take much interest in affairs of Government as long as affairs go on well and properously, and are content to leave questions of state to their ruling classes." He was completely opposed to the idea of people having a say in government by electing someone to represent their views and opinions as to how they, the people, should be governed. In fact, just as he raised his large family using loving but stern rules, so he dealt with his colonists.

Douglas did much more than establish the British tradition of law and order. He gave Britain a firm foothold on the Pacific Coast at a time when the United States seemed destined to take over much of western North America. And also did the same thing for the Canada-to-be. Like the ancient, fur-trade artery of the St. Lawrence in the east, the gold-rich artery of the Fraser had nourished Canadian settlement. Both river systems had given the future nation a solid territorial claim at each end of the continent.

Metis hunter-traders in the early 1870s, when it was
still possible to make a living by selling buffalo meat,
marrow and hides to eager American buyers.

6 The First Prairie Province

The surprising thing about the development of the Red River settlement was its transformation from a colony of European immigrants into a centre inhabited mainly by people of mixed Indian and European ancestry. By 1870, the population of the settlement amounted to some 5000 French Metis, 4000 English and Scots Metis, 1500 British and American immigrants, and 600 Indians. The French-speaking Metis were mainly nomadic hunters, or guides and canoemen for the Hudson's Bay Company, whereas English-speaking Metis were more often farmers, storekeepers, traders and, in some instances, lawyers and doctors. Roughly half of population was Catholic, half Protestant.

The British settlers lived mostly north of the Forks [the junction of the Red and Assiniboine rivers], the French mostly south. This linear development of the settlement necessitated a rather astonishing number of churches. Ten Anglican . . . churches were strung out along the upper Red and the north side of the Assiniboine, with three Presbyterian churches among them. The Presbyterians and the Methodists also had "preaching stations" spotted westwards to Portage la Prairie. The Roman Catholics were served by seven churches along the lower Red and the south bank of the Assiniboine. The Church of England parishes each contained at least one small day school; the Catholics had a sizeable school, an orphanage and a convent in St. Boniface. . . . it should be added here that two bishops reigned in Red River: the Anglican Bishop of Rupert's Land, who governed the missionaries scattered across the emptiness . . . and the Catholic bishop of St. Boniface, who oversaw the same immense diocese.

This radical change stemmed from the union of the two fur-trading organizations in 1821. The North West and Hudson's Bay companies had dotted the west with trading posts, many of which faced each other across a short stretch of water or stood side-by-side in immediate rivalry. After the merger such coverage was senseless, and many posts were closed down. As a result, several hundred men suddenly found themselves without employment, while others were discharged year by year because of Governor George Simpson's zealous "oeconomy" in managing HBC affairs. Many of these traders, canoemen, storekeepers and labourers were transported to Red River at Company expense to "maintain themselves and be civilized." Simpson's remark is easily explained; it had been a condition of Selkirk's grant that one tenth of Assiniboia should be set apart "to the use of such person and persons being or having been in the service or employ of the . . . Company for a term not less than three years." These newcomers doubly swelled the population because they were, of course, married to Indian or to mixed-blood women. Similarly, those chief factors and chief traders of the Company who built homes for their retirement years in the Red River parishes of St. Andrew, St. James and St. John had also contracted, in the words of James Douglas, "tender ties" with mixed-blood women.

Simpson's approval of ex-Company settlers and the Kildonan Scots — "steady . . . and consider Red River as much their home as the land of their nativity" — was one thing; his opinion of freemen and Metis was notably otherwise. He warned the governor and committee in London that:

The freemen and half-breed population is now growing very formidable in . . . numbers . . . the produce of their hunts, Buffalo meat, has hitherto met a ready sale in the colony, but . . . the stock of domestic cattle will render the inhabitants perfectly independent of the plain; these people will then. . . . be the greatest danger the colony has to fear. . . . They possess all the savage ferocity of the Indians with all the cunning and knowledge of the whites.

This is Simpson at his most cynical and, in this particular instance, at his most erroneous.

Far from being "the greatest danger," the Metis became a shield — notably under the leadership of Cuthbert Grant — against bands of marauding Sioux, and were the suppliers of meat and pemmican in lean seasons. Far from being ferocious and cunning, they were a generous-hearted, peaceable people, whose lives were greatly influenced by Roman Catholic missionaries. Indeed, the arrival of fathers Joseph-Norbert Provencher and Severe-Joseph-Nicholas Dumoulin in 1818 did much to persuade many Metis to make the settlement their home. Some became typical river-lot farmers; others built houses for their families, though they themselves were often away trapping or working on northern waters as HBC guides and boatmen.

In time, the once-roving Metis formed more or less permanent riverside communities all the way from Pembina to St. Boniface at the junction of the Red and Assiniboine rivers, and west on the Assiniboine as far as Portage la Prairie. These communities eventually became the parishes of St. Vital, St. Norbert and St. Agathe.

The real reason for Simpson's disapproval of the French-speaking Metis was his recognition of them as the major element in Red River society that resisted his manipulation and control. They lived a life neither civilized nor savage and had no intention of knuckling under to his personal regulation of Assiniboia. They were relatively unaffected by the price of land as dictated by Simpson because they were not as interested in farming as other settlers. They were not captive customers of the company-store situation because their still nomadic life style took them over the border into the United States where they traded or sold hides and pemmican. In fact, as surpluses in the agricultural and buffalo harvests of Assiniboia became more than the HBC could absorb, these particular Metis succeeded in forcing Simpson to recognize free trade — and also their right of representation on the Council of Assiniboia, Red River's appointed form of government.

*

The darkish skins and jet black hair of the Metis were the only visible signs of their Indian ancestry. A British aristocrat who lived among the Metis in the course of a big-game hunting expedition on the prairies doubted "if a half-breed, dressed and educated like an Englishman, would seem at all remarkable in London society." He also noted that "in all respects they are not more uneducated, immoral, or disorderly, than many communities in the Old World." Of their physical appearance, he wrote: "they are a fine race, tall, straight, and well-proportioned, lightly formed but strong and extremely active and enduring. Their chests, shoulders, and waists are of that symmetrical shape so seldom found among the broad-waisted, short-necked English, or the flat-chested, long-necked Scotch."

According to the settlement's earliest historian, Alexander Ross, the Metis "cherish freedom as they cherish life." Nonetheless, they did submit themselves to a form of self-government: the buffalo hunt. For many years, the rendezvous for the start of the summer and fall hunts was the village of Pembina, where the Metis of Red River joined up with their brethren, the Metis of Dakota. Here, the hunters elected ten captains of the hunt, one of whom was named "the great war chief or head of the camp; and on all public occasions he occupied the place of president." Also in attendance was a priest, for the Metis were a religious people and very devoted in their worship. A hunter would always reserve the best cut of meat for his priest, just as a woman would keep aside as a church offering a particularly fine piece of cloth obtained in trading.

By the time of the great hunt of 1840, the war chief was responsible for the well-being of a mobile community composed, Ross says, of 620 hunters, 650 women, 360 boys and girls, 403 hunting horses, 1210 Red River carts drawn by draft horses or oxen, and several hundred dogs. It was also a community armed to meet both buffalo and the ever-hostile Sioux, with 740 muskets and several hundred knives and axes.

The war chief delegated authority, first to his captains, each of whom had ten soldiers under his orders. Then he appointed ten guides, each of whom took his turn as the scouting leader of the expedition for a day. "Captains are subject to him," Ross remarks, "and the soldiers of the day are his messengers: he commands all." Upon the signal to camp, "the captains' and soldiers' duties commence. They point out the order of the camp, and every cart, as it arrives, moves to its appointed place."

Ross, who spent many years working for the rigidly stratified, rank-conscious Hudson's Bay Company, was astonished by the individualistic, independent-minded Metis, who nonetheless formed an orderly, supportive society. An excellent example was the "free runs" made through a herd by hunters for the benefit of needy families with no man to secure meat, fat and hides for them.

Ross also noted something else that explained an important aspect of the Metis personality. At the end of the day, the captains and elders usually got together outside the ring of Red River carts that surrounded the encampment Sitting there on the prairie, each with a gun in his lap — in case any Sioux unexpectedly happened by — they puffed at their pipes and discussed the events of the day's march or the hunt, if they had been lucky enough to find a herd. Listening to their talk, Ross found that the Metis detested "all the laws and restraints of civilized life, believing all men were born to be free. . . . Feeling their strength, from being constantly armed, and free from control . . . they are marvellously tenacious of their own original habits." A frontier society, why would they be anything else? Just like their Indian kin, they believed in a simple, direct form of government in which the power and authority of a chief lasted only as long as his followers respected his decisions.

But the most significant feature about the Metis was their conception of themselves. The community discipline of the buffalo hunt and their skill in checking and defeating Sioux raids gave them a strong sense of identity, a belief that they were a new nation. When the crisis of 1869-70 came, most Metis stuck by each other. And it is interesting to note that many mixed-bloods of Scots or English origin, though Protestant in outlook and behaviour, rallied behind their Roman Catholic brethren.

*

For several decades the inhabitants of Red River had little contact with the rest of North America. Hundreds of kilometres of prairie separated them from an American frontier advancing in the south; thousands of kilometres of prairie and many mountain ranges lay between them and the Pacific colony of British Columbia; and the granite-and-timber wilderness of the Canadian Shield prevented easy communication with the British colonies in the east. Their only connections with the outside world were the HBC supply line that led to and from Hudson Bay in the north, and Red River cart trails that meandered south into the Minnesota Territory of the United States. Here, in the city of St. Paul, Metis regularly exchanged buffalo robes, furs, pemmican, cattle and horses for cotton goods, groceries, ammunition and tobacco.

The HBC's Pembina post, next to the international boundary. Metis cartloads of pelts were not sold here: the hides fetched higher prices in neighbouring Minnesota.

Red River carts used no axle grease, because prairie dust would have made it an abrasive mud. The result was a high-decibel wailing of wood on wood.

TO RED RIVER & BEYOND.

113

In fact, the St. Paul-Pembina-Red River trail became a well-worn route to and from Rupert's Land. Along it passed many travellers: wealthy English noblemen in search of sport and adventure; French-Canadian nuns and priests stationed at Red River or farther west in Metis settlements springing up in the valley of the South Saskatchewan River; British scientists eager to observe an eclipse, plot the magnetic north, or chart the barren lands of the Arctic. Even most HBC merchandise was eventually freighted over this winding trail to points where steamboats and railroads connected with the Atlantic Ocean: the delicate balance between costs and profits obliged even Governor Simpson to overcome his deep distaste and distrust of everything American and use this easier, cheaper route to import supplies from Britain.

American settlers, however, gradually began to occupy the upper Red River valley. Part of the ever-advancing western frontier of the United States was veering across the international boundary of the 49th parallel into Rupert's Land via the Red River valley, for the simple reason that there was nothing to stop this intrusion. There were no policemen to warn off the intruders, no garrisons of red-coated regulars to drive them back. Nor was the HBC a counterforce: its personnel were located in the fur-bearing forests of the north. British Columbia had been saved from American clutches, but the Oregon country had been lost to the United States by a steady infiltration of frontiersmen and farmers. Was Rupert's Land going to be taken over in similar fashion?

It was this casual but steady northwesterly drift of American settlement that alerted some Canadians to the value of the prairie interior, the more so as, in the East, there was a land problem. Along the lower Great Lakes and in the St. Lawrence valley, the best arable land had already been occupied; the sons of many farm families were leaving home to seek the more available, more fertile lands of the American west. Businessmen, too, showed a revived interest in Rupert's Land. They wanted a share of the fur trade, notably a group of Torontonians, who were characterized by a fiercely indignant George Simpson as politicians and adventurers inventing fanciful claims to the HBC's ancient fiefdom in order to gain their own "electioneering and commercial ends." And then there were the idealists (and the pragmatists) who dreamed of a Canada extending from sea to sea.

When a British parliamentary select committee was investigating the HBC's trade monopoly and the question of its renewal, Chief Justice "Sweet William" Draper, a one-time political ally of John A. Macdonald and the official Canadian observer at the committee's hearings, volunteered an opinion held by many of his contemporaries. "I hope you will not laugh at me as very visionary but I hope to see the time, or that my children may live to see the time, when there is a railway going across all that country and ending at the Pacific."

In 1857, this select committee recommended that the HBC's monopoly of trade be limited to northern regions where there was no likelihood of settlement. The committee also recommended that Canadians be allowed to acquire, in due course, the valleys of the Red and Saskatchewan rivers.

At the hearings it became apparent that neither Canadian nor British witnesses appearing before the select committee knew very much about Rupert's Land. As for HBC witnesses — notably Sir George Simpson himself — they seemed remarkably reluctant to share their considerable knowledge of the region. So, in 1857, a Canadian-sponsored expedition set out to discover more about the western interior, specifically the best route for both trade and immigration from Lake Superior to the Red River settlement and the nature of "the great tracts of cultivable land beyond them." This group was led by University of Toronto professor Henry Youle Hind, a youthful, English-born chemist and geologist, and Simon Dawson, a Scots-born civil engineer. That same year, a second expedition set out, a British-sponsored group led by sportsman and explorer Capt. John Palliser; it crisscrossed the prairies and roamed the Rocky Mountains in its efforts to report back to London on the possibility of agriculture, mining, settlement and transportation routes.

In the course of their travels, both expeditions received considerable help and hospitality from the HBC, which hoped that these explorers would point out the uselessness of opening up any communication between Lake Superior and Red River and the unsuitability of its territories to settlement. The Company attitude was that of its London governor, who huffed and puffed to a British official, "Let in all kinds of people to squat and settle, and frighten away the fur-bearing animals they don't hunt and kill! Impossible!"

The reports of Hind and Palliser, however, disappointed the HBC. According to Hind, an all-Canadian transportation route north of Superior, while not without such construction problems as raging rivers, rugged rocks and miles of muskeg, was a good deal shorter than any journey to Red River via the Minnesota Territory. In Palliser's opinion, a route around Superior would be extremely expensive to build, but he admitted that, without an all-Canadian connection, a political union of the eastern provinces and British settlements west of the Great Lakes would be impossible. Both expeditions noted clear evidence of threats to British sovereignty: American merchants in business in Red River; a steamboat service that connected St. Paul, Min-

nesota, with the settlement; and a prairie trail to the railhead at the American border town of St. Cloud, where Red River folk now did much of their shopping. As to whether land and climate would support extensive farming, both explorers agreed on two things. The well-watered valleys of the Red, Assiniboine and the North Saskatchewan formed a great corridor of potential settlement — plus a practicable railway route to the Rocky Mountains. This was, as Palliser termed it, a "Fertile Belt." To the south, in the southern portions of the future provinces of Saskatchewan and Alberta, there was, in his opinion, an "Arid Belt" (later known as Palliser's Triangle). At least it was semidesert to Palliser. Hind, the scientist, could see great possibilities if some of its rivers were dammed to feed irrigation works.

*

Although for years it had enjoyed a trade monopoly in Rupert's Land and in those territories west and north of Rupert's Land, the Hudson's Bay Company empire had already begun to disintegrate. In 1858, HBC mainland territory west of the Rocky Mountains had become the crown colony of British Columbia. That same year, the Company-controlled territory of Vancouver Island was added to British Columbia. In 1859, the HBC's official monopoly in those lands whose rivers drained down to the Arctic Ocean, and its licence to trade north of the 60th parallel, were not renewed by the British Parliament. After almost two centuries, the Company was right back where it had started — as "true and absolute Lordes and Proprietors" of Rupert's Land.

Within a decade, the Company's position worsened. In those years, it fought off attempts by the British government to make Rupert's Land a crown colony. The Company also stalled an attempt to hand over Rupert's Land to the four

The HBC depot of Old (Upper) Fort Garry stood in what is now downtown Winnipeg, almost on the site of the modern headquarters of the Company.

eastern provinces that had federated to form the Dominion of Canada. But the new nation was determined to possess the prairie west. The British North America Act of 1867 that created the Dominion included – at the insistence of John A. Macdonald, George Brown and their follow Confederationists – provisions for the annexation. To that end, in 1867, Ottawa began constructing the Dawson Road between Lake Superior and Red River – without advising either the HBC or the Council of Assiniboia.

The Hudson's Bay Company could delay, but not postpone, the inevitable. Early in 1869, after much argument, Canada and Britain agreed on the terms under which Rupert's Land, and what was called the North-Western Territory, would be purchased from the HBC. It wanted one million pound sterling in bonds, but had to settle for £300 000 in hard money and one-twentieth of the Fertile Belt, together with specified blocks of land adjoining HBC posts (all in all, about 452 000 hectares). However, the Comapny shrewdly insisted on receiving both land and mineral rights, which were to give it a new lease on life in the form of department stores, the real-estate business and, ultimately, the mining of oil and gas.

The date of transfer of ownership was set for 1 December 1869, in the hope that by that date the British Parliament would have approved the transfer and made it legal. In Ottawa that summer, Prime Minister Macdonald had much satisfaction in telling an old political colleague that Canada had "annexed all the country between here and the Rocky Mountains." He was referring to what many of his fellow Canadians called the North West, a wilderness empire almost as large as the United States. Early in 1869, however, the normally astute Macdonald completely misread his political situation. The problem seemed to be the strong separatist feeling

resurfacing in Nova Scotia, but his real troubles were in Red River.

In the course of the transfer negotiations, nobody in London or Ottawa had bothered to consult the HBC's senior personnel in Rupert's Land – or its residents. Despite warnings from the West, nobody in Ottawa was in the least concerned about any trouble that this might create. On his way to Rome, Bishop Alexandre-Antonin Taché of St. Boniface had stopped off in Ottawa to warn Sir George Etienne Cartier, Macdonald's long-time Québécois partner, of the considerable unrest over the transfer. Cartier replied that he knew more about the situation than the bishop and did not want any information. Robert Machray, the Anglican bishop of Rupert's Land, and William Mactavish, the HBC governor of Assiniboia, both went to Ottawa to advise the cabinet of impending trouble. Mactavish later told Taché, "I have just returned from Ottawa, and although I have been forty years in the country, and governor for fifteen years, I have not been able to cause any of my recommendations to be accepted by the government. These gentlemen are of the opinion that they know a great deal more about this country than we do."

Thus, for some residents of Rupert's Land, the first indication of the impending transfer of authority was the abrupt appearance in the Red River valley in August 1869 of Canadian surveyors.

This was a mistake twice over. First, Canada had no legal right to make surveys before the transfer of ownership had taken place. Second, the Macdonald government had ordered the use of an American survey system that divided land into one-mile-square townships of sixty-four sections. This system, which cut across the long, ribbonlike farms fronting on the Red and Assiniboine rivers, took no account of a basic factor of

Interior of Fort Garry by H. A. Strong. When Upper Fort Garry was badly damaged by the Red River flood of 1826, the new depot of Lower Fort Garry was built twenty kilometres downstream.

life on the semiarid prairies: water. The American rectangular township had originated in moist regions, where distance from a river did not matter; but, in Assiniboia, without access to running water, no one could raise cattle or grow grains or vegetables.

On 11 October 1869, a team of surveyors had worked its way north from Pembina and finally reached the Red River settlement. These men started making their calculations on the land to the rear of the river-lot farms in a heavily settled Metis section. A few of its inhabitants, led by a pale-skinned, dark-haired young man, approached the survey team. He stopped its work by placing a moccasined foot on the survey chain and declaring that the surrounding territory belonged to the people of Red River, not the people of Canada. As he was to say on many later occasions, "the Canadian government has no right to make surveys . . . without the express permission of the people of the Settlement." The name of the young man was Louis Riel.

*

Surveyors from Canada were just one warning of change. There had been others.

Ten years before, two ambitious young newspapermen, William Buckingham and William Coldwell, had arrived in Red River. Former employees of George Brown, the editor-owner of the Toronto *Globe*, they shared Brown's dream that "Providence has entrusted to us the building of a great northern people." They had brought a printing press with them to publish their own newspaper, the *Nor'Wester*. Supposedly serving the "rapidly growing interests" of the Red River country, one of its favourite editorials was a demand for an end to HBC rule in Assiniboia and for union with Canada. Another was the imminent danger of the Americanization of Rupert's Land, a topic kept alive by regular reports of progress in the commercial expansion of neighbouring Minnesota.

From 1865 on, when the paper was owned by another Canadian, Dr. John Christian Schultz, the *Nor'Wester* became virulently antagonistic towards the Hudson's Bay Company. Schultz, who had earlier gained some success as a medical man, freemason, free trader and amateur scientist in the frontier society of Red River, was a highly partisan supporter of the Dominion's takeover of Rupert's Land. His propagandist editorials, widely reprinted in Canadian newspapers, gave readers the impression that the HBC was a cruel, oppressive overlord. Like his Canadian Party (formed by a group of immigrants from Ontario who would eventually dominate Manitoba politics), the *Nor'Wester* roused fear among the Metis with its obvious desire for immediate annexation to Canada.

As it was, the Metis had worries enough. Money for one. Buffalo robes and pemmican, sold at Red River to the HBC or to American merchants, had been a steady source of income, but were becoming harder to obtain. Each summer and fall hunters had to journey farther and farther out onto the prairies to find the great beasts. The herds were already dimishing in number, and there were years when none were to be found. It they died out, hunters would be unable to earn a living. Those Metis who traded furs were in much the same situation. The Lake Winnipeg region and the long valley of the North Saskatchewan River were just about trapped out. The fur trade in which they had long worked was now confined to regions hundreds of kilometres north of Red River.

Another Metis concern — a major one — was property ownership. Land had always been occupied by the first person who decided to inhabit a particular section of river front or a particular fishing spot. To those Metis busy with the hunt or freighting furs and goods for the HBC, home was only a place to rest from time to time. They built their shacks and cabins where they liked and, when the local fuel supply had been used up, moved somewhere else. To them, as to their Indian cousins, land was simply something to be used. Through their Indian blood, the Metis felt that they had the right to claim ownership of any piece of the prairies; but they began to wonder if they did have this right. The Canadian newcomers did not look at land in the same way. To them, land was something to be identified like a pack of furs or a bale of goods. They established ownership by dividing it up into clearly marked lots and then obtaining a legal paper that certified ownership. And the Canadian Party in Red River was loudly denying the right of the Metis — or anybody else without a clear title — to occupy land. Its members even scorned holdings that had been given by Selkirk himself or the few lots sold by the HBC.

As in the days of the Selkirk settlers, the same question was being asked again and again: "Are these outsiders coming to steal our homeland?" Louis Riel explained this fear in 1869 to the HBC's Council of Assiniboia, the only authoritative body in the Red River country. His people, he said, "were uneducated, and only half-civilized and feared that if a large immigration were to take place, they would probably be crowded out of a country which they claimed as their own." And, of course, the unannounced arrival of survey teams in the late summer of 1869 only increased suspicions aroused by *Nor'Wester* editorials. Other factors — ethnicity, language, religion and American attempts at intervention — complicated events, but, from the start, the Red River resistance to the takeover by Canada was centred on the issue of land ownership. It was motivation enough for Metis and other mixed-bloods to halt the takeover.

Macdonald's cabinet had prepared the way by issuing an *Act for the Temporary Government of Rupert's Land and the North-Western Territories when United with Canada*, which provided for a lieutenant-governor and a council of advisors, both to be appointed by Ottawa. But, politically, the next action was incredibly careless. Macdonald's choice of lieutenant-governor-designate was his minister of public works, William McDougall, the man responsible for the construction of the Dawson Road and the premature start of surveying in Rupert's Land. He was the worst possible appointee. The Canadians in Red River would welcome him as one of their own; the Metis would resist him as a notable annexationist member of Macdonald's cabinet.

Ottawa's initial western policy of blithely imposing a government on people who already had a form of self-rule was rejected politely but pointedly. When William McDougall arrived at the border village of Pembina with orders to effect the *anticipated* transfer of ownership, a Metis handed him a note, written in French, which read:

Sir,

The National Committee of the Metis of Red River orders Mr. William McDougall not to enter the Territory of the Northwest without special permission of this Committee.

By order of the President John Bruce.

Louis Riel, Secretary.

McDougall ignored the warning and journeyed to an HBC post on the north side of the border, where an armed patrol of Metis gave him until sundown to return to the United States. McDougall retreated to Pembina, cursing what he, and later many others, called "rebels." Without knowing it, he was including most of the English-speaking settlers, who had no reason to disagree with their French-speaking neighbours about the high-handed manner in which Ottawa was organizing their future.

The Red River Metis, under Louis Riel's leadership, have often been accused of organizing a rebellion, of offering armed resistance to the rightful owner of Rupert's Land. But the awkward question for seven months in 1869-70 was who *did* own Rupert's Land? The 1 December 1869 transfer of ownership needed the formal approval of the British government, an approval that was withheld until June 1870. Ottawa was quick to insist that the Hudson's Bay Company still owned it, and Macdonald refused to accept the transfer until law and order had been restored. For their part, the HBC governor and committee argued that Macdonald's government had at least some responsibility to deal with the "rebels." Yet the politicians in London were uncertain as to what to do about the whole situation, except to remind the HBC that it had been requested to maintain law and order until the takeover by Canada.

As matters turned out, Louis Riel answered the awkward question.

*

Louis Riel was born in 1844 in St. Boniface, in what is today part of metropolitan Winnipeg. Although he had only one-eighth Indian blood in his veins, he always thought of himself as a Metis and was proud of his heritage. Named after his farmer father, Louis was an intelligent, sensitive, religious boy who seemed likely to become a priest and was one of three Metis youngsters picked by Bishop Taché of St. Boniface to be educated in Quebec for the priesthood and then serve in the North-West as missionaries.

Riel spent ten years in Montreal and then returned to Red River but not as planned. A few months before graduation, something made him change his mind; he abandoned his studies and became a clerk in a law firm. A year later, he

On 4 March 1870, Thomas Scott was forced to kneel before a Metis firing squad. Only wounded by the first volley, he was finished off with a revolver shot.

left Montreal, driven out by the refusal of his fiancée's parents to permit their marriage. After a succession of casual jobs in the United States, he returned to his birthplace in 1868, lacking both money and a career. In the words of one of his biographers, "Louis Riel was home again. . . . He was almost twenty-four years of age, educated, imbued with a strong sense of pride in himself and in his own people, and unemployed. It was an explosive mixture."

The explosion was triggered by the transfer of Rupert's Land from the HBC to the Dominion of Canada. Riel did not begin the Red River resistance but quickly became the power behind it. The election of the National Committee of the Metis of Red River had been conducted along the lines of the buffalo hunt, and, officially, Riel was only the committee's secretary. In reality, he was the "great war chief" of the buffalo hunt whose orders had to be obeyed at all times.

While Schultz's *Nor'Wester* was issuing hysterical editorials about the need for "loyal" people to put down the "rebels," Riel was thinking about firepower. He knew that McDougall had three hundred rifles stored in a border warehouse, and that the HBC's Fort Garry depot contained several hundred more, plus several six-pounder cannon. Fort Garry was a prime problem because the members of the Canadian Party were McDougall supporters and might well commandeer its artillery on his behalf. So, on the same day that McDougall retreated to Pembina, Riel ordered his followers to take over the HBC depot to forestall Schultz and his fellow Canadians from starting a civil war. Then he had a barricade erected on the Pembina-Fort Garry trail so that Metis guards could check all goods and persons coming into Red River — in case McDougall tried to smuggle arms to his supporters in the settlement.

The struggle at Red River in 1869-70 is a

Copyrighted R.P. Meade

Red and Assiniboine Rivers, 1867 by Don Anderson.

story complicated by many personalities and events. However, it was basically a series of moves and countermoves by Riel and the Canadian Party to win the support of the settlement's inhabitants.

Riel's aim, from start to finish, was to have most of the settlers, Metis and non-Metis, support his efforts to negotiate with Ottawa the terms of the takeover. He knew that the only safeguard, particularly for his own people, was a set of agreements written into law by Ottawa and approved by London. In this he succeeded, though not without the help of two belated Macdonald emissaries. Chief Factor Donald Smith of the HBC convinced the inhabitants of Red River that they could send delegates to Ottawa "to give expression to their views, and to treat for the transfer of the territory to Canada." Bishop Taché, hastily recalled by the prime minister from a conference in Rome, reassured his flock that Ottawa intended "to grant the same free institutions which they themselves enjoy." With the approval of many settlers, Riel put together a list of rights, and early in 1870, delegates set off for Ottawa to present these to the Canadian government. In fact, these rights formed the basis for the creation of the Province of Manitoba. Riel, however, made a terrible blunder when he later allowed one member of the Canadian Party to be executed.

The chain of events that led to this execution started on 7 December 1869, when Schultz decided on a showdown with Riel. On the excuse that government stores in his possession required protection, he gathered forty-eight members of the Canadian Party at a warehouse and armed them. Riel reponded to this challenge by surrounding the warehouse with his men, pointing two cannon at it, and giving its occupants fifteen minutes to surrender. They did — and the doctor and his men were placed in cells at Fort

Garry. Also being held in the fort were several fellow Canadians taken prisoner earlier, one of whom was a young man called Thomas Scott.

Early in January, Scott and two companions escaped. Despite stormy, below-zero weather and huge snowdrifts, the trio succeeded in reaching Portage la Prairie, a Canadian settlement that was markedly anti-Metis. Here, Scott helped Maj. Charles Boulton, a member of one of the survey teams and a friend of Schultz, to round up a band of men to liberate Fort Garry. Their attack failed, and all were captured and held captive in the fort.

Thomas Scott was a labourer on the Dawson Road who had a reputation for violence and foul language. He showed a contempt for the Metis second only to that displayed by Schultz, and the humiliation of his second imprisonment only made him worse. He taunted his guards by screaming curses at them, their religion and their leader, and provoked Riel himself by mocking the provisional government he had organized in December to maintain law and order in the settlement. Scott was punished by being put in chains, but the curses and the insults continued. In the end, Riel's followers persuaded him to make an example of Scott. After the manner of the buffalo hunt, six captains and a president were chosen to form a court, with Riel acting as translator. Scott was tried on charges of having taken up arms against the provisional government and striking one of the captains of the guard. On the evening of 3 March 1870, he was found guilty by a decision of four to two and sentenced to death. The next morning, a dazed, disbelieving Thomas Scott was led outside the walls of the fort and shot by a firing squad.

Scott's offences did not merit the death penalty. But when a local resident, the Rev. George Young, pleaded with Riel several times to save Scott, Riel could not be persuaded. The reason, spoken in a sharp voice, was "We must make Canada respect us." Riel had convinced himself that, unless his government frightened all those against it into taking him and his aims seriously, the transfer of authority from the HBC to Canada could never be made in a manner fair to everyone affected by it. Later, Riel would beg for understanding. "If there was one single act of severity, one must not lose sight of the long course of moderate conduct which gives us the right to say that we sought to disarm, rather than fight, the lawless strangers who were making war against us."

He was both right and wrong. The surveyors had been allowed to carry on their work in the English-speaking parishes of Red River. Lieutenant-Governor McDougall had been warned to request the permission of its inhabitants before entering Rupert's Land. In the months during which they controlled Assiniboia, Riel and his Metis had arrested, instead of fighting, their opponents. Riel had even been persuaded to arrange a pardon for Major Boulton, the leader of his Portage la Prairie enemies, after a Metis court had found him guilty of treason against the provisional government. Thomas Scott, however, had been killed — and in cold blood.

Riel would never be forgiven for this execution in the fanatically Protestant province of Ontario, where Scott's brother and Schultz — who had managed to escape from Fort Garry — were loudly demanding vengeance. Religious hatred reached the boiling point when it was learned that Scott, a Protestant from Ontario, had been shot to death by Roman Catholics. A reward of $5000 was promptly offered for the capture of Riel. (It was one indication of the Ontario influence in the early affairs of Manitoba that Schultz lived to become lieutenant-governor of the province and give his official assent to legislation eliminating separate schools and the French language from the education system.)

By an odd coincidence, the day after the death of Scott, Ottawa decided to send a group of British and Canadian soldiers to restore order at Red River and placate Orange Ontario with a show of force. When they finally arrived at the settlement late in August, Fort Garry was deserted. The hunters were once again out on the prairies in search of buffalo, and Louis Riel had slipped away across the border to safety. He had been warned that at least two-thirds of the military expedition contained Ontario men, many of whom had enlisted with a desire to pay back the "French" for the death of Thomas Scott.

Meanwhile, the transfer of ownership of Rupert's Land had, at last, taken place. In June, the British government officially announced that both Rupert's Land and the North-Western Territory could become part of the Dominion of Canada.

On 15 July 1870, the "postage stamp province" of Manitoba, scarcely one-tenth its modern size, was officially born. The name Manitoba was derived from an Indian word for "water-prairie" or "prairie lake." Manitoba, however, also meant self-government and rights for the inhabitants of the former Assiniboia. They were guaranteed that existing land holdings in the province would be recognized and that a land grant of 240 acres (96 ha) would be made to each unmarried son or daughter in a Metis family. And Manitobans would have a say both in their own government and in that of Canada. They could elect members to their new legislative council and assembly, and elect four members to the Parliament of Canada. French, as well as English, was declared an official language, and separate schools were authorized for the education of the children of Roman Catholic parents. Unlike the eastern provinces, however,

Manitoba did not get control over the sale of its lands, which remained in Ottawa's possession "for the purposes of the Dominion," meaning railway building and land settlement. Macdonald made no secret of the fact that "the land could not be handed over . . . for the Pacific Railway must be built by means of the land through which it has to pass."

Upon learning that troops were advancing on Red River, Riel wisely took refuge in St. Joseph in the Dakota Territory. The militiamen from Ontario brawled with Metis in the streets and saloons of Red River, where fist fights and knife duels became commonplace. There were also murders and an attempted murder. Elzéar Goulet, a member of the court that had sentenced Scott, was stoned to death while trying to swim across the Red River to the safety of the St. Boniface side. François Guillemette, who had finished off the dying Scott with a pistol shot, was found dead on a stretch of prairie south of Red River. André Nault, who had given the signal to the firing squad, was pursued to Pembina, bayoneted, and left to bleed to death. (He survived his wounds.) A group of militiamen burst into Louis Riel's home, threatening the lives of his mother and sister in an attempt to discover his whereabouts. Metis women and girls were molested. But no one was ever punished, let alone brought into court, for these crimes.

In the very year in which Manitoba was created, a group of Canadians occupied a farming area staked out by Metis and defied them to take back their property. Then these Canadians named it the Boyne, for the battle in Ireland in 1690 by which Protestantism became the dominant religion in Great Britain. Only the intervention of Bishop Taché prevented a bloody fight — and these Metis never did regain that particular piece of land. The incident was a foretaste of what was in store for their people.

Ojibwa encamped at Lake Winnipeg in 1884.
Alongside the birchbark tepee is a dome-shaped
lodge of poles tied with basswood fibre.

7 "From Sea to Sea"

In 1870, the takeover of Rupert's Land and the North-Western Territory added about a quarter of North America to the Dominion of Canada. There was so much land that, as one prairie traveller discovered, he could wander 800 kilometres in a direct line and not meet a single human being. Government surveyors had years of work ahead of them. Millions of hectares would have to be surveyed, plotted and mapped. Some sections would be handed back to the Hudson's Bay Company as part of the purchase agreement; other even more enormous blocks of land would be granted to railway builders and sold to settlers. The Dominion was determined to live up to its motto of *A mari usque ad mare*.

Smarting from its experience with Riel and his Metis, the first thing Ottawa did was to deal with Indian ownership of the land.

In 1871, the lieutenant-governor of the newly created Province of Manitoba – who had also been made lieutenant-governor of the North-Western Territory – received blunt instructions from the Macdonald government to

turn your attention promptly to the condition of the country outside of the Province of Manitoba, on the North and West; and while assuring the Indians of your desire to establish friendly relations with them, you will ascertain and report to His Excellency [the Governor General of Canada] the course you may think the most advisable to pursue, whether by Treaty or otherwise, for the removal of any obstructions that might be presented to the flow of population into the fertile lands that lie between Manitoba and the Rocky Mountains.

Canadians have often criticized the American treatment of native peoples while lauding their own, yet the difference was only one of method, not of intent. In 1871, Washington stopped making treaties with Indians and used the U.S. army to grab territories from their original inhabitants. In Canada, between 1871 and 1877, seven agreements made with prairie tribes secured their hunting grounds, rivers and lakes in return for minor gifts of various kinds and the promise of modest annual payments of money. In the name of the monarch of Canada, Ottawa employed treaties in order, as the law puts it, to extinguish all rights to land ownership. Officials called commissioners travelled treaty regions by horse or canoe to meet Indian bands. With the aid of Metis interpreters, Mounted Police, missionaries and HBC officers, these commissioners explained Queen Victoria's need of land for farming, ranching, lumbering and transportation. The general native impression was that the Great White Mother was asking for two things: their loyalty and the use of large tracts of land. Puzzled though they were by the promise that they would be paid for both, Indians were more concerned about their rights to hunt, trap and fish. As a result, these were guaranteed. Payment, in money and in land in the form of reserves, sealed the transaction – at least in the minds of those government officials who drew up the treaties. Basically, the deal included the payment of $5.00 a year to every Indian man, woman and child, the grant of one square mile [2.6 km^2] per family of five, and the supply of twine for nets or ammunition for hunting.

So the "obstructions" to settlement on the prairies were relocated, and these lands exploited peacably. And not a little profitably. As for territories lying north of the prairies, which were unsuited to farming or ranching, treaties with Indian owners could wait; despite appeals from HBC officers and missionaries in times of want and famine, Ottawa ignored its many other Indian wards. In the years 1870-90, the government attitude was "no treaty, no help." As Macdonald noted in the margin of a letter sent in 1884 by the lieutenant-governor of the Territories to the Superintendent General of Indian

133

Treaty No. 7 by A. B. Stapleton. In 1877, the federal government made treaty with the Blackfoot, Blood, Peigan, Sarcee and Stoney tribes in what is now Alberta.

The Buckboard by John Innes.

A prairie encampment in 1887. The Red River carts indicate that some Metis were either travelling in company with these Indians or sharing the same campsite.

Affairs, "the making of a treaty may be postponed for some years, or until there is a likelihood of the country being requested for settlement purposes." However, between 1899 and 1921, two treaties were signed with northern Indians. In each case, there were money-making reasons for Ottawa to do something about establishing its ownership of land in the drainage basin of the Mackenzie River.

By 1899, the Klondike gold rush was in full swing. A spin-off activity was the invasion of the Lake Athabasca and Great Slave Lake regions by prospectors seeking gold and any other precious metals that could be found there, activities that produced frightening change. Mounted Police patrols into the Territories at this time reported a substantial traffic in illegal liquor, the widespread use of poisoned bait by Canadian trappers and hunters, and a blatant disregard for Indian territorial and property rights. In 1898, Winnipeg and Ottawa newspapers had reported that Indians encamped at Fort St. John, in northeastern British Columbia, refused to let miners — or the police — go farther north until a treaty had been signed. Their horses were being stolen, sled dogs were being shot, and bear traps were being destroyed. Thus, there was reason for government to step in, extinguish title to land, and enforce law and order. However, another underlying consideration influenced the treaty-making; overland routes to the Klondike gold fields had to be kept trouble-free. The Territory of the Yukon had just been created (in 1898), the Mounted Police had firm charge of the region, and gold was flowing south in gratifying quantities. Years later, confirmation came from David Laird, an Indian commissioner who had been working out of Winnipeg at the turn of the century. In a letter to the Indian Affairs Department, Laird explained that, during the treaty-making, boundary decisions had been made in order "to

Uniformed Indian schoolboys in Metlakatla, B.C., at the turn of the century, one example of Ottawa's policy of de-Indianizing: no native studies, no native teachers.

Fort Whoop-Up (flying the American flag) was the main whisky fort in Blackfoot territory. There were others in the foothills country of the Rocky Mountains. It was built near what is now Lethbridge, Alberta.

protect and control whites who were going into the country as traders, travellers to the Klondike, explorers and miners.''

Thus, in the summers of 1899 and 1900, the Dominion of Canada obtained another excellent bargain. It was made between Her Most Gracious Majesty the Queen and "the Cree, Beaver, Chipewyan, and other Indians, inhabitants of the territory within the limits hereinafter defined and described." In return for the ownership of their lands, they were guaranteed hunting, trapping, and fishing rights and annual payments of $25 to each chief, $15 to a headman, and $5 to every other Indian. There were also sundry handouts: silver medals, flags, a suit of clothing for chiefs and headmen, salaries for any schoolteachers appointed, axes, handsaws, various agricultural tools, animals and seed supplies.

The entire treaty-making process, which began in 1763, is suspect, because it was not treaty-making in the normal sense of the term. Treaty terms were imposed, not negotiated. Had Indians refused the terms, their land would have been taken from them. Yet, when they made their mark on a piece of paper, it is extremely doubtful that they understood they were literally handing over ancestral lands to others. To an Indian, the ownership of a dog, a sled, hunting equipment or cooking utensils is one thing, but the earth belongs to no one individual or group. A family, band or tribe might have long-established, clearly-recognized hunting and fishing rights in a particular territory, but the exclusive, personal possession of land is alien to native thought and experience. To them, land is a perpetual inheritance: everyone has the use of it. To them, no one has a right to destroy it and thus deny its benefits to successive generations.

It is this radical difference in outlook and way of life that is still at the root of conflicts between the native peoples and officialdom.

*

The Red River resistance of 1869-70 had clearly demonstrated that a few determined men could defy the authority of the Dominion of Canada. Since there was no system of law enforcement on the prairies, the West was liable to further disturbances. In the early 1870s, two investigations of life in the region warned federal authorities of impending trouble.

In 1871, Capt. William F. Butler of the British army spent a leave of absence exploring the prairies and noted that the buffalo, the Indians' chief source of food, was rapidly disappearing. He rode all the way from the Red River settlement to the Rocky Mountains without seeing a single buffalo. Hide hunters, armed with repeating rifles, were threatening to make the animal extinct. Butler also noted that there were no HBC posts between the international border and the North Saskatchewan River. As a result, American traders based in Montana were operating their own outlets north of the border and selling rotgut whisky to the Blackfoot, while other free traders were supplying whisky to Indians along the South Saskatchewan River. In 1872, Lt.-Col. Patrick Robertson-Ross reported that

at Fort Edmonton during the present summer whisky was openly sold to the Blackfoot and other Indians trading at the post by some smugglers from the United States who derive large profit thereby, and on these traders being remonstrated with by the gentleman in charge of the Hudson's Bay post, they coolly replied that they knew very well what they were doing was contrary to the law of both countries, but as there was no force to prevent them, *they would do just as they pleased.*

Butler, too, had observed that the Saskatchewan region was without law and order and that robbery and murder were not being punished. Both Butler and Robertson-Ross recommended the creation of a police force to deal with the lawlessness, but Prime Minister Macdonald resisted the suggestion. Ottawa was always short of money. And Macdonald well knew that Washington was spending about $20 million a year subduing Indians, a sum much greater than the annual Canadian federal budget. But the only West he wanted was a quiet one in which a transcontinental railway could be quickly constructed and in which immigrant settlers would be able to farm peacefully, so Macdonald was finally persuaded to create a federal constabulary.

In May 1873, Parliament passed "An act respecting the Administration of Justice, and for the establishment of a Police Force in the North West Territories" — the North-West Mounted Police (NWMP). (Later, the name was changed to Royal North-West Mounted Police, later still to Royal Canadian Mounted Police.) And the first place the Mounted Police headed for was the notorious Fort Whoop-Up, the main whisky fort of several maintained on Canadian territory by traders from Montana.

The reputation of the NWMP was not earned by pursuing criminals in the dramatic tradition of "They always get their man," nor, equally dramatically, by confronting and gentling the touchy-tempered Sioux who sought refuge in Canada from the "Long Knives," the United States cavalry. That reputation was earned in the course of all the unglamorous, day-to-day work. In villages, towns and construction camps, it was the prompt arrest of thousands of cases of assault and battery, theft, liquor smuggling, or plain "drunk and disorderly" that produced respect. On the open plains, it was the endless routine of patrol duty that produced admiration.

Patrols were of two kinds: regular and flying patrols. The former followed a fixed route at regular intervals. Constables on regular patrols carried a book that was signed by all settlers on their route and in which any complaints were recorded. Flying patrols were random in their timing and did not follow fixed routes. They were intended to plug gaps in the coverage and prevent lawbreakers from taking advantage of the predictability of the regular patrols.

Information gathered by the patrols was compiled into reports and forwarded to headquarters in Regina. This gave an immediate picture of conditions in the various districts of the Territories.

The reports noted the state of crops and livestock, weather conditions, cases of poverty and destitution, movements in and out of the area; in short, the general social and economic condition of the district. . . . Families in need of relief could be given a little money to tide them over or temporary work around the barracks. Neighborhood quarrels could be settled before they escalated into violence. New settlers could be given advice on local conditions, and dangerous rumors could be nipped in the bud.

The basic task of the NWMP was to occupy the prairie west until large numbers of settlers made it undeniably Canadian. This meant keeping the peace between settlers and Indians, work for which officers and men alike showed a remarkable aptitude. Blending firmness with good humour and patience, above all motivated by a sense of fair dealing, the Mounted Police lived by their motto, *Maintiens le droit* ("Uphold the Right"). Some settlers seemed to think that the only good Indian was a dead one. If a cow strayed, they immediately jumped to the conclusion that Indians had stolen it and had to be talked out of attacking the nearest native encampment. Others were made to understand that if Indians appeared on their farms and ranches, they had every right to do so: the treaties had given them unrestricted hunting privileges. As for occasional itinerant whisky traders, they were tracked down and arrested.

141

Crowfoot, a Blood Indian who became chief of the Blackfoot nation, was a statesman. During years of semistarvation and subjugation, he persuaded his people to accept the reserve as a way of life.

The Indian gratitude for this is recorded in the touching tribute paid by Chief Crowfoot of the Blackfoot: "If the Police had not come to this country, where would we all be now? Bad men and whisky were killing us so fast that very few of us would have been alive today. The Mounted Police have protected us as the feathers of the bird protect it from the frosts of winter."

Some years later, the Mounted Police showed a similar concern for the welfare of thousands of labourers constructing the Canadian Pacific Railway. Keeping them sober was a job in itself, since no liquor was supposed to be sold within ten miles (16 km) of the right of way. And constables often acted as mediators in labour disputes, persuading construction bosses to improve working and living conditions, or helping workers to secure overdue wages.

For many prairie residents, the Mounted Police were the only source of information about what was happening in the Territories, and the patrol system brought to isolated families a sense of security and a brief break in the loneliness of homesteading. Whether as uniformed members or as time-expired veterans who took up farming or ranching, they quickly established themselves as social leaders in the growing settlements.

*

By 1880, Indian treaties had made available millions of hectares of fertile land, and the Mounted Police were enforcing law and order from Winnipeg to the Rockies. The prairie west, the centre span of the future nation, had been saved from an American takeover. Or had it? What supported the centre span on either side? To the east, the primordial waste of the Canadian Shield isolated the "postage stamp province" of Manitoba from its nearest Canadian neighbour, Ontario, so Manitoba's trade continued to flow

Sir John A. Macdonald, Canada's first prime minister. His personal life was tragic: his beloved first wife died after a long illness; their first son died at thirteen months; and his only child by his second marriage was mentally retarded.

south to the United States. In the far west, the colony of British Columbia seemed destined to become American territory. The 10 000 inhabitants of British Columbia had no links of trade or transportation with Canada, thousands of kilometres away on the other side of the continent. Americans had already built a transcontinental railroad (the Union Pacific) and a spur line reaching northward from it would connect the colony and its natural resources with the heavily populated eastern United States. Moreover, British Columbia was now sandwiched between two American territories: Alaska, which the United States had purchased from Russia in 1867, and Oregon. The crown colony was the obvious corridor that Americans needed to link their Pacific possessions.

Sensing profits, a number of businessmen in British Columbia began promoting the benefits of annexation and presented their argument to an incredulous Colonial Office in 1867, the year of Confederation. The time seemed ripe because a bill had been introduced into Congress, proposing that all the provinces and territories north of the international border be admitted to the Union as states or states-to-be.

Two men in particular saved the Pacific colony — and the rest of Canada, for that matter — from American clutches: John A. Macdonald, and a Nova Scotian with the dramatic name of Amor de Cosmos, "Lover of the World."

De Cosmos was born and raised plain William Alexander Smith in Windsor, Nova Scotia, and later emigrated to the goldfields of California, where he earned a living of sorts as a photographer and journalist. Becoming disgusted by the American way of life, he moved on to the tiny capital of British Columbia, Victoria, where he became the owner and editor of the *British Colonist*. In the initial issue of his newspaper, de Cosmos described the policies he would later support as a member of the legislative assembly: the unification of British North America; communication links between its constituent parts; and, in British Columbia, a form of government answerable to the people as exemplified by the Westminster parliament. To this end, in his editorial columns, he vilified the autocratic rule of Governor James Douglas and castigated the administration of his successor, Frederick Seymour. He told anyone willing to listen (and some not so willing) that his aim was to expand Confederation as soon as possible and also to "secure representation for the colony, and thus get rid of the present one-man government, with its huge staff of overpaid and do-nothing officials." De Cosmos even organized a Confederation League and stumped the colony to promote union with Canada.

Governor Seymour happened to die of dysentery in June 1869, and for once Macdonald was paying attention to western affairs. He advised London to make Anthony Musgrave, who was just finishing a term as lieutenant-governor of Newfoundland, the next governor of British Columbia. Macdonald had been impressed by Musgrave's "prudence, discretion, and loyalty to the cause of Confederation," and recommended him as just the man to "put the screws" on the executive council that, under Seymour, had rejected Confederation.

Musgrave justified Macdonald's confidence. He applied the screws so gently but steadily that, within two years of his appointment, his executive council, without a single dissenting opinion, voted to seek terms of union with Canada.

Macdonald routed the annexationists, a minority in the colony, by making an offer too good to refuse. Ottawa would take over British Columbia's debts, pay the province an annual subsidy of $1,000,000 and build a railway to the Pacific. Victoria would have happily settled for a wagon road through the Cordillera and the promise of a start, within three years, on the construction of a transcontinental railway. Macdonald, however, delighted British Columbians and dismayed his own Conservatives by insisting on starting the rail line within two years and completing it within ten.

The promise to construct a Pacific railway was easily made and easily accepted because neither Victoria nor Ottawa understood the magnitude of the task. Only a handful of surveyors appreciated the awesome realities of Canada's geography, and not even the roughest reconnaissance of a possible route had been made. Between Ottawa and Winnipeg lay 1920 kilometres of rock and forest, innumerable lakes and rivers, and then a 1600-kilometre stretch of prairie. The Hind and Palliser expeditions had discovered a feasible route across the northern prairies to the Yellowhead Pass in the Rocky Mountains. But beyond that was barrier after barrier of mountains, whose bases were slashed by the deep, dark canyons of rivers racing to the sea. There was also the nagging problem of how a 4000-kilometre-long railway, constructed through regions that contained few settlers, was going to pay its way. A world depression had defeated Macdonald's plans to organize massive immigration. Without grain and lumber going east, and manufactured goods going west, how could the railway earn the money to pay its operating expenses and show a profit?

Yet Macdonald stubbornly stuck to his argument that until a rail line was built, the gigantic gap between Ontario and British Columbia would never be bridged, and the enormous agricultural potential of the prairies would never be tapped. Until that potential was conjoined with the industrial strength of Ontario and Quebec, he warned, Canada would never be a nation from sea to sea. It would remain a disunited, disconnected Dominion.

Macdonald was, in fact, staking the continued existence of Canada on the craziest gamble of his political career. But if he did not gamble, British Columbia would be forced to accept the alternative of annexation. The telegrams exchanged between Ottawa and Victoria were one proof of this: the messages had to be relayed via telegraph wires in the United States. The prime minister was convinced that Americans were "resolved to do all they can short of war to get possession of the western territory, and we must take immediate and vigorous steps to counteract them. One of the first things to be done is to show unmistakably our resolve to build the Pacific Railway."

*

Ask anybody in Canada what name he or she associates with the construction of the Canadian Pacific Railway (CPR) and the answer will likely be William Cornelius Van Horne, the general manager who drove his construction crews as hard as he drove himself. Another answer might be Major Rogers, the tiny, tobacco-chewing surveyor who discovered the vital pass in the Selkirk Mountains that now bears his name. A railway enthusiast might mention Sandford Fleming, the brilliant chief engineer who coordinated the work of survey parties scattered like confetti between the shores of the Pacific and the valley of the Ottawa River. Or James Jerome "Big Jim" Hill from Ontario, who knew everything about running a railway line and everybody, American or Canadian, who was a railroad man. (It was Big Jim who considered the American-born Van Horne the best boss in the

business and had him put on the CPR payroll.) The man least likely to be mentioned is George Stephen, the mastermind behind the miracle of the CPR.

Stephen is a classic example of the immigrant success story. The son of a carpenter in a Highland village, he left home at the age of fourteen to work as a clerk in a dry-goods store in London. Offered a similar position in Montreal, it was not long before he was a partner in the business. In what little spare time he had, Stephen studied banking and the stock market. By taking carefully calculated financial risks, he was able to purchase his own store and, later, to invest in various manufacturing companies. He became a prominent member of the Montreal Board of Trade and, in 1876, president of the Bank of Montreal.

While Stephen, a self-made but strangely shy man, was busy acquiring a fortune, he met his equally shrewd but egotistic cousin, Donald A. Smith, who introduced him to the fascinating risks and rewards of railroading.

Smith, too, was an important, influential man, another Scots-born immigrant with a rags-to-riches story. He started out as an HBC trader in the wilds of Labrador, where he had been exiled by Governor George Simpson for sweet-talking Mrs. George Simpson. Living as frugally as possible, Smith cannily invested in such sectors of the burgeoning Canadian economy as banking and manufacturing. He became commissioner (chief Canadian official) of the Hudson's Bay Company after the death of Simpson in 1860. Smith's hunger for recognition was such that, while commissioner, he became the representative for Winnipeg in the Manitoba legislature *and* the member of Parliament for the Manitoba constituency of Selkirk.

To fulfil his various responsibilities, Smith

had to make many a time-consuming, round-about journey between Ottawa and Winnipeg via the United States. On one of these journeys, he met and became friendly with James J. Hill, who was investigating the tangled business affairs of a bankrupt Minnesota company, the St. Paul and Pacific Railroad. The St. Paul and Pacific — or, as local people called it, "two streaks of rust and a right of way" — was deeply in debt and hopelessly disorganized. The line was uncompleted and its rolling stock was over twenty years old and unreliable, but Hill confided to Smith that whoever bought the line would get the land originally granted it by the territorial legislature of Minnesota — one million hectares of fertile soil. This land could be sold at a very nice profit to the land-hungry settlers crowding into Minnesota, who would then become customers for the railroad's freight services. The shrewd Smith realized that a renovated St. Paul and Pacific could be extended to join the growing city of Winnipeg with the Minnesota capital of St. Paul.

Donald Smith called on his cousin Stephen to beg for advice. The challenge of the whole financial manoeuvre intrigued Stephen, who decided to help Smith gain control of the St. Paul and Pacific. Stephen had always enjoyed the calculated gamble. If the venture succeeded, it would make him a millionaire several times over.

In partnership with Smith, James J. Hill and Norman Kittson (an associate of Smith and Hill), Stephen supervised the intricate moves that led to the purchase of the bankrupt company in 1879. Characteristically, he bore the greater share of the risk, pledging more of his own money and sources of credit that did his partners. (Stephen dreaded that anyone should suffer financial loss in an enterprise in which he himself was involved.) As Smith had foreseen, everything worked out well. Hill proved to be a genius at reorganizing the line and extending its operations into Manitoba. The partners sold most of the one million hectares for almost double the price they had paid for the company, now christened the St. Paul, Minneapolis, and Manitoba Railroad Company. Settlers produced bumper crops, and freight haulage soared. The railroad's earnings rapidly reduced its debts. Suddenly, George Stephen and his colleagues acquired the reputation of men experienced in the intricacies of financing and constructing railways.

*

Meanwhile, the Pacific railway remained a dream. Macdonald's first attempt at construction had ended in disaster. Sir Hugh Allan, president of the Allan Steamship Line and the wealthiest man in Canada, had been given a government charter to build a line to the Pacific. However, during the general election of 1872, the prime minister and several of his colleagues had accepted large sums of campaign-expense monies from Allan. When this Pacific Scandal leaked out a year later, Macdonald was forced to resign. In the ensuing election, his Conservatives were badly beaten by Alexander Mackenzie's Liberals.

Railway building in Canada has always been exorbitantly expensive and thus government-subsidized, but the world depression that had stalled Macdonald's immigration plans was also undercutting trade and commerce. Mackenzie's government was sadly strapped for money; it spent a great deal on survey work, but had little left over for construction. When Macdonald won the next election in 1878, only a hundred or so kilometres of track had been laid, graded and bridged. But bad times forced him to continue the Liberal railway policy of construction on the instalment plan. Then, in the summer of 1880,

Forging slowly but steadily eastward from the Pacific, a CPR construction crew builds a cantilever bridge.

Building a snowshed in the Rogers Pass, a major avalanche location. *See previous page.*

his luck changed when he was approached by a group of Canadian businessmen, led by George Stephen.

Stephen, like Macdonald, could not resist the twin challenges of railway building and nation building. For once recklessly altruistic, he had great faith in what Macdonald and his Conservatives promoted as the National Policy. If large numbers of farm and ranch families were settled in the West, they would be a market for clothing, agricultural machinery and manufactures produced in eastern Canada, and the demand for these goods would quicken the expansion of industry in Ontario and Quebec. A transcontinental railway would facilitate the exchange of grain and cattle for manufactured products. The problem, of course, was that in order for thousands of settlers to make the prairies their home, there had to be a railway first.

Stephen realized the tremendous odds against success and even wrote Macdonald that both friends and enemies in Montreal were convinced that the venture "will be the ruin of us all." In the same letter, however, he advised that "Unless we can have the cars running over a long piece of road, west of Winnipeg, by this time next year, both the Government and the contractor will be put into discredit with the public." Stephen was telling the prime minister that he was not a promoter trying to make a quick profit: he was a businessman willing to pledge his wealth and reputation in an effort to make an impractical dream into a working reality.

In February 1881, after seven weeks of angry argument and corrosive criticism in Parliament about the "giveaways" and "handouts" in the railway contract — even Macdonald's followers from Manitoba objected to the much-debated monopoly clause that precluded competition — the Canadian Pacific Railway Company received permission to build the line.

The first Canadian Pacific Railway Company, led by Sir Hugh Allan, was to have received subsidies of $30 million and fifty million acres (20 Mha) of land before the Pacific Scandal destroyed Allan's company. Stephen's Canadian Pacific Railway Company was to get subsidies of $25 million and twenty-five million acres (10 Mha). However, profitable extras were included in the contract: land grants would be free of taxes for twenty years; land for stations, workshops, railyards, docks, etc., would be given free of charge and be free of taxes forever; the transfer to the CPR, without charge, of sections already under contract to be completed at government expense; an exemption from duties on imported construction materials. And, for twenty years, Ottawa would not permit any other line to be constructed south of the CPR within fifteen miles (22.5 km) of the Canada-U.S. border.

The CPR, for its part, promised completion and perpetual operation of the railway. The whole project was to be finished by 1 May 1891. Stephen and Macdonald were now committed to achieving what many people considered to be the impossible.

Impossible is the only word to describe the work of construction. The riblike ridges and rubble of the Canadian Shield almost broke men's hearts as well as their backs. One particular bad mile, which had to be dynamited out of the oldest and hardest rock anywhere on earth, cost $700,000. In winter, construction crews floundered in two metres of snow, often in temperatures well minus zero; in summer, there was no escape from millions of voracious black flies and mosquitoes. The rapid progress of track laying on the prairies in 1882 and 1883 was offset by rising costs once the CPR reached the mountains. The route had been changed from a northwesterly one across the Fertile Belt and through the Yellowhead Pass to a route across a much drier, southern section of the prairies, in order to discourage any branch-line invasions by ambitious Americans. Once in the Rockies, locomotives had to be teamed to haul trains up the steep gradients of the Kicking Horse Pass, and many bridges had to be built as the line was forced to switch from one side to the other of the steep-walled valley and gorge of the Kicking Horse River. In the next mountain barrier, the snow-laden Selkirks, avalanches regularly ripped out large chunks of the line. Enormously tall trestles had to be constructed to cross the near-vertical gulches made by mountain streams tumbling down from the many glaciers.

Construction in the canyons of British Columbia's Fraser and North Thompson rivers was another nightmare. Nonetheless, under the cool direction of Andrew Onderdonk, the job was done. His native Indian, Chinese, American and Canadian labourers drilled and blasted twenty-seven tunnels and manhandled several million cubic metres of lumber to construct six hundred trestles and bridges. As in the Shield section, men were blown to bits by dynamite and nitro-glycerine, crushed to death by falling and flying rock, drowned in spring-swollen rivers, and killed by slipping off cliffs. But the track steadily advanced to Savona's Ferry on Kamloops Lake. Here, Onderdonk's men would link up with Van Horne's sweating crews, who were inching their way between the pointed peaks of the Selkirks towards yet another mountain barrier, the rounded bulk of the Gold Range (now the Monashees), where surveyor Walter Moberly had discovered the all-important Eagle Pass.

If the work of construction was dangerous, the financial side was also hard on the nerves. Owing to the CPR's snaillike progress in the mountain and Shield sections, the sums of money required to pay several thousand men and purchase construction materials were enormous. Onderdonk's subcontractors in the mountains were laying a mile (1.6 km) of track at an average cost of about $185,000, and Van Horne's men, in the Shield, at anywhere from $185,000 to $435,000. At times, both bosses thought themselves lucky to advance six feet (1.8 m) in one day. Yet, under the terms of the contract, the government doled out the cash subsidy — $13,000 per mile in the mountains and $15,000 in the Shield — only every 20 miles (32 km) of completed track, and sections of land every 15 miles (24 km). Land sales to settlers were disappointingly slow, a grim development since Stephen had counted on these sales to provide further financing.

For a time, Stephen was able to raise money in London and New York by selling CPR stock, but by the end of 1883 the railway was headed for trouble. Investors — worried by stories of the difficulties of construction, disheartened by the slow progress of laying track and discouraged by rumours of disaster — stopped buying shares. Early in 1884, all Stephen could do to bridge the steadily widening gap between income and expenditure was to badger the prime minister into persuading Parliament to lend the CPR $22.5 million in return for a first mortgage on all the company's property. Even this money was not enough. Stephen and Smith had to raise more by secretly pledging every last item of personal property, from stock holdings to the very sheets and blankets in which they slept.

All this was still not enough to pay the bills, and Macdonald refused to do any more for the company. On 15 April 1885, Van Horne sent a telegraph message to Stephen's mortgaged mansion in Montreal: "Have no means paying wages. Pay car can't be sent out, and unless we get immediate relief we must stop." The CPR was broke.

LOUIS RIEL.

COMPLIMENTS OF

S. Davis & Sons, Montreal,

LARGEST CIGAR MANUFACTURERS IN THE
DOMINION.

152

This photograph of Riel was taken about 1876. There being a price on his head at the time, this package "premium" was, in effect, a wanted notice.

In later years, Van Horne often remarked that the Canadian Pacific Railway ought to raise a monument to Louis Riel as its saviour. Riel, he claimed, saved the CPR from bankruptcy.

*

Fifteen years earlier, Riel had hurried out the front gate of Fort Garry, as British soldiers and Canadian militiamen hammered with their rifle butts on the back gate. For the next few years, his life was one of frustration and fear. He was twice elected to Parliament by his loyal followers, but a scandalized Commons refused to accept him as a member. A marked man, liable to arrest and the target of murder plots, he had to hide for months in the United States, upset at being separated from his mother and sister whom he had to visit secretly in St. Boniface. Eventually, he only felt safe among French-Canadian sympathizers in Montreal and across the border in New York State.

In 1874, the Liberal government of Alexander Mackenzie had decided to give Riel amnesty on condition that he stay out of Canada for five years. This was small comfort to a man who had become subject to religious visions and alternated between moods of mystic rapture and brooding despair. From 1876 to 1878, under an assumed name, Riel spent various periods of time in lunatic asylums in Quebec and was discharged, in his doctor's words, "more or less cured." He eventually settled down as a school teacher in the tiny Roman Catholic mission settlement of Sun River, Montana, married, and became the father of two children. Riel seemed to have found peace — until the morning of 4 June 1884, when four men rode into Sun River after a journey of almost 1220 kilometres.

Gabriel Dumont, Moise Ouelette and Michel Dumas represented the French-speaking inhabitants of the Saskatchewan River country, and James Isbister its English-speaking residents. They had come to ask Riel to make Ottawa listen to their complaints and to redress their grievances. Five days later, Louis Riel and his family set out in a Red River cart for the Metis village of Batoche.

In the prairie west to which Riel was returning, there were any number of disappointed, angry people. Many Metis, resenting the Canadian settlers who kept crowding into Manitoba, had moved farther west into the valley of the South Saskatchewan River. Here, life was more like the old days. The surrounding prairies were nearly empty except for a few Indian bands and the ever-wandering buffalo. The Metis founded new communities — Qu'Appelle, Batoche, Duck Lake and St. Albert — on the banks of the South Saskatchewan and enjoyed the buffalo hunt, combined with a little farming. By the winter of 1879, however, the last of the great buffalo herds had been slaughtered. The only alternative was full-time farming in a region where locusts, drought, hail or frost could wipe out a whole summer's work in a few hours. Farming was an uncertain occupation in another way, too: the Metis were squatters, not landowners.

Title to land was what the Metis wanted above all else. In 1878, Ottawa had passed a Dominion Lands Act that included a clause by which the government could grant land to the Metis, but no such grants had been made. Petitions had been sent to Ottawa year after year. But Macdonald could not make up his mind whether to treat the Metis as Indians and give them reserves, or to treat them like new settlers and give them land.

Some 30 000 Indians were only a little better off. They lived on reserves, land that was unquestionably theirs by treaty, but, with the disappearance of the buffalo, had no option except to till the soil and raise livestock. Frustrated by the difficulties of changing over from a life of hunting to one of farming, they often slaughtered the cattle and ate the seed supplied by Ottawa. This situation was made worse in the early 1880s by a government policy of economy, which reduced the rations of flour and bacon given to these Indians. For the first time, the Mounted Police began to experience encounters with hostile Indians, some of whom defiantly broke into government food warehouses.

As for newcomers to the Territories, many a farmer and businessman was facing ruin. Some had emigrated to Prince Albert, Battleford and Edmonton, confident that the CPR would go through the Fertile Belt of the valley of the North Saskatchewan River. Instead, the railway headed straight west of Winnipeg, leaving these communities isolated. This turn of events coincided with a fall in grain prices and with several successive years of bad weather at harvest time. Late in 1883, the Manitoba and North-West Farmers' Protective Union had been formed to send representatives to Ottawa to protest the high costs of CPR freight and farming machinery manufactured in Ontario, and the drastic drop in the price of grain. Other organizations — the Settlers' Rights Association at Qu'Appelle and the Settlers' Union at Prince Albert — made similar complaints. All failed to make any impression on the federal government. Not for the first time, the prairie west found itself ignored and left to make out as best it could.

In December 1884, a petition of rights, signed by Saskatchewan settlers and Metis, was sent to Ottawa. Written this time with the help of Riel, the list of grievances was not limited to the complaint that "the Half-breeds of the Territory have not received 240 acres [96 ha] of land each, as did the Manitoba Half-breeds." It requested that the government of Canada do something about the worsening living conditions of the In-dians, pointing out that "the settlers in many localities are compelled to furnish them with food, partly to prevent them from dying at their door, partly to preserve the peace of the Territory." It protested taxes levied on "timber, rails, and firewood required for home use." It asked why Manitoba, with a population of 12 000, governed itself, while the Territories, with a population of 60 000, were still subject to decisions made in Ottawa. It included a polite reminder that the people of the Territories were still not allowed to elect members of Parliament. And the petition ended with the bold suggestion that the Territorial District of Saskatchewan be organized as a province.

The petition was duly acknowledged by one of Macdonald's cabinet ministers. Macdonald later denied that it had ever been received, but the Metis had always been a blind spot in his continental vision. Like Indians, he considered them of no account.

Riel now spoke of going back to Montana. He had done what he had come to do: bring Metis and settlers together and make their common interests known to Ottawa. However, his followers would not hear of his returning to the United States. To them, he was the "true father of the French people of the North West." They told him that they could not win their rights without his leadership.

Riel was persuaded to stay — but he was a changed man. The calm, self-possessed leader who for months had been content to depend on the charity of others to support him and his family now became bitter about his penniless condition. Was he not entitled to a grant of land like all the Metis living in Manitoba at the time it became a province? Did not Ottawa owe him a reward for bringing Manitoba into Confederation? Having been exiled from his native land and having lived under the threat of as-

Maple Creek, District of Saskatchewan, 1884. A Metis
and an Indian bridegroom (r.), who consented to be
photographed only if he could keep his rifle handy.

sassination, was he not entitled to compensation for his services and suffering?

Riel's diaries record "conversations with God" — presumably prayers and answering revelations — and suggest that, after the dispatch of the petition of rights, he considered himself an agent of God charged with a divine mandate to reform the Roman Catholic Church. Informing the Metis that he was a prophet, he announced the creation of a "Catholic, Apostolic, and Living Church of the New World" and declared that Bishop Grandin of St. Albert (to that good man's surprise and horror) was its pope.

As week after week passed without any action from Ottawa except the promise of a "commission of investigation," Riel began to talk to the Metis about "a blow to gain their rights." On March 5 he held a secret meeting with a small group of Metis, which included Gabriel Dumont; and those present signed an oath "to save our country from a wicked government by taking up arms if necessary." A few days later, Riel proclaimed the formation of a "Provisional Government of the Saskatchewan," with a president, secretary and councillors. He appointed Gabriel Dumont "Adjutant-General of the Metis nation . . . at the head of the army." Dumont rode out to Batoche, St. Laurent, Duck Lake and Fish Creek to recruit fighting men to the Metis cause, and Riel sent couriers to rally the other Metis settlements and Indians on reserves. The Cree under their leaders Big Bear and Poundmaker supported Riel, but Crowfoot, chief of the Blackfoot, kept his people out of the conflict.

Riel was, of course, deluding himself. In 1885, he could not take the same position that he had in 1869. He did not have the support of the Roman Catholic Church, the English-speaking Metis or many Indians. The prairie west was no longer an isolated region: the railway was being built, and the Mounted Police were keeping close watch on him. Most important of all, he was challenging the authority of the *legal* owner of the West, the federal government. This time, he would be rebelling against lawful authority and thus committing treason. So why did his followers stay with him to the bitter end? "They chose to fight because their freedom and pride as a people seemed to be threatened, and that has been the motive of all the resistance movements which in history have gained more lustre than common wars."

The tragedy of Louis Riel and his Metis began at Duck Lake in a March snowstorm. Alongside the muddy trail leading to the village, Dumont and his sharpshooters ambushed a small force of Mounted Police and volunteers who were trying to prevent provisions at Duck Lake from falling into rebel hands. The end came barely two months later at Batoche, where the outnumbered, outgunned rebels were overrun by Canadian troops commanded by an uninspired, if brave, British general. But the man who really defeated Riel was William Cornelius Van Horne.

As soon as Van Horne heard the news of the massacre at Duck Lake, he saw a way to both solve the military transport problem and to save the CPR. In 1870, Colonel Wolseley and his force of regulars and militia had taken three months to travel from Montreal to Red River. Van Horne assured the Macdonald government he could transport troops from Ontario to Qu'Appelle in ten days — and he kept his word. The first units, which entrained on March 28, were in Winnipeg within a week; two days later they were at Qu'Appelle, just 400 kilometres south of Batoche, Riel's headquarters.

No personality in Canadian history has inspired so much love and hatred, respect and contempt, as Louis Riel. In his lifetime, he was a self-sacrificing hero and patriot to some, a blood-

A soldier's life is spent preparing for, then waiting and waiting for, battle. Here, at Batoche in 1885, a group of Canadian militiamen sleep in the spring sunshine.

thirsty rebel and mad messiah to others. To this day, Riel remains a controversial man: intelligent and masterful, yet capable of peculiar behaviour and passionate rages; gentle and peace-loving by nature, his name is forever linked with violence. Even his end was controversial. Arrested and tried for high treason, he refused the efforts of his lawyers to save his life on the grounds that he was insane. "I cannot abandon my dignity," he cried out in the Regina courtroom. "Here I have to defend myself against the accusation of high treason, or I have to consent to the animal life of an asylum." He preferred to die with dignity rather than live with what he called "the stain of insanity."

A jury of six men found Riel guilty, but recommended the prisoner "to the mercy of the Crown." Not one of the jurors was a French Canadian, a Roman Catholic or a Metis, yet they asked for a commutation of the death penalty. Later, one juror explained:

In recommending him to the mercy of the court, we did so because we considered that while the prisoner was guilty . . . at the same time we felt that had the Government done their duty and redressed the grievances of the half-breeds of the Saskatchewan, as they had been requested time and again to do, there never would have been a second Riel rebellion, and consequently no prisoner to try and condemn. We could not but condemn in the strongest terms possible the extraordinary dilatoriness of Sir John Macdonald, Sir David McPherson [Minister of the Interior] and Lieutenant Governor Dewdney [of the North-West Territories].

Perhaps the last, ironic word belongs to Louis Riel: "I have been quarrelling with an insane and irresponsible government."

Macdonald, however, could not be persuaded to show mercy to Riel. Twice, the prime minister was obliged to postpone the execution so that the condemned man's lawyers could ar-

Stoney Mountain Penitentiary, Manitoba. Cree chiefs Big Bear (2) and Poundmaker (5) supported Riel in 1885. Captured and sentenced to three years apiece, neither survived for long the shock of imprisonment.

gue against the death sentence. Each time, there was rejoicing in the French-speaking Catholic province of Quebec and rage in English-speaking Protestant Ontario, where the death of Thomas Scott would never be forgiven. A third stay of execution so that three doctors could examine Riel was simply an effort by Macdonald to win over his French-Canadian colleagues. After the examination, the doctors agreed — as Macdonald knew they would — that on matters other than politics and religion, Riel was aware of the difference between right and wrong. He was neither violently insane nor an obvious idiot. Therefore, by the legal definition of sanity in that day, he was not insane. Therefore, he was guilty of treason. Therefore, he could be executed.

Macdonald's cabinet had the power to cancel the death sentence. All its English-speaking members, however, insisted that Riel must die. And its French-speaking members, mainly out of loyalty to their longtime leader, went along with the majority decision. Thus, the lieutenant-governor of the North-West Territories was informed that the execution would take place.

On the sunny, frosty morning of November 16, in the Mounted Police barracks in Regina, Louis Riel stepped calmly onto the scaffold. He had renounced his mission to found a new church, confessed his sins, and was at peace with himself. As the hangman drew a white cap over the condemned man's head and adjusted the knot of the noose under the left ear, Riel repeated after his priest the Lord's Prayer in a quiet, steady voice. He got as far as "And lead us not into temptation, but deliver us," and the trap door dropped open beneath his moccasined feet.

*

In November 1885, the headlines in Canadian newspapers were about either the execution of Riel or the imminent completion of the railway.

In the summer of that year, Macdonald had been persuaded to coax yet another loan from Parliament to aid the CPR. He had been loath to do so, but may have been convinced of the bitter necessity by a perceptive comment once made by a cabinet colleague: "The day the Canadian Pacific busts, the Conservative party busts the day after!" Fortunately, Parliament had been impressed by the speed and efficiency with which Van Horne had rushed troops west to crush the rebellion, so it approved the loan. The pay cars went out, and Van Horne's men went back to work on the uncompleted sections north of Lake Superior in Ontario and in the interior mountains of British Columbia.

The last spike of the transcontinental railway was ceremonially tapped into place in British Columbia's Eagle Pass on the dull, misty morning of November 7. At last, Canada was linked "from sea to sea."

8 "The Last, Best West"

In order to populate the practically empty prairies, John A. Macdonald adopted the American homesteading practice of offering 160 acres (64 ha) to each head of a family or to any person over the age of twenty-one. After living on this quarter section for three years and cultivating some part of it — and also after becoming a British subject — the homesteader was given clear title to his or her land.

From the 1870s to the early 1890s, few people took up Macdonald's offer. These were years of worldwide economic depression, and most would-be immigrants were reluctant to leave home — with the notable exception of some who came all the way from Russia. The first group to immigrate to the West was a Mennonite community, which arrived in 1874 to settle in Manitoba.

While the first or "East" reserve (east of the Red River) contained some low-quality land, the later reserves took up rich and fecund prairie lands. In an astonishingly short time Mennonite expertise made that fecundity bear fruit.

Though they lacked wood for log houses or fencing, they knew how to build mud huts until they could afford lumber for frame buildings. They planted trees extensively. . . . As for farming methods, they introduced crop rotation and summer fallowing. . . . And they prospered — in spite of some drought and frost in the early years.

. . . The west may not have realized it, but the Mennonites had established two vital aspects of the settlement and immigration pattern that was to come. First, they had proved that the open prairie was cultivable; second, they had shown that Canada would welcome the immigration of ethnic groups, and would make the way easy for them.

Compared to the size of the land that lay empty, the westward flow of newcomers was a trickle: Mennonites and Icelanders in the province of Manitoba; Mennonites, Swedes and Finns in the Territorial District of Saskatchewan; and a few cattlemen in the Territorial District of Alberta. What was needed was a flood of settlers. And the flood did not occur until the election in 1896 of the Liberal government of Wilfrid Laurier, which happened to coincide with a revival of prosperity in the western world. Another fortunate circumstance was Laurier's appointment of Clifford Sifton as minister of the interior. Sifton was an Ontario-born lawyer who had made a name for himself in Manitoba politics and a small fortune in local business ventures. Tough, tireless, almost machinelike in his competence and supremely self-confident, Sifton made his mark on the national scene by promoting what he called, in one of his felicitous catch phrases, "The Last, Best West."

*

Activated by crisp memos from their new minister and his deputy (fellow Manitoban James A. Smart), Canadian immigration officials blanketed Europe with posters that promised free land. (The land was not actually free, since a fee of $10 had to be paid when filing a claim.) Journalists churned out admiring articles on the "Land of Opportunity"; agents rented community halls in hundreds of towns and villages to spread the word to farm folk of a prairie paradise blessed by an invigorating climate, fertile soils and bumper crops. Tours of the prairies were organized for influential American and European politicians and newspapermen, either as guests of the federal government or of an equally interested landowner, the CPR.

The success of all this advertising took Canada — and the whole western world — by surprise. A major reason was that the immigrants themselves became unofficial promoters of settlement. Their accounts of Sifton's "Wondrous West" turned out to be the most successful propaganda of all.

In 1874, at Winnipeg, the first of some 7500 Mennonites arrive to homestead.

Well into the twentieth century, it was the muscle power of humans and horses that broke the prairie sod — and levelled a dirt road to a grain elevator.

It was so often letters. What people today call word-of-mouth. . . . Canada . . . all that land. My God!

So if it was Germany or Russia or England you came from, you'd send letters to your home town and the letters would get passed around. Talked about. Soon another family would pack up, sell what they couldn't carry, and be off to Canada.

. . . the land was the thing. Free land. Cheap land. No cossacks riding you down, no landlord, no lord, no boss. No man was a peasant or serf in Canada. Every man was free. The letters told it all.

. . . the immigrant . . . might start on a farm and find he was a lousy farmer, didn't like it and become a baker in town. Or go to a town and then wind up on a farm or a big garden patch. Same with the city. A big anthill. In and out, back and forth. Be a shoemaker. Be a carpenter. Run a café. A man could do anything. Everybody always wound up doing the thing that usually turned out right for him.

"Free land" was the irresistible offer that motivated one of the greatest human migrations in history. The offer drew people from Britain, Denmark, Finland, Greece, Holland, Italy, Norway, Poland, Sweden, Russia and Iceland. "Free land" lured Sifton's favoured "stalwart peasant in a sheepskin coat . . . with a stout wife and a half-dozen children" from the Austro-Hungarian empire's provinces of Galicia, Ruthenia and Bukhovina, a group of people who were to become known, collectively, as Ukrainians. Some immigrants came from as far away as Tasmania, some from just next door: Ontario and the United States.

Gone were the days when European immigrants headed for the United States with its bountiful acres. There were none left: all the arable land had been occupied. Now, the land-hungry flocked to Canada. In 1881, the prairies had only 66 000 settlers; by 1901, there were 420 000, most of them "bustin' sod." A decade later, thousands of immigrants were still rolling westward by rail coach or covered wagon. In those years, the area of settled land in Manitoba and in what became the provinces of Saskatchewan and Alberta leaped from six to twenty million hectares.

Statistics obscure the stark realities of life for the newcomers. The first problem for these optimistic farmers-to-be was to locate their particular quarter section on the vast emptiness between Winnipeg and the Rockies. As soon as they got there, the next task was finding water. Few quarter sections had a regular supply; many had sloughs, which dried out as the summer grew hotter and hotter. So a well had to be dug. In fact, if there was no water supply in the immediate vicinity, the quarter section had to be abandoned and another obtained.

Settlers started out farming with the bare essentials bought at the village where they got off the train: a yoke of oxen, a milch cow, a wagon, a chilled-steel breaking plough and some seed. A fortunate few arrived with trunk loads of personal possessions, but many with just the clothes they wore. Americans and British commonly brought a little capital with them; immigrants from Europe had to earn the cash to buy necessities by hiring themselves out to well-established farmers or as railway labourers, while their women and children ran the homestead as best they could.

Homesteaders not only worked the earth but lived in it: a "soddy," or shack made of earth. All that was needed was a frame of willow or poplar poles, against which big pieces of sod, ten centimetres thick, were stacked like bricks to form walls. The roof was made of poles laid closely together and covered with alternating layers of hay and sod. It leaked, of course. One oldtimer commented that a three-day rain outside meant a five-day rain inside. But rain is rare on the prairies, and the soddy was warm in winter and cool in summer. Inside, rooms were created by

On the northern prairies, the distinctive, thatch-roofed homes of Ukrainians dotted the landscape.

Building a "soddy" around the framed-in door and windows. The roof was made of "government shingles" — more sod laid on poplar poles.

Cowboys on a roundup near Cochrane, Alberta.

hanging blankets on a line; crates and boxes served as tables and chairs. About the only store-bought item would be a squat-legged, sheetmetal or cast-iron stove for cooking and heating. Water was hauled daily from the nearest slough or stream, and the toilet was a hole dug in the ground every other month until there was time and energy enough to build an outhouse.

Food was the plainest possible fare. One pioneer remembered the first winter's menu as oatmeal without milk and tea without sugar, while another recalled a diet of jackrabbit — fried, stewed, roasted and boiled. Kitchen gardens were planted; turnips, potatoes, onions, corn and beans. Some of the produce was put by in a root cellar, some was sold in the nearest town to buy flour, oatmeal, salt, sugar, dried fruit and coffee.

Prairie farming was a never-ending round of work for man, woman and child. Land had to be cleared, but, with its millions of tiny, interlaced roots, prairie sod was as tough as board lumber and resisted even the power of a pair of sturdy oxen yoked to a steel plough. The result was often a crooked furrow — or a wrecked plough. Clearing five acres (2 ha) a year was considered steady progress. Stock had to be fed and watered daily, a chore commonly done by eleven- and twelve-year-olds. When the settler's wife was not cooking, baking and canning, spinning, knitting and sewing, she was feeding pigs and chickens and milking the cow. As for her husband, there was always a ploughing, seeding, harvesting and threshing season. In between times, he repaired the house and barn, mended equipment, perhaps began construction of a log home, and cut enough wood to keep the family warm through the winter.

That was the worst season. Paralyzing cold, blowing or drifting snow, short days and long

Montgomery

nights isolated the homestead. Winter was a sort of seven-month imprisonment. Even if only a day's wagon ride from the nearest neighbour, the hazard of storm and blizzard made visiting risky. For that matter, just going into the backyard to feed and water stock could be dangerous without the lifeline of a rope from the house to the barn.

The development of ranching is a different story. Its beginnings were casual, often accidental. In the 1870s, an enterprising man and his partner would bring some cattle, horses or sheep from the States or Manitoba and sell them for a profit or graze them on some section of lush prairie.

Ranching in Alberta began in 1881 when the federal government made it possible for a man or a company to lease up to 100 000 acres (40 000 ha) for a yearly rental of one cent an acre. Senator M. H. Cochrane of Quebec started a trend when he established the Cochrane Ranche Company with 3000 head of cattle. Three years later, there were about fifty ranches leasing nearly 800 000 hectares. Many of them failed, but among those that survived some bad winters were the North-West Cattle Company (owned by the Allan family of Montreal) and a number of cattle empires financed by British syndicates: the Oxley, Walrond, Quorn, Maunsell and Cypress companies. The British ranches were run by upper-class "gentlemen emigrants" who built homes that resembled English country houses and who kept up the practices of a genteel life, complete with afternoon tea and cricket matches.

In British Columbia, ranching got its start when American and British entrepreneurs drove in herds of cattle and sheep to sell to hungry gold miners. One of these drovers, Joseph Greaves, eventually set up a ranch in the Nicola valley that became the famed Douglas Lake Cattle Company in 1886, with 12 000 head.

At this time, there was a minor vogue for setting up special communities of British gentry in the West. The failure of all such settlements in the United States did not deter an English country squire named Edward Pierce from setting up Cannington Manor (with a mansion surrounded by gracious homes and tennis courts) in the Territorial District of Assiniboia. The project failed because the settlers were more interested in social and sporting activities than in farming. Two decades later, the Barr Colony (later the town of Lloydminster), which had settlers from a variety of social classes, played less, farmed more, and was generally successful. However, the group of Edwardian gentlefolk who set up fruit farming at Walhachin in the sage-brush Thompson valley of British Columbia was less fortunate.

*

The CPR largely determined the urban geography of western Canada by spawning towns where its divisional offices, yards and repair shops were located. It created Brandon, Regina, Moose Jaw, Swift Current, Medicine Hat and Calgary. The same phenomenon occurred west of the mountains: Golden, Farwell (renamed Revelstoke), Ashcroft and Haney sprang into existence with the coming of steel. At the junction of the Thompson and North Thompson rivers, the town of Kamloops was transformed into a prosperous service centre for a fast-developing cattle industry. But the most spectacular metamorphosis of all took place near the mouth of the Fraser River. Here, on the southern shore of Burrard Inlet, a small sawmill community whose magnificent lumber built an imperial palace in China and several stately homes in England was

171

English settlers detraining at Saskatoon and loading up wagons for the final leg of their trip to the Barr Colony (later Lloydminster).

In May 1887, the first transcontinental passenger train steamed into Vancouver, bearing the proud motto "From Ocean to Ocean" (though the train had actually set out from Montreal).

First Train in Vancouver.

The CPR boosted tourism. And, thanks to its fleet of "Empress" liners, it could take a passenger to and from the Far East, "Down Under" or around the world.

turned into a metropolis. Officially, this backwoods shanty-town neighbour of the dignified, anglicized town of New Westminster was named Granville. However, everybody in the Fraser valley referred to it as Gastown because its preeminent citizen was a true Falstaff in girth and garrulity, a river pilot-turned-saloon owner called "Gassy Jack" Deighton.

In November 1885, when the famous last spike was ceremonially tapped in place in British Columbia's Eagle Pass by Donald Smith, there was track almost all the way from Montreal to Port Moody, another Burrard Inlet sawmill community. The line was completed the following summer, and on 4 July 1886 the first scheduled passenger train from Montreal puffed into Port Moody — only one minute late after a journey of 4650 kilometres. Port Moody's inhabitants gawked at the arrival of the "Pacific Express." They anticipated that their town would become the most important rail and ship terminus in British Columbia. However, the CPR, in the person of William Van Horne, had decided differently.

As part of the transportation empire he was building to link Europe and the East, Van Horne wanted a large, deep-water harbour. In addition, it had to have ample shoreline for docks to handle large freighters and plenty of space for railyards and sheds. In fact, he had already squeezed permission from the British Columbia government to extend the main line nineteen kilometres west from Port Moody to just such an anchorage and acreage: Coal Harbour. (A year before the end of steel arrived at Port Moody, he had demanded from Premier William Smith almost half the peninsula on which Vancouver now stands, but had to be content with about 2400 hectares of waterside property to the east of Stanley Park.) In his usual brusque manner, Van Horne announced that nobody would know

what the name Granville meant. And he insisted that the politicians in Victoria change the name to Vancouver.

Thus, on 23 May 1887, there was yet another transcontinental first as a gaudily decorated train — complete with a transparency of Queen Victoria fixed over its headlight in anticipation of her birthday the next day — clanked into the newly incorporated City of Vancouver. As newly elected mayor Malcolm A. MacLean and sundry citizens cheered the train's arrival, construction crews were busy hammering into shape a wharf to receive the first CPR passenger ship, the chartered steamship *Abyssinia*, at that moment making ready to leave its berth in Yokohama, Japan.

The *Abyssinia* put to sea May 31, and after a speedy passage of 13 days, arrived in the Strait of Georgia June 13, anchoring in English Bay. . . . A special train stood on the dock to take 65 bales of raw silk, consigned to Montreal, New York and London. With some tea added to its load, and all other traffic yielding way, the train reached New York June 21. The London consignment was transferred to a fast passenger ship and arrived there June 29.

. . . Suddenly, on that twenty-ninth of June, 1887, the globe had shrunk to half its size and the CPR made good a boast its trains and ships maintained for 50 years — "Spans the World!" . . . as the veteran *Abyssinia* edged through the Narrows in that far-off June dawn, she carried in her holds Vancouver's charter to be one of the great ports of the Seven Seas.

Every CPR train and ship brought eager arrivals to the bustling "Terminal City" of Vancouver. From the nearby prairies and from the eastern provinces came lawyers and engineers, bankers and merchants, speculators and promoters, farmers and miners, lumbermen and fishermen, wives and sweethearts — and prostitutes. From Hong Kong and Japan came "houseboys", storekeepers and market gardeners. Within six months of the arrival of the first passenger train,

A trader at Fort Chipewyan sorts fox, beaver, mink
and other precious furs worth, in all, $35,000.

Mining for coal near Nanaimo, B.C., originally an HBC
activity.

Vancouver boasted a population of 5000 and was being touted as "the seaport of the twentieth century." Some ships steamed from its harbour to coastal logging camps, coal mines and salmon canneries. Others carried away cargoes of fir, pine, cedar, spruce and canned salmon to China, South America, Australia and Britain. To the annoyance of Victoria and New Westminster, the upstart Vancouver was becoming the province's prime port and, consequently, the centre of business and commerce.

The development of British Columbia was accelerated further by the discovery and exploitation — underwritten by British and American capital — of the rich resources of the province's interior. Silver, gold, zinc and lead mines led to the founding of Rossland, Nelson and Slocan. At Kimberley, the Sullivan Mine became a leading world producer of lead, zinc and silver. And coal deposits in the Fernie district provided coke for smelters in both southern British Columbia and neighbouring Montana. Farmers with capital were beginning to buy glowingly advertised "fruit ranches" in the Okanagan valley.

*

The last great gold rush in North America took place in the Yukon and in the Atlin district of northwestern British Columbia. It came at a time when, like much of Europe and North America, British Columbia had been hard hit by the depression of the early 1890s. Many of its residents were moving to the United States. Banks reported that businessmen who had borrowed money were falling behind in their payments. Vacant houses were a common sight in Vancouver and New Westminster. Unemployed men walked the streets and queued up for handouts of bread and soup in church halls. Then came a succession of whispers that finally changed to shouts of "Gold!" By the summer of 1897, every-body in the province had heard a story about a prospector panning frozen gravel and happening upon a vein worth hundreds, even thousands, of dollars. The result was a stampede from at least half the countries of the world to an isolated bay in the strip of territory called the Alaska Panhandle. From Skagway, the town at the head of the bay, feverish fortune hunters climbed passes in the coastal mountains that led to the Yukon and the Atlin district.

In August 1896, George Washington Carmack had arrived at the Mounted Police post in the Yukon town of Forty Mile to register a mining claim. His discovery of gold-bearing gravel in a section of Rabbit Creek (Bonanza Creek) — a tiny tributary of the Klondike River — lured thousands of men and women to the Canadian north. Two years later, at the height of the rush to find a rich mother lode like the one that Carmack had literally stumbled upon, Prime Minister Wilfrid Laurier faced his first serious problem in Canada-U.S. relations.

When the United States had bought Alaska from Russia in 1867, the purchase included the Panhandle, a strip of coastline extending a considerable distance south. For years, Ottawa and Washington had disagreed as to the exact location of the border between British Columbia and the Alaska Panhandle, but neither country cared strongly about this boundary — until the sudden arrival of gold-mad adventurers raised awkward questions. When were the newcomers on American soil and when on Canadian soil? Which nation had the right to enforce law and order along the Panhandle route to the Klondike? Clifford Sifton had already sent Mounted Police detachments to the Chilkoot and White passes, where they were busy turning back those tenderfeet without a year's supply of food. The most important matter of all, however, stemmed from the gold itself. Canada and the United States had

Prospectors labouring up the Chilkoot Pass on their way to the Yukon: the Mounted Police checked that each brought in a year's food supply.

to work out their zones of power and potential profit.

Ottawa argued that the Alaska Panhandle boundary should follow the general curve of the coast, cutting across the heads of its long fiords: a boundary away from the coast would shut off northwestern British Columbia and the Yukon from the Pacific and a shipping connection with Canadian and American ports in the south. Washington insisted that the boundary lay along the summits of the mountains parallel to the coast, ignoring the awkward fact that the mountains did not always parallel the coast.

A settlement of the dispute being preferable to war, the problem was referred to a commission appointed by the U.S. and Britain. President Roosevelt got his way by applying his diplomatic principle of speaking softly but carrying a big stick. He made sure that at least half the members appointed to the commission shared his view of how the boundary should be defined — and ordered the dispatch of troops to Alaska. In 1903, the commission's decision in favour of the United States isolated northwestern British Columbia and the Yukon from the Pacific coast.

Sometimes, visitors who came to Canada in the early years of the new century declared that British Columbia was the most "British" of all the Canadian provinces. In some communities on Vancouver Island and in the Interior, private schools modelled on English public schools flourished as never before; "ranchers' clubs" and "bachelors' clubs" served as a haven for English "Bank-boys" and others; and meetings of hunt clubs, cricket matches, croquet tourneys, garden parties and band concerts were more popular diversions than a Canadian sport like lacrosse, which was so much enjoyed at New Westminster. Yet public reaction to the Alaskan Boundary Award in 1903 revealed a deep sense of national humiliation. The Vancouver *Province* wrote of the grievous wrong done to "every self-respecting and patriotic Canadian" by the sacrifice of Canadian territory and Canadian rights "on the altar of American friendship". And more than one loyal British Columbian felt with the Rossland *Miner* that "perhaps we should be thankful that there is left no territory which grasping Americans can reach for and complaisant British commissioners can give away".

The truth of the matter was that British Columbians were beginning to think of themselves at Canadians.

Picnics were a popular pastime for those Britishers
who tried to keep up appearances in an outpost of
Empire: Victoria, B.C.

9 "The twentieth century belongs to Canada!"

The period from 1900 to 1913 was one of rapid recovery in Canada from the low prices for agricultural products in the 1880s and 1890s. At long last, the farm business boomed. The new century brought to the prairies not only waves of immigrants but a steady stream of orders for barley, flaxseed, oats and wheat — particularly wheat. In the factories of the United States, Canada and Europe, growing numbers of workers needed bread: the demand was for wheat, wheat and more wheat. And the granary of the prairie west responded in astounding fashion. By 1905, Manitoba's annual wheat production had climbed from the one million bushels of 1885 to thirty-three million, and between there and the Rocky Mountains from five to thirty-five million bushels. All of which posed the problem of how to transport this massive output to market.

The CPR line to Fort William was the only outlet to the east, and as early as 1901 that freight system, together with its backup storage and shipping facilities, was breaking down. Farmers needed more boxcars to move their ever-mounting production of grain. Even Van Horne — now president of the CPR — admitted that "the hopper is too big for the spout." Another related problem was that, with the discovery of hardier, frost-beating strains of wheat, settlers were homesteading well north of the transcontinental line; CPR branch lines to Saskatoon and Edmonton could not keep pace with the steady surge of settlement. Saskatoon, a village of 113 people in 1901, had become a city of 12 000 by 1911. That same year, Edmonton, once a small stopover point on the way to the Yukon gold fields, had 30 000 inhabitants.

There was angry agreement all over the West that one railway was far from enough. Added to which, Westerners had long been saying that the CPR needed competition to force down its oppressive freight rates.

Prime Minister Laurier announced that he wanted to build a "larger Canada," and that railways were the means to develop and exploit the nation's vast natural resources. Being as shrewd a political opportunist as Macdonald, Laurier planned to use railway expansion both to pacify western farmers and to mollify those Quebec politicians who wanted French Canadians to have their frontier opportunities in the forests and mines of central Canada.

Donald Mann of the Canadian Northern Railway was quick to agree with the prime minister's vision of a larger Canada. He maintained that his company, unlike the CPR, was worth only "what the soil will yield, what the mines will produce; the timber and the fisheries."

*

Donald Mann was an Ontario farm boy, with an aversion to agriculture, who had ventured westward and wangled a small construction contract on the CPR line being built west of Winnipeg. In 1884, he picked up a subcontract to build snowsheds in the Kicking Horse Pass, where he met another farmboy-turned-contractor from Ontario, William Mackenzie, his future partner. (There's a tale that their first meeting was a shouting match over the ownership of a particular boxcar-load of pack mules.) The two men worked together for a time on CPR lines in eastern Canada, but eventually parted company. Mackenzie went to Toronto where, with a group of entrepreneurs, he financed the electrification of that city's streetcar system. Mann, after a brief, frustrating attempt at railway construction in Chile, returned to the prairies; he had a feeling that something would turn up there.

Mann's hunch was right. The Manitoba government needed someone to get the Lake Manitoba Railway and Canal Company, a prairie

WESTERN CANADA
THE NEW ELDORADO

HOMES FOR EVERYBODY
EASY TO REACH
NOTHING TO FEAR
PROTECTED BY THE GOVERNMENT

WHEAT LAND
RICH VIRGIN SOIL
LAND FOR MIXED FARMING
LAND FOR CATTLE RAISING

A WHEAT FARM IN THE CANADIAN WEST

MARKETING HIS CROP IN WESTERN CANADA

THE OLD AND THE NEW HOME

"WESTWARD THE STAR OF EMPIRE TAKES ITS WAY"

THIS IS YOUR OPPORTUNITY WHY NOT EMBRACE IT?

FREE 160 ACRES WESTERN CANADA FARM LANDS

INFORMATION AND ADVICE CAN BE OBTAINED FROM
W.D. SCOTT
SUPERINTENDENT OF IMMIGRATION
OTTAWA, CANADA
J. OBED SMITH
ASST. SUPERINTENDENT OF IMMIGRATION
11-12 CHARING CROSS
LONDON, ENG.

Federal government poster promoting the "New Eldorado." *See previous page.*

Grand Trunk Pacific (GTP) tracklayers work westward through Manitoba in 1906. Much GTP and Canadian Northern trackage paralleled the Winnipeg-Edmonton Trail, today's Yellowhead Highway.

branch line that existed only on paper, constructed and operating. He claimed he could do the job, obtained the contract, and promptly invited his old buddy Mackenzie to help him.

Beginning in 1895, the dazzling combination of Mann's construction experience and Mackenzie's golden tongue persuaded politicans and businessmen to put money into their rail projects. The two made an unbeatable team. They built the Lake Manitoba Railway by getting a bank to guarantee some of the costs and local farm women to help construct embankments. Within nine months of starting, the Gladstone-Dauphin section of the line was open for business. "Service" was the company motto, though at first there was only sufficient rolling stock to operate one train. As one of Mann and Mackenzie's employees noted afterwards, "We had more stopping places to the ten miles, I think, than any railway in the world. Only a few of them were on the timetable." Families in the Dauphin Lake district, however, were ecstatic; they were being served by a railway that, in contrast to the CPR, acted more like a servant and less like a master. They promptly christened it "The Farmers' Friend."

Mann and Mackenzie were successful in most of their ventures because they knew how to trim costs to turn a profit. A typical example was the Manitoba and South Eastern Railway Company (MSER), another line the provincial government was eager to establish. This one was to run from St. Boniface eastward through some settled country and then through the soupy muskeg of the Canadian Shield to the Lake of the Woods. The two partners, figuring that it would someday be a link between the Dauphin line they had taken over and their most recent acquisiton, the Ontario and Rainy River Railway, decided that the MSER had possibilities. To add to the project's attraction, the Manitoba govern-ment was willing to guarantee part of the construction costs and include in the railway's charter a land grant of almost 300 000 hectares. Moreover, timber along the right of way could be cut and sold to feed the fireplaces of homes in St. Boniface and a fast-growing Winnipeg. (Eventually, the MSER's "Muskeg Special" chugged into St. Boniface several times a week with flatcars stacked with cordwood.) Although some sections of track constructed in Shield country proved to be expensive, Mann and Mackenzie made money on the MSER almost from the start.

In 1899, the ambitious partners started expanding east of Winnipeg, gambling that thousands of immigrants would homestead the northern sections of the Fertile Belt, survive the hazards of prairie weather, and harvest large crops of the latest frost-beating strains of wheat. In anticipation of this expansion, they negotiated railway deals with Manitoba and Ontario in order to connect with the grain ships that hauled cargoes through the Great Lakes from Superior to Montreal. Manitoba even agreed to guarantee construction costs to a maximum of $20,000 a mile on the *Ontario* section of the Winnipeg-Port Arthur line, in return for special low freight rates for wheat, so great was the value placed by the prairie province on an alternative to the CPR route to the Lakehead. Soon, freight traffic on Mann-Mackenzie lines leading to Lake Superior was so heavy that a million-bushel grain elevator at Port Arthur had hardly been completed before the construction of another had to be begun.

Next, the Canadian Northern expanded in the opposite direction, arriving in Edmonton in 1905. This time, the persuasive Mackenzie induced the federal government to guarantee some construction costs. Alongside its right of way were numerous railway stations, the focal points of collections of stores, post offices, banks and boarding houses serving the settlers that

185

Tête Jaune Cache, B.C., 1912. Whisky was a forbidden item in railway workers' bunkhouses but, during the construction of the transcontinentals, someone tried to smuggle into camp these "blind pigs" stuffed with bottles.

A prairie blacksmith's shop in 1910. Like the village store, it was an unofficial social centre, a place to catch up on world events — and local gossip.

poured out of every westbound train. A typical new town in Saskatchewan was North Battleford, which was "ushered into existence in June 1905 with one house to its credit"; six months later, when the Canadian Northern reached Edmonton, North Battleford's population was 500. A total of 132 settlements, Mann claimed, owed their existence to his railway.

Mackenzie and Mann then decided that they could achieve an even greater railway feat and proclaimed their intention of extending the Canadian Northern into a transcontinental system. They could do so because they had been building eastward from Port Arthur on the Lakehead to link up with lines they had bought (or leased running rights on) in Ontario, Quebec and the Maritime provinces. They had already made arrangements with British Columbia for crossing the province to the Pacific coast. The major reason for this dramatic decision was serious competition in 1903 from an unexpected source, a combination of the federal government and the Grand Trunk Railway (GTR).

The Grand Trunk, long established in Ontario and Quebec, had been repeatedly invited by John A. Macdonald in the 1870s and 1880s to build the first transcontinental, but had refused. Its insistence on building in American territory south of Lake Superior had clashed with Macdonald's even more stubborn desire for an all-Canadian route. Now, in the early 1900s, the GTR wanted to expand into a wheat-rich western Canada. Unfortunately, despite some nudging by Prime Minister Laurier, neither the GTR nor the Canadian Northern would take the obvious action and amalgamate or co-operate. Even more unfortunately, there was much disagreement on Parliament Hill as to which railway company should receive Ottawa's support, though Liberals and Conservatives alike agreed that Canada needed a second transcontinental. In that era of giddy prosperity, epitomized by Laurier's clarion call that the twentieth century belonged to Canada, few Canadians questioned the wisdom of ultimately allowing the construction of *two* more transcontinental railway systems.

Laurier, who had always favoured the Grand Trunk, obtained reluctant approval from his cabinet and Parliament for a GTR line from New Brunswick to the Pacific. The line's eastern section, called the National Transcontinental Railway, would be built from Moncton, New Brunswick, to Winnipeg — some 2880 kilometres — at public expense and would be leased to a subsidiary of the GTR, the Grand Trunk Pacific Railway (GTPR). The western section, from Winnipeg to British Columbia's northern coast (at the new terminus of Prince Rupert), would be built by the GTPR, with the assistance of certain government guarantees. So, in 1905, construction began on both the eastern and western sections of the Grand Trunk's transcontinental. In the course of nine years of track laying, costs exceeded estimates by a staggering 160 per cent, averaging $88,300 a mile, mainly because the GTR executive insisted on building a main line of high quality, while ignoring interim revenue that could have been earned from local feeder extensions.

Meanwhile, nothing daunted, Mann went right on building his transcontinental, financed by millions of dollars borrowed in Britain and other European countries by Mackenzie. And they obliged Laurier, the public champion of national development, to guarantee construction bonds of $35,000 a mile on the Port Arthur-Montreal section of their route. Sensibly, the two kept to their proven principle of building high-quality tracks only through heavy traffic areas;

The John Deere Company is a famous name in agricultural machinery. Here, Deere binders, hitched up to gasoline-driven tractors, make short work of a grain field in 1911. *See next page.*

unlike the GTR, they built stretches of inexpensive track, which were improved and upgraded as revenues increased. By 1918, the Canadian Northern was operating from Quebec City to Vancouver. The spectacular success of Mann and Mackenzie was due to their acumen. Their trans continental was a collection of many small railway companies linked by complicated financial arrangements: cash subsidies from all three levels of government, land grants, loans and bond issues.

The insanity of three national lines became most apparent in the near-parallel rails of the Canadian Northern and the GTPR in their Winnipeg-Edmonton-Yellowhead Pass divisions, and the Canadian Northern and CPR trackage between Kamloops and Vancouver, which duplicated one another on opposite sides of the Thompson and Fraser rivers. By 1915, Canada had the greatest rail mileage per head of population of any country in the world. But a price for this extravagant coverage had to be paid – and is, in fact, still being paid – by Canadian taxpayers. Large stretches of track ran through the unpopulated, unprofitable regions of the Shield and the mountainous interior of B.C. Thus income earned from freight traffic on the prairies or in southern Ontario and southern Quebec had to be used to meet interest charges on the enormous amounts of money borrowed to build the GTPR and Canadian Northern. The war that raged in Europe in 1914-18 only made matters worse. Immigration virtually ceased, Britain was no longer able to invest in Canada, and these two transcontinentals soon felt the lack of new customers, new freight and new capital. In 1914, both companies were still laying track in the mountains of B.C. when the flow of people and pounds dried up. Even after the completion of each line, neither company could pay its way

and was only kept going by subsidies from Victoria and Ottawa.

The outcome was predictable. In 1917, Ottawa was forced to take over ownership of the debt-ridden Canadian Northern. In 1919, the Canadian National Railway Company (CNR) was incorporated, the beginnings of today's CN. Within six years, Ottawa also had to take over a bankrupt National Transcontinental, *and* a bankrupt Grand Trunk Pacific, *and* a bankrupt Grand Trunk.

*

While immigrants were eagerly welcomed by the Dominion of Canada, they were received with restrained enthusiasm by the government of the North-West Territories. The basic reason was the inability of that government to act with the powers of a province.

The Manitoba Act of 1870 that created the Province of Manitoba and the NWT gave them the same lieutenant-governor. Five years later, the NWT was given its own lieutenant-governor; but all legislative and executive powers were vested in this official, who answered to the federal cabinet. Ottawa divided the NWT into nine districts in 1882 for postal and legal purposes, but could not be persuaded to create a territorial legislature until 1888. The legislature was little more than a debating society; any law it proposed was subject to the approval of the lieutenant-governor and Ottawa. Not until 1897, when Clifford Sifton pushed through a bill for true representative government in the Territories, was an executive council established.

Meanwhile, many of the newcomers to the NWT bypassed existing settlements, fanned out to create communities far removed from towns and rail facilities, and promptly demanded such services as roads, schools and ferries. Since the

189

Following an old community-help tradition, neighbours raise a family's barn at Roland, Manitoba.

Rivalries in bareback riding, saddle-bronc riding, calf roping and steer roping were formalized in such special events as rodeos and stampedes. Women competed as roughriders as well as ropers.

land was semiarid, they also demanded wells and reservoirs. In addition, the territorial government was always being petitioned to hand out monies for such varied purposes as exterminating wolves, constructing fireguards, and supporting the poor and aged.

The territorial government never had enough funds to meet all these needs, yet was unwilling to impose a heavy burden of taxes on pioneers struggling to build a new life in a new land. The root of the problem lay in the fact that, unlike the five eastern provinces and British Columbia, the NWT did not possess the land, timber and mineral rights within its boundaries, so could not generate revenue by selling these rights. The federal government had kept these rights to itself "for the purposes of the Dominion" — to give land grants to settlers and railways. And, by 1900, Ottawa had granted millions of hectares of land in the Territories, sixteen million of them to railways alone. In addition, the CPR had been exempted from taxation on its lands in the Territories "for 20 years after the grant thereof." Worse still from the Territories' point of view, the CPR was "forever free from taxation" in respect to all its stations, grounds, workshops, buildings and yards. Yet the only money the NWT government had to work with came from various local licences and taxes and an annual grant by Parliament. In fact, the legislative assembly of the NWT complained to Ottawa in 1896 that that grant was not enough: the population had increased by fifty-six per cent in five years, but, in the same period, the grant had increased by only sixteen per cent.

In no matter was the Territories so helpless as that of railways. After 1896, when immigration and grain production were increasing at fantastic rates, many a pioneer community was eighty or more kilometres from the nearest branch line. Yet the NWT government had no power to authorize the construction of lines or to give railway companies incentives in the form of land grants or cash. The transportation and grain storage facilities of the CPR and other smaller lines were totally inadequate: thousands of bushels of wheat often lay rotting in the fields or clogging grain elevators. The NWT's legislative assembly regularly accused the CPR of failing to meet the necessity for grain transportation and of causing enormous losses to grain growers.

Despite constant reminders about the lack of money and poor transportation facilities, Parliament did not respond to the territorial government's requests. Despite the prosperity of the years from 1898 to 1904, when the Dominion treasury was reporting a surplus of income over expenditure, Ottawa ignored NWT appeals for larger grants.

As early as 1896, debates in the territorial legislative assembly introduced the idea of provincial status. Dr. R. G. Brett, the member for Banff in the District of Alberta, argued that it was "high time" for the western portion of the NWT to demand provincehood. Premier Frederick W. G. Haultain took matters a stage further: with help from Clifford Sifton, he tried for almost two years to persuade Laurier to grant provincial status to the Territories. The prime minister declined to do so. In Laurier's opinion, there were not yet enough people to justify the creation of a province. He also had a general election coming up in 1904 and had no desire to annoy eastern voters with a western issue.

By 1904, the composition of the North-West Territories had changed. One of the original nine districts, the Yukon, had been severed from the NWT in 1898 and made into a separate territory under the administration of a commissioner and an advisory council. The Districts of Assiniboia,

A ten-dollar payment at the Dominion Lands Office in Saskatoon allowed homesteader Albert Andrew to begin "proving up" his 160 acres.

No. 61607

DEPARTMENT OF THE INTERIOR.

Dominion Lands--Sub-Agent's Receipt,

Amount, $ *10* F.   *Saskatoon* Sub-Agency *Aug 21* 19 *06*

RECEIVED from *Albert Andrew* of *Saskatoon* P.O.

the sum of *Ten* Dollars in payment of

homestead entry fee for *N W* Section *16* Township *33* Range *28* West *2* Meridian

NOTICE.—This payment above acknowledged is received subject for its acceptance by the Agent of Dominion Lands at *Regina* who will refund it if it cannot be applied to the purpose for which it was made owing to the land not being vacant and available.

Robt McCulΓ‘¡och

Sub-Agent.

Saskatchewan and Alberta had become prime agricultural areas and centres of population. The more northerly, heavily forested District of Athabasca possessed mineral resources of great potential, but was sparsely settled. And the northern and northeastern Districts of Mackenzie, Keewatin, Ungava and Franklin could not be developed or settled.

Haultain and his colleagues wanted to unite the Districts of Assiniboia, Saskatchewan, Alberta and the southern portion of Athabasca into one province. Some of their opponents in the legislature wanted to make these same districts into two provinces of equal size, and one member was in favour of the creation of three provinces.

Arguments for provincial status were substantiated by the incredibly rapid development of the southernmost disricts. The demands of a population that had swelled from 160 000 in 1901 to nearly 500 000 by 1905 were too great even for Ottawa to ignore. Such massive immigration and settlement emphasized the need for more schools, more roads, more rail lines — and, of course, highlighted the NWT government's inability to meet just its day-to-day expenses. Provincial status was the obvious solution, in order to be able to borrow money, receive a provincial subsidy from Ottawa, charter railway companies, and possibly even receive compensation for lands given away by Ottawa.

*

In February 1905, Prime Minister Wilfrid Laurier made an important speech in the House of Commons. He reminded the members of the House that a frontier region, originally administered by the government of the Province of Manitoba, was now a prosperous society that only needed to be given certain powers of self-government to complete the chain of provinces from sea to sea envisaged by the Fathers of Confederation in 1867. He informed the House that only four main matters had to be settled: the number of provinces to be created; the ownership of the public (unoccupied) lands in the proposed provinces; the financial terms granted to the new provinces; and the school system to be established there.

If the ghost of Louis Riel was present that day, it must have been pleased to hear the prime minister comment on what he termed "perhaps the most important question": education. True to his French-Canadian birth, Laurier insisted that the Roman Catholic minority have the power to establish their own schools and receive a share of public monies.

In proposing a dual system of government-supported schools, one anglophone and Protestant, the other francophone and Roman Catholic, Laurier touched off an eruption of wrath. As in Riel's time, religious passions and cultural prejudices boiled over. The "North-West School Question," as it came to be called, infuriated the anglophone majority in the Territories. The Orange Order of Canada, sundry Protestant ministers, Robert Borden's Conservative opposition, and even many Liberal MPs refused to accept a twin system of education. Clifford Sifton was so outraged by Laurier's proposal that he resigned from the cabinet. Newspapers across the country pointed out that though Riel had obliged Macdonald to include separate schools in the Manitoba Act, Manitoba had later made its schools into a single, nonreligious provincial system.

In the end, Laurier backed down and agreed that the existing educational system in the Territories would continue unchanged. The political price of the controversy, however, was high — two prices, to be exact. Sifton, the strongest voice the West had sent to Ottawa, remained estranged by the episode, a factor in his ultimate retirement from politics. And a Quebec still resentful over the treatment of French-speaking Catholic schoolchildren in Manitoba had been further alienated.

After the fuss and furor of the North-West School Question, the other three main matters — the number of provinces, land ownership and financial terms — were, by comparison, quickly settled.

Canada's provinces, Laurier reasoned, should be as near as possible the same size. Setting aside the northern half of the NWT as "absolutely unfit for agriculture," his government decided to give provincial status to the 1 430 000 square kilometres between Manitoba and the Rockies, and between the international border and the sixtieth parallel of latitude. This immense region would become two provinces of approximately the same size (750 000 square kilometres) and approximately the same population (250 000). The dividing line was to be the fourth meridian of longitude — which surprised the inhabitants of Lloydminister, for the Alberta-Saskatchewan border sliced right through the middle of their town.

Like Macdonald before him when Manitoba was created, Laurier refused to hand over ownership of public lands and forest and mineral rights. The homesteading system that was making a reality of Sifton's "Last, Best West" would continue to be administered by the Dominion. No territorial protest, argument or appeal could change the prime minister's mind on this matter. But he was prepared to pay some compensation for federal ownership of public lands (plus the normal, annual provincial subsidy). The payment "in lieu of lands" proved to be a disappointing one. For each province, it was calculated by Ottawa on the basis of twenty-five million acres (10 Mha) at $1.50 an acre — at a time when the HBC and the CPR were selling land for four to five dollars an acre.

*

In 1905, at Edmonton and Regina, the provinces of Alberta and Saskatchewan were officially welcomed into Confederation, on September 1 and 4 respectively. If the negotiations for provincehood had been difficult and disappointing, at least the birthday of each province was celebrated with picnics and pageantry. The scene at Edmonton was typical of the occasion, and one matter touched on by Laurier in his speech was very significant. "We do not anticipate, and we do not want, that any individuals should forget the land of their origin or their ancestors. Let them look to the past, but let them also look to the future; . . . let them look to the land of their ancestors, but let them also look to the land of their children." A devoted disciple of British liberal principles, it was characteristic of Laurier that he should advise the prairie newcomers to "Canadianize" themselves, to become basically British in outlook. He may also have been reassuring them that they lived in a democratic country, because the reception given immigrants depended very much on their country of origin.

*

In 1905, Edmontonian Frank Oliver succeeded Clifford Sifton as minister of the interior and soon made it clear that he did not favour his predecessor's "open door" immigration policy. He amended the Immigration Act by increasing the scope of ministerial powers to reject or deport immigrants. Oliver was not the only politician with an isolationist outlook; his actions did not satisfy some of his Conservative critics across the floor of the Commons, a number of whom condemned communal or group settle-

Doukhobors labouring for a railway company to earn extra dollars often took their horses with them as draft animals, so their womenfolk had to hitch themselves to the plough.

ment as a prime obstacle to what they called "Canadianization." They distrusted Mennonites and Mormons, Doukhobors and Hutterites. They wanted the Immigration Act made restrictive, exclusive and selective. One of them even expressed the opinion that "Canada is today the dumping ground for the refuse of every country in the world." Yet a religious and cultural separateness was the reason why these groups had come to Canada in the first place — often with the co-operation of federal authorities.

Settlers from Britain were easily assimilated into the predominantly Protestant, English-speaking society of the prairies and British Columbia. Also absorbed with little difficulty were American businessmen or farmers, particularly those with a knowledge of dry-farming techniques, which they put to good use in the arid areas of southern Alberta and Saskatchewan. The only Americans who were not welcomed by immigration officials were blacks. Climate was the reason usually given to discourage any enquiries by black leaders, but colour was the real one. This became clear in 1911, when a large number of blacks in Oklahoma tried to arrange group entry; they did not encounter an official ban on black immigration but were kept out by suspiciously strict regulations in such matters as health and reserves of money.

Eastern Europeans, with their curious costume and culture, were automatically regarded as foreigners. Of these particular newcomers, the greatest number were from the southern reaches of the polyglot Hapsburg empire. Officially classed as Ukrainians, these people formed compact settlements near Dauphin, Yorkton, Innisfree, and in the Edna-Star district northeast of Edmonton. They earned a grudging respect among farmers and railwaymen for determination and hard work, but, among tem-

198

During the rioting provoked by the Asiatic Exclusion League in downtown Vancouver in 1907, this wrecked store was typical of the vandalism to property owned by Japanese and Chinese.

Prime Minister Laurier's Inaugural Day address in Edmonton upon the creation of Alberta. Three days later, in Regina, he gave a similar speech about the new province of Saskatchewan.

ERNEST BROWN
COPYRIGHT

Dickering with the Factor by Frank E. Schoonover, circa 1912.

perance advocates and Methodist missionaries, earned a reputation for overly long, overly alcoholic wedding celebrations and an un-Canadian religion (Greek Catholic or Russian Orthodox).

However, it was the Chinese, Japanese, Sikhs (and other Indians) — the most obviously "un-Canadian" of all newcomers – who were regarded as quite unassimilable and, therefore, quite undesirable. And the centre of controversy over immigration from Asia was British Columbia. Here, there was a resident population of several thousand Chinese, the relatives and descendants of the 15 000 Chinese imported to help construct the CPR. John A. Macdonald had expressed the prevalent view of the Chinese when he spoke of them as "an alien race," but he refused to deny them entry, informing his fellow members in the Commons that "either you must have this labour or you cannot have the railway."

Public resentment of Asian immigrants found a violent release in Vancouver in 1907. It was a year of high unemployment and recession in British Columbia, coinciding with an exceptional number of Asian immigrants: 8000 Japanese, 2000 Sikhs from India and 1500 Chinese. And as lawyer-turned politician Richard Bedford Bennett (a future prime minister) told a British Columbia audience, "We must not allow our shores to be overrun by Asiatics, and become dominated by an alien race." An Asiatic Exclusion League was formed in Vancouver, and one of its mass meetings degenerated into a mob invasion of Chinatown and "Little Tokyo." Stones were thrown through the windows of Japanese stores, which roused their owners and families to grab stones, sticks and bottles to rout the invaders. In later fighting the next day, rowdy Leaguers were again worsted. The Immigration Act was tightened up to cut off the flow of Japenese and Indian immigrants, but even the continuation of a head tax of $550 on each Chinese immigrant did not stem that inflow.

Slights and sneers were the immigrants lot, and World War I brought out prejudice on a massive scale. The nearly 500 000 immigrants of German or Austro-Hungarian birth were treated with suspicion, resentment and even hate. Prime Minister Robert Borden reminded Canadians that, having invited immigrants of enemy origin to become citizens of Canada, "we owe to them in the trying circumstances in which they are placed the duty of fairness and consideration." To no avail. Public opinion forced his government to pass stringent legislation. Failure to report monthly and register as an alien, or suspicion of complicity with the German or Austrian enemy, would result in internment in one of the work camps organized by the federal Department of Militia and Defence. About 8000 Ukrainian men were eventually interned, of whom 3000 were classified as reservists in the Austro-Hungarian army and treated as prisoners of war. The remainder were paroled daily for labour outside the work camps, most of which were set up in Ontario and British Columbia.

The problems of prejudice that immigrants encountered in the West raised awkward questions in the minds of Canadians. How could all these newcomers be assimilated into a culture that was essentially British? Would western Canada become a melting pot like the United States, or would it become a motley mosaic of peoples?

203

In 1914, East Indian immigrants aboard the S.S. *Komagata Maru* were prevented from landing by police and immigration officials, so these Sikhs refused authorities permission to board by bombarding them with coal.

10   War and Peace

The summer of 1914 was extremely hot and dry, and prairie farmers watched their crops wither under a searing sun. For many families in southern Alberta and Saskatchewan, it was the fourth successive year of drought, a hint of things to come. In Manitoba, prospectors were fanning out from the town of The Pas to stake thousands of claims in the province's newly discovered mineral belt. In British Columbia, the focus of attention was Vancouver harbour, where 376 East Indian immigrants aboard the *Komagata Maru* were determined to enter the country; and a handful of federal immigration officials were equally determined that they would not. A detachment of militiamen and HMCS *Rainbow* were rushed to Vancouver as visible signs of Ottawa's refusal to accept the "foreigners." After two months of legal battles, these Sikhs were forced to return to their homeland after their Japanese charter vessel was restocked with food and water.

In Europe that same summer, an obscure student in an obscure town shot and killed the heir to the throne of the Austro-Hungarian Empire, thus aggravating a mixture of economic and national rivalries that ranged Europe into two armed camps. The Triple Alliance of Germany, Austro-Hungary and Italy prepared to do battle with the Triple Entente of France, Russia and Britain. By August 4, the British Empire was at war, and Canada, being part of the Empire, was too. This news spread through western Canada the next day and produced delirious demonstrations of loyalty ranging from parades to gifts of thousands of bushels of grain, 1500 horses and thousands of cases of canned salmon.

For Canada, the conflict was very much a soldiers' war. At Ypres in 1915, the First Canadian Division was exposed to the first poison-gas attack of the war. Its infantrymen and gunners helped to halt and fling back the hordes of German infantry trying to capture the Channel ports through which Britain and the Empire sent reinforcements and supplies to the battlefields of France and Belgium. That same year, two more divisions were formed and sent overseas to form the Canadian Corps, which gained a tremendous fighting reputation in such battles as the Somme, Vimy Ridge and Passchendaele.

Many Canadians who left home to join the army transferred to the Royal Flying Corps (RFC) or the Royal Naval Air Service (RNAS). When these two groups were joined together to form the Royal Air Force (RAF) in 1917, about twenty-five per cent of the pilots and observers were Canadian. Although Canadians distinguished themselves in the aerial bombing pioneered by the RNAS, it was the aces of the RFC who caught the attention of the press and public. One of the great stories of World War I is the encounter between the doyen of German flyers, Baron Manfred von Richthofen, and a young RAF lieutenant from Edmonton named Wilfred R. "Wop" May. In anticipation of his eighty-first victory, Richthofen harried May — whose guns had jammed — and chased him over the war-torn surface of the Somme. The youngster expected to die from the bursts of bullets that were turning his plane into a sieve, but was saved by a boyhood friend, Roy Brown, who got on Richthofen's tail and killed Germany's "Red Knight."

The war effort was, of course, also a production battle waged in fields and factories, in mines and forests.

The conflict created a huge demand for one particular export: wheat. Encouraged by the federal government, by the return of regular rains, and by the fact that the price of No. 1 Northern was climbing towards two dollars a bushel, prairie farmers brought eighty per cent more land under cultivation. In Saskatchewan,

Immigrants from Colorado arrive at Bassano, Alberta, in 1914. As a popular ditty of the time revealed, "The Yankees in the land abound/For Uncle Sam gets all around/And with his push and grit and go/Is sure to make the country grow."

Servicewomen on inspection parade at Hastings Park Race Track, Vancouver, 1915. Of the 600 000 Canadian men and women who served overseas, 60 000 were killed and 180 000 wounded.

A threshing gang near Prince Albert, Saskatchewan, circa 1915. Many men came from eastern Canada on CPR "harvest trains" to work the grain fields for a couple of dollars a day and keep.

where there was a great deal of fresh land-breaking, even school students had parts to play in the war effort.

In 1917 the Saskatchewan Department of Agriculture estimated that gophers destroyed on the average of a quarter of a million acres [100 000 ha] of crop each year. . . . Municipal and farm organization officials together with school teachers were urged to encourage the children to snare, trap, and shoot gophers. Competitions, among schools and children, were stimulated by awards of 37 inscribed shields, 36 medals and a gold watch. May 1 was Gopher Day when 880 schools accounted for more than half a million gophers.

To encourage high school lads from the towns and cities to help in seed-time and harvest, the Canadian government issued bronze buttons inscribed "Son of the Soil". While these miniature medallions were favourably received and proudly displayed on lapels of Sunday suits, a major inducement was the folding money for pants pockets and bank accounts. Wage rates from threshing hovered around $5 a day, rising in exceptional instances to $10 per day plus food and shelter before the war ended. The soldier, enlisted in Canada's army, received $1.10 per day.

The war did not, however, increase the West's manufacturing output. The production of guns and other military equipment took place in factories in Ontario, Quebec and, to a limited extent, in British Columbia. By accident or design — and the prairie west suspected that it was due to the powerful, persuasive voices of Toronto and Montreal manufacturers — it was eastern Canada that got the profitable war contracts from Ottawa. If anything, the prairie west became more dependent than ever on the sale of field produce. The one comforting factor was that, by 1917, wheat was $2.21 a bushel, three times its prewar level.

*

One direct result of the war was that it accelerated the achievement of women's right to vote and hold public office. Since the turn of the century, more and more women had been entering the work force, usually as domestics, teachers and typists. The trend of employment outside the home was quickened by war.

As suffragist organizations were quick to publicize, many Canadian women were making their sacrifice for the war effort. In offices, stores, warehouses, factories and gas stations, women took the place of men who had enlisted. Women drove streetcars, serviced rolling stock in railroad shops, kept farms producing — and worked extra hours at every job. They gave up their leisure time to serve in the Red Cross, to knit and sew in local bees for the men in uniform, to make up food parcels for the Canadian Corps, and were the first to promote meatless and breadless days in order to conserve foodstuffs to send to Europe. And, of course, women were expected to "carry on as if nothing had happened" after a husband or father, son or brother had been killed or maimed.

The part that women played in the war made it difficult for men to argue that women did not deserve equal citizenship, a subject that was particularly difficult to argue with Mrs. Nellie McClung. A popular writer and lecturer, she was as doughty a defender of women's rights as she was a strong supporter of the temperance movement.

Born Helen Letitia Mooney in Ontario in 1873, she was educated in the Souris River valley of Manitoba and at the Normal School in Winnipeg. In 1907, she began to take an active part in the Women's Christian Temperance Union and in the Political Equality League. In time, she became Canada's best known suffragist. Her argument for votes for women was unanswerable. Women were not asking for, she stated, "a reform, or a gift, or a favour but for a *right* – not for mercy but for justice."

Wartime conditions provided just the circumstances needed by Mrs. McClung and her associates to organize protest parades and badger western premiers with demands for the female franchise. Provincial legislatures were deluged by petitions signed by thousands of determined women, and Nellie McClung's dramatic lectures converted many a male listener. And so it was four western governments that acted ahead of Ottawa in the matter of women's suffrage. In the early months of 1916, each prairie province granted its female residents the franchise. A year later, British Columbia passed the same legislation. In fact, by 1922, all provinces, except Quebec, had granted women the vote.

In 1917, the women's rights movement scored other successes in the West. In Saskatchewan, Joan Ethel MacLachlan became the first woman justice of the peace and, later, the first woman judge of juvenile court. In Alberta, Louise McKinney and Roberta MacAdams were elected to the legislature, and Emily Murphy became the first woman in the entire British Empire to be appointed a magistrate.

On her first day in court, she was challenged by a defence lawyer who argued that her decisions were invalid because of her sex. His precedent was a decision of an English court in 1876: "women are persons in matters of pains and penalties, but are not persons in matters of right and privileges." Since being a magistrate was a privilege, Mrs. Murphy, a non-person, was ineligible. This taunt, the so-called "persons argument," was used repeatedly against both Judge Murphy and her Calgary colleague Alice Jamieson until 1917, when the provincial Supreme Court silenced it on the grounds of "reason and good sense."

Despite requests from women's organizations, the federal government refused to appoint

In 1917, at Westcott, Alberta, several women vote for the first time in their lives. It was in this province that the female franchise was first exercised in Canada.

Michel, B.C. A mine rescue team, circa 1912.

Clearing track in the Carlyle (southeastern Saskatchewan) subdivision of the Canadian Northern Railway
in 1916.

a woman senator, using the familiar "persons argument." But five particular Alberta women would not be denied. Emily Murphy, Nellie McClung, Henrietta Edwards, Louise McKinney and Irene Parlby asked the Supreme Court of Canada for an interpretation of the constitution. The Court ruled that women were not "fit and qualified persons" for appointment to the Senate. So the "Famous Five," as they came to be known, then carried their cause to the Privy Council in London — and this time the decision was in their favour. The Privy Council noted that there was no specific mention of sex in the clause of the British North America Act describing the qualifications of a senator, and that in the act the word "persons" included both sexes. In 1929, the Liberal government in Ottawa appointed Canada's first woman senator; it was not Emily Murphy, who had led the long legal fight for recognition, but Liberal party worker Cairine Wilson of Ontario.

*

The soldiers came home, their uniforms specially cleaned, their boots specially shined, for home-town victory marches — only to find jobs scarce and getting scarcer. Many men, lately valued members of the famous Canadian Corps, found themselves moneyless, jobless, and classified as unskilled labour. Few Canadians realized that the war had merely postponed a recession. Throughout the nation, the plight of working men and women drew public attention to a number of basic problems as soon as the war ended.

In western Canada, the seeds of the "troubled twenties" had been sown in the 1890s, when the prairies and British Columbia had experienced a tremendous boom in railway expansion, plus growth in the production and sometimes processing of grains, minerals and timber.

Winnipeg, Calgary, Edmonton and Vancouver gradually became manufacturing centres and acquired large populations of factory, construction and railway workers. Between 1891 and 1921, Winnipeg's population rose from 25 640 to 136 000, Calgary's from 4390 to 43 700, Edmonton's from 4170 to 31 060, and Vancouver's from 13 700 to 120 800.

The enormous profits being made by businessmen encouraged workers to form trade unions to seek higher wage rates and better working conditions. Men, women and children frequently worked twelve hours a day, seven days a week, for subsistence wages. And the conditions in which many of them lived in boom-time western Canada were both depressing and degrading. The bunkhouses of railway construction gangs or lumberjacks were gloomy, dirty and bug-ridden; sanitary facilities were poor or nonexistent. In British Columbia, mining corporations built the infamous "company towns," where workers and their families lived in housing that lacked lighting, water or sewage systems, and shopped at a company store that sold food at outrageous prices. The worst urban slum area was probably Winnipeg's North End, a section of the city occupied by many immigrant workers. Half of its houses were not connected to the city's water system; the toilet was often a backyard privy, and outbreaks of dysentery and typhoid were frequent.

Western employers countered union demands for legislative help by persuading politicians that employees were just one of a number of resources used in the manufacturing process. Workers had to be paid as little as possible to keep costs low, so that products would sell well in foreign markets. Even when governments did pass industrial legislation, their departments of labour seldom took the time or trouble to enforce the laws. One result was that the coal

Trans-Canada Flight, 1920 by R. W. Bradford. This painting is based on photos taken during the flight. The Canadian Air Force de Havilland 9a is flying over the mountains from Calgary, Alberta, to Revelstoke, B.C.

The chuckwagon routine was unpacking, cooking, repacking (stoves and pipes lashed to the rear) and driving like mad to the next bunch of hungry cow-hands.

Homesteading family in southern Alberta, 1918.

mines of British Columbia and Alberta acquired the reputation of being among the world's worst for gas explosions and cave-ins. In fact, in 1914, Canada's worst mine disaster to that time occurred at Hillcrest, Alberta, when 189 men were blown to pieces in a single explosion.

Above all, the great complaint of Canadian workers was that they were not getting their share of wartime prosperity. They maintained that wages were not keeping pace with prices. And they were right. Food prices alone had increased by sixty-five per cent between the outbreak of hostilities in 1914 and December 1917 — while the owners of many businesses and factories boasted of large profits from their "war efforts." Thus, when employers refused to discuss wage increases, workers resorted to their only weapon. Strikes took place all over Canada, but most of them occurred in the West. A series of strikes that began in 1916 in the coalfields of the Crowsnest Pass district of Alberta and British Columbia accounted for the greatest loss of production time. And in 1918, major work stoppages broke out in Winnipeg, Calgary and Vancouver.

Trade union membership in Canada had grown enormously by 1918, though a split had developed between the western and eastern sections of the labour movement. The Trades and Labour Congress (TLC), Canada's first major labour organization, was composed mainly of unions in Ontario in Quebec. TLC officials had always urged members to conduct peaceful bargaining, insisting that strikes were no substitute for patient negotiations to obtain shorter hours, safety regulations and fair-wage agreements. Western labour leaders, however, were much more hostile towards both employers and governments. During the annual convention of the TLC in 1918, many western delegates scorned the tradition of negotiation, pointing to the suc-

cess of the Bolshevik takeover of tsarist Russia the year before. If Soviet revolutionaries could set up a government in the interests of the working class, why couldn't the same be done in Canada? Why not seize control of the federal government and make all "capitalistic property" into the "collective property" of the workers?

Western hard-line unionists decided to hold their own conference in March 1919 in Calgary, where they began to organize the One Big Union (OBU), a Canadian version of the militant American labour organization of the same name. Shouts of revolution echoed through the meeting hall as delegates lambasted the Canadian political and economic systems and demanded an end to production based on the profit principle. They called for a people's government based on the Soviet model and a thirty-hour work week. Among other things, the Calgary conference announced June 1 as the date for a nation-wide strike to publicize labour's distrust of Ottawa.

It was against this frenetic background of OBU demands for a labour takeover of Canada that workers in the Winnipeg building and metal trades happened to go on strike on 1 May 1919. They were seeking higher wages, reduced working hours and recognition of the principle of collective bargaining. Two weeks later, the Winnipeg Trades and Labour Council, a conservative body committed to operating within the free-enterprise system, conducted a vote of the city's union members to determine whether or not they wanted a general strike in support of the construction and metal workers. The decision was overwhelmingly in favour of a strike. Overnight, business in the "Chicago of Canada," the nation's third-largest city and fourth-largest manufacturing centre, came to a halt as 30 000 male and female workers (including some 12 000 who were not even union members) left

In Winnipeg, on 21 June 1919, many people were injured in a Mounted Police charge, motivating these men to topple a streetcar. Later, they tried to set it on fire.

their jobs. Streetcars stopped running. Postmen no longer made their rounds. Cooks, waiters, butchers, bakers and store clerks quit. So did street cleaners, garbagemen, telegraph and telephone operators, and the vanmen who made home deliveries of bread and milk.

The Central Strike Committee realized that essential goods and services such as milk, bread, water and fuel could not be discontinued, and made sure that these were maintained. For the same reason, the committee urged city police to stay on the job, and replaced striking firemen with volunteers. And also ordered movie theatres and restaurants to reopen to help keep the streets clear of people who suddenly had nothing to do and nowhere to go. With all the newspapers closed down, the Strike Committee published its own journal, *The Western Labour News*, though telegraph companies were allowed to send out stories approved by the committee's board of censors.

Sympathy strikes broke out in Brandon, Edmonton, Calgary, Vancouver, Port Arthur and Toronto. This produced panic throughout the country — particularly in Ottawa, where politicians feared that this was a planned series of strikes similar to those that had led to the overthrow of the Russian government by "Red revolutionaries." However, the nation-wide general strike called for by the OBU did not take place, and people began to realize that the nation was not going to be seized by revolutionaries. As the stunning shock of the Winnipeg General Strike began to wear off, countermeasures were taken. Ottawa quietly reinforced army and Mounted Police garrisons in the city. The mayor and city council fired prostrike policemen and replaced them by enrolling university students and Canadian Corps veterans as special constables. Business and professional people formed a Citizens' Committee of One Thousand and subsidized an antistrike campaign. About one-third of the city's population was foreign-born, and much of the antistrike propaganda was aimed at what the Citizens' Committee called "bolsheviks and bohunks." Newspaper owners rounded up sufficient staff to print small editions that denounced the strikers as revolutionaries determined to replace the Canadian way of life "with the Russian Bolshevik system." Influenced by all this, many nonunion strikers began drifting back to their jobs.

Despite the strident antilabour attitude of Winnipeg's business community, negotiations between the metal workers and their employers had been continuing on in mutual good faith. On June 16, this resulted in the recognition of the principle of collective bargaining. Then, the very next day, a still-nervous federal government blundered.

Several so-called strike leaders were arrested and charged with sedition. To protest these arrests, there was a silent, orderly parade of ex-servicemen along Winnipeg's Main Street, though the mayor had forbidden such a demonstration. A force of Mounted Police and special constables armed with baseball bats charged again and again into the crowd of would-be marchers. By the time the street had been cleared, one man was dead, another was badly wounded (and later died), thirty people had been taken to hospital, and ninety-one put in jail.

Towards the end of June, the Winnipeg Trades and Labour Council declared an end to the strike. Its aftermath was very revealing. Of the so-called strike leaders and others taken into custody, four were of foreign birth but had had nothing to do with starting or conducting the strike. (Nonetheless, they were speedily deported.) The remaining ten were reputable citizens: James S. Woodsworth and William J. Ivens were Methodist ministers; John Queen and A. A.

Heaps were city aldermen; F. J. Dixon was a member of the Manitoba legislature and coeditor with Woodsworth of *The Western Labour News*; and the remaining five were union officials of considerable seniority. The trials of the ten on serious charges that included an attempt to "introduce a Soviet system of government" resulted in a tacit victory for the accused. Three were acquitted. Six received sentences of a year or less each, and one received a two-year prison sentence.

A commission of enquiry under lawyer H. A. Robson was appointed by the Manitoba government to investigate the causes of the strike and reported that there had been no intent to overthrow the federal government. Indeed, it was the commission's opinion that the real causes of the strike were the high cost of living, long work hours, low wages, poor working conditions, war profiteering, and the refusal of employers to recognize the principle of collective bargaining.

*

At the time of the Winnipeg General Strike, the minister of justice in the Conservative government of Robert Borden was a politician from the West. Arthur Meighen (1874-1960) was an Ontario farm boy who had migrated on a harvest excursion train to Manitoba, where he ultimately became a lawyer, real-estate investor and prominent member of the provincial legislature. Later, ambition led him into federal politics. Brilliant of mind, caustic of tongue, he was a distinct oddity — a right-wing protectionist from a radical, free-trade West. Meighen completely misread the nature of the Winnipeg strike and paid for his lack of understanding. In ordering the arrest of the strike leaders — and the prosecution of James S. Woodsworth, in particular — he managed to sever what few connections there were between the Canadian labour movement and the Conservative party.

After Borden's retirement in 1920, Meighen became prime minister and proceeded to lose the rural vote in Ontario and the farm vote on the prairies by favouring a high-tariff policy. (He had already alienated the inhabitants of Quebec with his fervour for conscription in World War I and his denigration of them in the Commons as a "backward people.") A man of political principle as rigidly honest as his Presbyterian belief, Meighen could not compete in the election of 1921 with the man of no fixed political principle: William Lyon Mackenzie King.

*

The story of western Canada's wheat fortunes and failures — and the resulting farm protest of the 1920s — begins in the nineteenth century.

David Fife was a farmer in Ontario who liked to experiment with new seeds. In 1844, he sowed two quarts of some unknown wheat that a friend had casually procured for him in Europe, but only three sprouts came up.

One day the family cow stretched her neck over the fence and started to eat the three stalks, and she had nibbled one of them when Mrs. Fife drove her off. Had she eaten the other two, we might have a different Canada today.

The remaining two heads of grain matured, ten days earlier than any other wheat that Fife had ever seen. Ten days meant the difference between safe maturity and freezing in such a climate. He harvested forty grains of this precious stuff, stored them in a teacup over the winter, and planted them in the spring. This time he harvested a pint of seed and, in the third year, half a bushel. He called it Red Fife, for its color.

Red Fife, shipped out of Ontario in 1876, was the foundation of the Canadian West. In many parts of the dry prairies only a desert plant can produce a crop, and it must mature in a little more than a hundred days of rapid growth before the fall frosts. The old wheat strains would be useless there. Without Fife's seed, grain might never have spread past the Red River Valley.

The next notable discovery, made by Dr. Charles Saunders of the federal government's experimental farms, was Marquis wheat. Marquis is a hard, high-quality wheat that matures in about one hundred days and also resists rust. Like Red Fife, it spread across the southern prairies, but Marquis could also be harvested on the northern prairies where the growing season is shorter. Canada's production of wheat soared.

However, the prairie farmer soon learned that just as he could not control frost, rust, hail, grasshoppers and drought, he could not control the price of his cash crop. Supply and demand in the world marketplace decided the price of his labours. If other countries managed to produce surpluses of wheat for sale, the price might be low. If there were few surpluses, then the price was high. Although the price of wheat fluctuated, the farmer had fixed expenses: a mortgage, as well as seed, machinery and maintenance costs.

While the wheat farmer had to accept the fact of supply and demand in the world market, he deeply resented having to pay an inflated price for farm machinery manufactured in eastern Canada. The National Policy of the Conservatives — continued by the Liberals as well as Macdonald's political heirs — protected Canadian industry by imposing high tariffs on American imports. Even spare parts were more expensive when made in Canada.

Once the farmer sowed his wheat and, God and nature willing, harvested it, he encountered a whole new set of problems. Since he was usually unable to store the grain on the farm, he took it to a railhead where there was a grain elevator. Here it was examined and graded, the top rating being given to the famous Manitoba No. 1 Hard. The grain was then either sold to the elevator company at the current price offered for that particular grading, or stored in the elevator for sale and shipment to a grain company. Farmers often questioned the grade given their wheat by elevator companies, but not until 1908 did they win the right to appeal a grading to the federal Board of Grain Commissioners. Farmers also suspected that railway companies, notably the CPR, and grain companies that owned elevators were working together to monopolize the transportation of grain and to fix freight charges.

One of the farmers' few consolations was the Crowsnest Pass Agreement. In 1897, the Laurier government partially subsidized the construction of a CPR branch line from Lethbridge, Alberta, through the Crowsnest Pass to Nelson, B.C. In return, the CPR agreed to reduce freight rates on grain and flour moving east, and on agricultural machinery and certain settlers' effects and supplies going west. The reductions were supposed to be in perpetuity, but the agreement was later broken.

For many years, the CPR refused to permit the loading of grain into rail cars at any place where there was not an elevator. (In 1900, Westerners in Parliament forced through an act that obliged all rail companies to provide a loading platform at every local point where a farmers' petition requested it.) For many years, only an elevator company had the right to order the delivery of rail cars to pick up grain, until this, too, was changed by amendments to the Manitoba Grain Act. The problem of allocation of boxcars at harvest time led, in fact, to the creation of powerful farm lobbies. In 1901, when the wheat harvest was the greatest to that time in

A tractor parade in Medicine Hat, Alberta, about
1920. Many farmers disliked these machines, claim-
ing they frightened livestock. But steam tractors,
then gasoline-powered ones, converted opponents.

prairie history, only one-third of the crop had been moved by the CPR by Christmas. Frustrated farmers in Assiniboia founded the Territorial Grain Growers' Association which, among other things, persuaded the CPR to put more grain cars into service. In 1906, the Manitoba Grain Growers' Association was created to lobby the federal government on behalf of the province's farm families. Four years later, the Grain Growers' Company, formed by rural leaders in Saskatchewan and Manitoba, secured a seat on the Winnipeg Grain Exchange, and began challenging the business methods of the exchange's grain merchants.

The long-standing grievance was that the farmer had no influence over the price at which he sold his wheat. That was decided by grain companies — notably a combination of elevator owners and grain dealers called the Northwest Grain Dealers' Association — which, via the local elevator agent, bought crops for resale to overseas purchasers. The prairie farmer distrusted this system of buying and selling wheat. Prices were usually low in the late summer and fall when he had to sell the year's crop because his debts were due for payment. All too often, however, the price went up late in the winter, after his delivery to the elevator, and he got no extra payment. Then there was the matter of charges made by elevator and grain companies for handling, storing and shipping grain — a huge amount of money since millions of bushels were handled each year. It seemed to the farmer that these companies were growing richer faster than the man who actually worked the land. The farmer much preferred the system finally introduced by the federal government in 1917, whereby a Canadian Wheat Board bought and sold wheat at a fixed price. Upon delivery, he received an initial payment. Later, he received interim and final payments based on the total monies received by the Wheat Board for the year's sales. (For various reasons, the Canadian Wheat Board was abolished in 1921 and, despite many pleas, was not revived as a permanent institution until 1943.)

During World War I, the rapid rise in demand for farm produce, specifically wheat, turned out to be a mixed blessing. For many farmers, the war brought their first real taste of prosperity. It put money in their pockets, though they often spent it and borrowed more to buy additional acres at high prices or to modernize equipment. When the price of wheat dropped drastically to $1.10 a bushel in 1921 — the result of a postwar slump in demand and a return to free trading — farmers were first puzzled and annoyed, then angered. Once again, they were trapped between a falling price for what they produced and a rising cost of living. Added to which, banks levied high interest rates on mortgages and loans, eastern manufacturers charged high prices for farm implements and machinery, and the CPR charged high freight rates.

The farm protest of the 1920s took root in 1919 when Prime Minister Robert Borden and his Conservatives refused the demands of farmers' organizations in western Canada and Ontario to lower the tariff and maintain the Canadian Wheat Board. As a direct result, Thomas Alexander Crerar, a former president of the Grain Growers' Grain Company and a much respected figure in western agricultural circles, resigned his position as minister of agriculture in the Borden cabinet. After decades of trying to get the Liberals and Conservatives to listen to them, with little success, the farmers decided to create a political party devoted to their own welfare. Such a party would lower tariff rates and reform the parasitic system of grain elevators, railways and the Grain Exchange. It would arrange a return to a state monopoly of buying and selling wheat, and revise bank legislation. And since farmers were still the nation's largest and most important economic group, they seemed just the people to change this iniquitous system.

In 1920, farmers' representatives in the House of Commons, led by Crerar, decided to form a National Progressive Party, committed to a New National Policy, a reversal of John A. Macdonald's National Policy. In general, the Progressives condemned high tariffs, advocated tariff-free trade with the United States and Great Britain, demanded a tax on profits, and promised the public ownership of all railways. In the election of 1921, William Lyon Mackenzie King's Liberals won enough seats (117) to become the government. But, to the astonishment of all Canada, the next strongest party was the Progressives with 65, including Ontario schoolteacher Agnes MacPhail, the first woman to become a member of Parliament. The Conservatives trailed last with a mere 50 seats. And, as a reminder of western labour's continuing discontent, J. S. Woodsworth of Winnipeg was elected as an independent.

The Progressives did not aim to become the ruling party. They knew they could not command the necessary votes at the polls to defeat the Liberals or the Conservatives, so they acted as a pressure group. Since they held the balance of power, they would force the old-line parties to change their ways as the mouthpieces of eastern business interests. So the Progressives allied themselves with an apparently remorseful Mackenzie King, having bargained for the restoration of the Crowsnest Pass freight rates and minor tariff rate reductions on agricultural implements as the initial price of their support of other Liberal policies. (One of the most important factors in the election of the Progressives was their promise to restore the Crowsnest Pass freight rates, which Borden's Conservatives had

cancelled on the grounds of inflation and the need to raise the rates to aid railway finances.)

Unfortunately, the Progressives broke up into opinionated groups and dissipated their strength. A despairing Crerar resigned the leadership, while some of his colleagues were persuaded by a crafty Mackenzie King to join the Liberal party.

The Progressives knew what they were united against, but were fatally divided as to whether they stood for farm politics or national politics. Canadians sensed this indecision and reduced their parliamentary strength to twenty-five seats in the next election. A year later, during yet another election, their membership in the House of Commons dropped to thirteen.

While the Progressive movement failed at the federal level, two of its provincial branches had a longer life. The United Farmers of Alberta governed their province from 1921 until 1935, and the United Farmers of Manitoba held office from 1922 to 1928, when the organization withdrew from politics. The aims of the United Farmers of Manitoba were, however, carried on by its political heirs, an alliance of the Liberals and Progressives that was in power from 1928 to 1958.

The decline and fall of the Progressives at the federal level had a strange sequel. Although they failed to have the Canadian Wheat Board re-established, that failure sparked a self-help movement in the prairie provinces, where farmers tried a new method of marketing: co-operative marketing by means of a pool, in which all wheat delivered was pooled by grade and sold together.

The farmers were thrown back upon themselves. Their response in that moment was magnificent. It carries the mind back to those old settlers who simply would not be beaten by famine, flood or war. If there could not be a Government pool, to which all farmers

In the 1920 and '30s, prairie roads were often mud traps. Here, a touring chautauqua (adult education) group, including the performers, has to give the horses a hand.

Great Bear Lake, NWT. The bush plane and the gasoline drum became the twin symbols of Canada's
development of its northland in the 1920s and '30s.

would send their wheat to be sold, there would be a voluntary pool. In the early summer of 1923, within two weeks after it was clear there would be no Wheat Board, the United Farmers [parties] of all three western provinces had met and declared for the voluntary pool idea.

The co-operative marketing of grains through these pools had much the same result as if there had been a Wheat Board. By contracting or promising his crop to a pool, the farmer was assured of two interim payments, each before seeding and harvesting to meet the expenses of these operations. Once the entire grain crop was sold, he was given a further payment based on the amount he had delivered, its grade, and the average price for that grade obtained by the pool, whose handling and storage costs were generally lower than those charged by grain companies. In 1924, the three provincial pools organized Canadian Co-operative Wheat Producers Limited, better known as the Central Selling Agency. It opened offices in several European countries, Mexico, Brazil and China, and soon proved itself a reliable supplier of high-quality export consignments.

*

The second half of the 1920s was as prosperous a time for the West as it was for the rest of the nation. Once again, depression had run its course, and the world was eager to buy wheat and livestock from the prairies, and lumber and minerals from British Columbia. Farm prices, especially those of coarse grains, rose. And 1928 saw the production of one of the prairie west's great harvests.

Hundreds of families began homesteading a new farm frontier in the Peace River country of Alberta and British Columbia. In the Pacific province, many fruit growers were cultivating newly irrigated sections of the Okanagan valley or farming the delta lands of the Fraser River. On the prairies, an expanding cattle and hog industry kept stockyards busy; a diversification in grain produced oats and barley in addition to wheat. The threshing machine was being replaced by the combine, and the horse by the tractor. Food processing plants, pulp mills and breweries belched busy clouds of smoke in communities between the Ontario-Manitoba border and Vancouver Island. Highway departments extended construction programs to accommodate increasing volumes of car and truck traffic. North of the prairies, thousands of men were moving into the Canadian Shield to harvest its pulpwood, nickel, copper, silver, lead, zinc and gold in amounts totalling almost a billion dollars annually. Smelters and metal-fabricating factories were established. And out of the northland came word of bush pilots opening up what had long been a remote but mineral-rich region. A railway-minded nation was about to become air-conscious.

In the early hours of 7 August 1919, a small war-surplus airplane took off from a rough-and-ready runway near Vancouver and headed eastward. The pilot, Capt. Ernest C. Hoy of Vancouver, a veteran of World War I, intended to reach Calgary by battling the tricky air currents and dangerous downdrafts of mountain passes. Sixteen hours and four refuelling stops later, he landed his "Little Red Devil" at Bowness Park, Calgary, with the aid of car headlights. About a year later, six aircraft of the Canadian Air Force (CAF) flew a cargo of mail from Halifax to Vancouver. Using CAF bases as stopover and servicing points, they took eleven days to cover the 5280 kilometres. Both flights made aviation history: Hoy was the first to cross the western mountains, and the CAF flyers were the first to travel coast to coast. Perhaps more importantly, they focused attention on the potential of air

Dance being performed by Northwest Coast native
people during a potlatch ceremony at Duncan, B.C.,
in 1920.

Morley, Alberta, 1926. Stoney Indians holding the Sun Dance, an annual religious festival, at a specially constructed lodge.

Trees in B.C. grow to monstrous proportions, as indicated in this photograph of a stump being used as a dance floor.

transportation in a land of long distances with numerous obstacles to cross-country travel.

In the 1920s, commercial aviation got its start in Canada in the form of aerial fire patrols, photographic survey work, and flights made by bush pilots to supply mining areas or to transport prospecting parties. These pioneer aviators worked in pairs. The pilot traversed the largely unmapped wilds using a mixture of calculated guesswork and sheer bravado. Fuel gauges rarely worked properly, and so he measured gasoline consumption by his watch. When rain or snow obscured visibility, he had to fly by the seat of his pants in order to maintain a level keel. The air engineer or mechanic performed miracles when up to his neck in freezing water repairing a punctured float or doing an engine overhaul — without gloves — in minus-zero conditions. He even managed to "manufacture" spare parts on the spot.

To a bush pilot and his mechanic, anything from eggs to dynamite and anybody from a baby to a trapper and his dogs was routine cargo. Indeed, livestock was handled as just another freighting chore. Frank Ellis, a mechanic-turned-pilot, tells of a normal business conversation in his experience:

"Doc Smith says that the baby in at Sturgeon needs cow's milk."
"What makes you think we're running a dairy?"
"Well, we're getting a cow in on Tuesday night's train."
"What do you want us do do — fly a cow in?"
"We'll pay you for it — whatever it's worth."
"A cow? A live cow? Sure, we can take her in, if Doc will give her a hypo[dermic injection]."

When machinery was too large or too unwieldy to carry in one trip, it was cut apart by oxyacetylene torch and then welded back together after it reached its destination. No other nation utilized bush flying as much or as successfully as Canada, and the roster of these "voyageurs of the air" is a long one. The exploits of just a few bush pilots – H. A. "Doc" Oaks, C. H. "Punch" Dickens and W. R. "Wop" May – made their names household words in the 1920s.

While some ex-servicemen made a living by flying in and out of the northland, others who had learned something about wireless broadcasting started to put the first private radio stations on the air. In those days, it was a poor man who could not afford to buy his family a "crystal set" to hear the latest radio programs. So, with earphones strapped to their heads, Canadians – particularly Westerners, who countered isolation by bringing the world into the kitchen via air waves – fingered a "cat's whisker" to a point on the crystal sensitive enough to pick up the elusive impulses of early broadcasting.

The prime feature of "The Roaring Twenties" as they were called was the remarkable improvement in living conditions in North America. Many Canadians were earning a great deal of money, particularly in Quebec, Ontario, Manitoba and British Columbia, the provinces with large mineral deposits, the finest stands of timber and the best hydroelectric sites. Indeed, the cheap, plentiful electric power that became available during this decade helped industries turn out relatively inexpensive, everday luxuries: radios, toasters, refrigerators, stoves, washing machines and vacuum cleaners. In Alberta, towards the end of the decade, the output of coal passed the seven-million-tonne mark, and Turner Valley was producing natural gas in billions of cubic metres.

Yet another sign of prosperity was the completion of the Hudson Bay Railway (HBR), which had long been a dream of escape from the high freight rates levied by the CPR. Although the HBR would have to be built over some of the world's worst terrain, the CPR had proved that treacherous muskeg could be conquered and a line blasted through even prehistoric rock. Thus, a railway north to Hudson Bay, an alternative outlet to the sea, had been a persistent prairie plea over the years. The problem was finding the necessary millions of dollars, so it was not until early in the twentieth century that construction got under way. By 1910, Mackenzie and Mann's Canadian Northern had built a branch line from Hudson Bay Junction in Saskatchewan to The Pas, Manitoba. But World War I slowed construction, and the opening of the Panama Canal in 1914 made it cheaper to ship grain by sea from Vancouver than by rail through Winnipeg to the east – or to the nebulous north. (This was a blow from which Manitoba's grain economy is still recovering.) Work on the line was halted in 1915, but the On-to-the-Bay Association pushed for completion of the railway, and the last spike was driven in at the port of Churchill in 1929. In the fall of that year, a token shipment of No. 1 Hard wheat went off to Europe on the HBC ship *Nascopie*.

*

The late 1920s were boom times that far exceeded anything experienced in Canada up to that time. Everybody was sure that the prevailing prosperity would continue indefinitely. Everything was going to get bigger and better.

The year is 1922, and a Manitoba Elks jazz band is pounding out a tune, perhaps the song "Yes, We Have No Bananas" that characterized a restless decade.

11   Poverty and Politics

The prosperity of the 1920s in North America is an example of one phase of the business cycle. The next phase is a period of recession which, in turn, is followed by another period of prosperity. Good times and bad times follow each in endless repetition, a cycle that has been going on for centuries. The recession that occurred in North America in the 1930s, however, was so severe that it earned the name of the Great Depression. And the collapse of the Wall Street stock market signalled the beginning of financial chaos.

Recession began in the usual way. Slowly but surely throughout the booming 1920s, there had been a buildup in storage yards and warehouses of huge quantities of unsold goods: building materials, cars and trucks, electrical appliances, clothing, foodstuffs and so on. Yet, due to the supreme confidence that is so common in easy times, manufacturers ignored this warning that production was outpacing consumption. And for a time this problem was obscured by the new and popular practice of buying on credit. People could be induced to buy just about any product from a washing machine to an automobile if the downpayment were small enough. Manufacturers and merchants also ignored the ultimate effect of raising the prices of their goods so that they could make quicker profits with which to expand their businesses. Some of these men honestly thought that their efforts — and greater spending on advertising — would break the historic pattern of boom and bust, and that prosperity would become a permanent state of affairs.

In reality, the good times of the 1920s were being enjoyed by too few people. Many farm families were not sharing in the general prosperity; neither were many miners, textile workers and clerks. Millions of Canadians were unable to purchase anything but the bare necessities.

Canada had long depended on the money earned by exporting wood pulp, wheat, lumber, fish, coal, meat and fruit. During the 1920s, pulp and paper companies had made more profits and employed more workers than any other industry in the country; these companies were exporting as much wood pulp as the rest of the world's producers combined. In fact, the raw material for fifty per cent of all newsprint used in the United States was produced in Canada. Much Canadian grain was being bought by the war-ravaged countries of Europe with dollars loaned to them by the United States, and the result was another farm boom. To meet this demand, more new land had been broken in northern Saskatchewan and Alberta, contributing to a record wheat crop of 567 million bushels in 1929. Selling to fifty per cent of the international market, Canada became the world's largest supplier of wheat, stimulating railways to construct new branch lines. This, in turn, meant new business for the producers of steel and agricultural machinery.

Meanwhile, overseas markets for these raw materials were beginning to shrink. In an effort to help their own forest workers and farmers, European countries were raising tariff rates in order to make imports more expensive than domestic products. Year by year in the 1920s, Canadian shipments overseas began to decline, but the biggest blow of all came between 1929 and 1932. Panicked by the growing force of the Depression, the United States government introduced the highest tariffs in that nation's history in order to shut out all foreign products. At the same time, Washington refused to make further loans to European countries. Partly in self-defence, partly in retaliation, the governments of twenty-five nations raised their tariffs to comparable levels. The result was the spread of depression around the world as nations reduced or

Picking a bumper crop of apples in the Okanagan area
of B.C. in 1929, with no hope of finding buyers. Yet,
tree fruits were becoming basic to the economy of the
southern interior at this time.

cancelled trading with each other.

The combination of vanishing markets and huge harvests caused grain prices to plummet. Wheat fell from $1.60 a bushel in 1929 to thirty-eight cents in 1932, the lowest price in three hundred years. Barley had already fallen in value from seventy cents a bushel to thirty-four cents, and oats from sixty cents to eighteen.

Like grain, the world demand for fish, lumber, fruit and minerals practically disappeared. The prairies and British Columbia lost their prosperity and much of their pride. The first breadlines appeared in Vancouver as early as December 1929, and conditions all over the province deteriorated rapidly. With the slump in lumber markets, logging camps and sawmills up and down the coast were forced to close. Dwindling demands for coal and metals forced mining and smelting companies to cut wages or lay off workers. In 1930, fish canneries were busy dealing with exceptionally large salmon runs and packed over two millions cases, most of which they were unable to sell. And in 1932, despite a long, hot summer that dried up irrigation reservoirs, the apple crop in the Okanagan was embarrassingly abundant. But who could buy it?

If the Depression hit the British Columbia miner, lumberjack, fruit grower or fisherman with particular force, it hit prairie people with extra severity. Wheat was hardly worth the time and trouble involved in growing it. In many cases, a farm family's earnings would not even meet the cost of repairs to buildings and equipment. And the crumbling of the agricultural economy had many ripple effects. At this time, one of every two Canadians was a farmer or worked on a farm, so the steep drop in farm income just about finished off a consumer-goods industry already badly hurt by the layoff of thousands of employees in the forest, fishing and mining industries. The farmer could not pay the storekeeper, who, in turn, could not pay his suppliers in eastern Canada. The farmer could not buy from the manufacturers of agricultural machinery and tools. So factories in eastern Canada closed down. The drastic drop in the volume of wheat being shipped east and goods being shipped west reduced railway revenues. So railwaymen were laid off.

At first Canadians did not understand the extent of the disaster. After all, there had been bad times before. Friends and acquaintances assured each other that "Prosperity is just around the corner." Sooner or later, business would return to normal.

But things did not return to normal. As 1930 became 1931 and then 1932, business did not get better. Unemployment got worse. That year, industrial production was half what it had been in 1929. Workers had their wages reduced or were laid off. Banks, which had loaned money for commercial and industrial expansion, were unable to collect debts and had to close. Railways, deprived of profitable freight and passenger revenues, went bankrupt. Yet few realized that Canada was undergoing something much worse than a typical North American depression. Economic conditions elsewhere were affecting the nation.

By 1933, close to twenty-five per cent of the Canadian work force was unemployed; by 1935, ten per cent of the entire population of Canada was living on relief.

Barry Broadfoot, himself a child of the Great Depression, explains why so many were forced to accept public charity to stay alive.

There came a time for hundreds of thousands when the mortgage had been surrendered, the insurance abandoned, savings gone, heirlooms sold for pennies, and they had no job, no money, very little food, only worn out clothing, and no hope.

Then they turned to relief, "the dole", "the pogey". This was a new concept in government help to the poor, an admission at last by the politicians that the poor were not to blame for the desperate plight they were in, and that they needed assistance . . .

Necessary legislation it was, but the shame and bitterness can never be legislated out of the recipient's mind. If he had been a proud and hard-working wage earner only a year or two before, the most shameful moment of his life was walking into the relief office for the first time. I know that to this day men still remember that moment.

Ironically, the Depression was a time when men could not find work but women could — if they were prepared to work long hours for low wages. As a Royal Commission on Price Spreads and Mass Buying later found out, thousands of Canadian women in the textile, canning and baking industries laboured for sixty or seventy hours a week to earn three or four dollars. Or they found work as housemaids and cooks in the homes of the well-to-do for $15 or $20 a month and board. But workers who were male and single had to leave home to try and find a job in some other town or city or region of Canada, not least because it meant one mouth less in the family to feed.

Since there was no work, many men ended up drifting back and forth across the country, hitching rides on top of rail freight cars and eating at soup kitchens along the way. In winter, the floor of a town hall or a jail was a place to sleep; in summer, a clump of bushes beside a railway track was an overnight resting place. As one drifter said long afterwards, "That's the way we were them days, in The Thirties. Coming from nowhere, going nowhere. Like gypsies." The only alternative was a federal government relief camp. There, men were clothed, fed and paid twenty cents a day to perform such make-work projects as building roads and bridges in national parks, clearing airstrips in the middle of forests, restoring historic sites, or cutting firewood. But to many who experienced them, they were slave camps. They were run by ex-army personnel employing army discipline and were deliberately located in isolated areas. The inmates felt that, as far as Ottawa was concerned, they were "out of sight, out of mind." And twenty cents a day was the worst humiliation of all. A newspaper reporter commented, "There was something about that twenty cents per day that came to symbolize everything that was wrong with the lives of everybody on relief. It affronted human dignity as little else could have done. It was just the right size to be insulting."

*

In the House of Commons, the hardhitting verbal attacks of Tory leader R. B. Bennett on a Mackenzie King administration baffled by tough times that were getting even worse revitalized the Tory party and produced victory in the federal election of 1930.

Richard Bedford Bennett was born and bred in New Brunswick of United Empire Loyalist stock. After earning enough money as a teacher and librarian to pay for his studies at Dalhousie University, he settled in the then cowtown of Calgary. Here, he formed a law partnership with Senator James A. Lougheed (the grandfather of Alberta Premier Peter Lougheed). Their numerous clients included the CPR and the HBC; the syndicate that raised the capital to develop natural-gas utilities in Calgary, Medicine Hat and Edmonton; the developers of coal mines in the Lethbridge area; the entrepreneurs who organized water, light, telephone and streetcar facilities in Calgary; plus the group of men who searched for natural gas and oil just south of the city in Turner Valley in 1914. Bennett made his own fortune in real estate, though unkind critics have suggested that the lifelong bachelor really

Many farm families, like this one en route to Spirit River, Alberta, in 1933, tried to find unoccupied land in the less arid northern areas.

did this by capturing the affections of a childhood playmate, the widow of industrialist E. B. Eddy. Bennett was the beneficiary in her will of control of the Eddy matches and toilet paper empire.

By 1927, an enthusiastic Bennett had determinedly worked his way up the political ladder from member of the Northwest Territories legislature to successor to Meighen as leader of the Conservative party. Big, bluff, Bible-quoting "R.B." was an enormous success as a businessman, but was destined to be a resounding failure as prime minister.

Bennett's answer to a deepening depression was to end unemployment by eliminating competition from abroad. In the next two years, the general tariff level was raised by almost fifty per cent, and he either persuaded or bullied the British government into negotiating preferential imperial tariffs. But even the hard-working "R.B." could not hope to reverse the course of economic and climatic vagaries that produced bankruptcies and breadlines, drought and dust. Added to which, he was insulated from the full force of these realities by a staggering self-confidence, a fervent faith in the capitalist system and a Methodist self-righteousness. At least until 1935, when he finally perceived the dimensions of the Depression and reversed political direction. In a series of CBC radio broadcasts, a radically repentant prime minister abruptly informed the nation of the solution to its problems: a Roosevelt-type New Deal of unemployment insurance, price controls, regulation of hours, wages and marketing, and central-bank control of the money system.

The result was predictable. In the election of 1935, given the choice between a suddenly socialist millionaire prime minister — and the Liberals' "King or Chaos!" slogan — Canadians voted overwhelmingly against Bennett and chaos.

241

*

The Dirty Thirties. That's what they called the Depression years in the southern parts of Saskatchewan and neighbouring districts in Alberta and Manitoba that formed the about-to-be infamous Palliser's Triangle. That's where the drought and dust years hit hardest.

In the winter of 1930-31, little or no snow fell in the Palliser Triangle, and the first of many windstorms began to tear away the surface of the land. The summer of 1931 was hot and dry. What rain there was fell everywhere except in southernmost Saskatchewan, in southern Alberta, and on the Souris and Portage plains of Manitoba. Strong westerly winds continued to take away topsoil. Between 1932 and 1937, the winters got steadily colder, the summers got steadily hotter and drier, and the wind never stopped carrying away fine particles of earth. (The CPR had to use snowploughs to clear the tracks of drifts of grey-black dunes up to three metres high.) The Triangle — and much of the Great Plains as far south as Texas — became a dust bowl where the hardy Russian thistle and tumbleweed became the predominant plants.

An exodus began from the land to towns and cities. When a farm had been sold and the various debts for supplies, machinery or bank loans paid, there might be a few hundred dollars left. With this money, a family would move to Winnipeg or Regina or Calgary, rent a room, and try to maintain themselves for a year in order to become eligible for relief. Or they loaded whatever possessions they had on a truck or a wagon and trekked north, where there was more chance of rain. But families were also driven off the land by something even worse than rock-bottom wheat prices: a change of climate that made it almost impossible to grow anything in a particular section of the prairies.

Those stubborn families still working the land in the Triangle had yet to experience nature at its worst. They battled grasshoppers in 1933 and wheat rust in 1935, but, in 1937, summer brought the worst dust storms of the entire decade. For days on end, the sun was obscured. Roads became impassable. Lakes, sloughs and wells that had contained water for as long as anyone could remember dried up. By the end of June, whatever wheat was being raised in the Triangle was dead on the stalk.

It was the wind, literally and figuratively, that killed the dreams of these particular prairie farmers. One of them remarked, "They was Dirty Thirties all right. . . . The land just blew away." Another recalled the tragedy in terms of human error:

The Palliser Triangle shouldn't have ever been broken to the plough. We know that now. Grazing, stock. The buffalo thrived like the green bay tree on it and so could cattle. We had this loose sub-soil that had no holding power and then we had the winds. Why them winds came, I'm not sure anyone knew, but I've seen them blow for two weeks at a time, blowing hard. Blowing the . . . country right out from under our feet and nothing we could do about it.

We got around to contour ploughing later but for an awful lot of people, later was a lot too late. That dust, which was our earth and our livelihood, would blow for dozens of miles, scores of miles, and airplane pilots used to have to fly higher to get over them, they were thousands of feet high. You mistreat the land, take away its essential goodness, and this will happen.

James Gray, born and brought up in Manitoba, experienced both sides of the Depression. He stood in line for relief vouchers to support his family and, later, as a reporter for the *Winnipeg Free Press*, described the misery of that dreadful decade. It was a time of bewilderment and anguish, but also, Gray remembers, one of compassion and generosity:

Until soil erosion in southern Saskatchewan was brought under control, farmhouses and barns appeared to be strangely adrift on a sea of sand and dirt.

Winnipeg financier James A. Richardson helped establish Western Canada Airways, which in 1930 introduced the Prairie Mail Service between Winnipeg, Regina, Saskatoon, Calgary and Edmonton.

contributions came from every province of Canada. The churches across the country became the gathering-points for the donations of clothing and blankets, sheets, etc. In 1931 the United Church sent 135 carloads of food, clothing, and other supplies into Saskatchewan; the Roman Catholics managed sixty-two cars, the Presbyterians ten, and the Lutherans eight. The total of 249 cars was beyond all expectations and these supplies were augmented generously by a flood of hampers into the province from friends and relatives across the country.

While the voluntary drive was being launched, the Saskatchewan government set up the Saskatchewan Relief Commission to take charge of making grants to municipalities, providing loans for seed grain, binder twine, feed, fodder, and repairs. It organized the multitude of volunteer agencies, which dispensed the donated supplies, into a province-wide Saskatchewan Voluntary Rural Relief Committee.

It was well that this was so, for during the next five years distribution of relief to the south country of Saskatchewan became the province's major industry. In one area, 890 out of a population of 895 were on relief. In the community of Minton, the disaster was so complete that even the chickens had to be supplied with relief feed. There was nothing edible left for them to scratch.

Weather conditions began to return to normal in the fall of 1937. Thereafter, snow came each winter and "starter" rains each spring and early summer. The Bennett government had already begun to help by passing the Prairie Farm Rehabilitation Act. It made available thousands of dollars each year for farmers and ranchers to conserve soil by windproof methods of ploughing, planting trees and drought-resistant strains of grass, irrigation projects, and the conversion of millions of hectares of ploughed land into pasturage. By 1939, Saskatchewan, for example, had a 250-million-bushel harvest, about seven times that of 1937. And the world price of wheat was starting to inch upwards.

The Great Depression was not a total national disaster: its impact varied from region to region, and many people never lost their jobs. In an age when annual wage and salary increases were by no means common, employees were not too bothered by cuts in their pay cheques. After all, the price of most necessities — food, clothing, shelter — kept falling through the 1930s, so that their reduced incomes had the same purchasing power. The people who bore the brunt of the Depression were workers in the resource and manufacturing industries, and prairie families.

Various levels of government kept people alive. For the first time in history, Ottawa gave large amounts of relief monies to the provinces, which, in turn, handed on funds to local governments in towns and cities. (At this time, responsibility for the unemployed lay with provincial and municipal governments, not the federal government.) But, as depressed conditions continued year after year, physical survival was not enough for men and women who could never get a job or never sell a crop for a decent sum of money. Something seemed to be badly wrong with the whole economic system. Nobody knew exactly how to put things right, but wasn't it the job of government to run things properly? Why didn't governments bring the Depression to an end? Would new, different philosophies of government get the economy back into working shape again? With these kinds of thoughts in western minds, the 1930s became a time of new ideas about leadership roles and the emergence of new political parties. Two of these were born in western Canada.

*

The Co-operative Commonwealth Federation (CCF) owed its existence to various groups of

Ontario-born James Shaver Woodsworth was a Methodist minister who worked in Winnipeg's immigrant North End. Later, as a politician, he became "the social conscience of Canada."

people. One was those Progressives in Parliament who had survived the collapse of their party as an effective opposition in the House of Commons; another was certain union leaders in western cities, notably Vancouver; yet another was a handful of university teachers in Montreal and Toronto. The most important group, however, was comprised of various farmers' organizations, which wanted lower tariffs on manufactured goods, reductions in freight rates, and lower interest charges on mortgages and loans. The very words of the party's name hinted at its aims. "Co-operative" recalled the farmers' belief in joint action; "Commonwealth" indicated the economic sharing that the party intended to create; "Federation" announced that it was composed of several political, economic and social groups.

The CCF believed that the answer to Canadians' problems was meeting needs, not making profits. The two major Canadian political parties supported the private-enterprise system, whereby businessmen employed workers to produce raw materials or manufacture goods for sale at a profit, some of the profits being used to expand a company's operations by taking on more workers to produce more raw materials or goods. The CCF totally disagreed. It wanted a socialist system in which most companies would be owned and operated by government. Thus, at the first CCF national convention held at Regina in 1933, the party announced details of "a social order from which the domination and exploitation of one class by another will be eliminated, in which economic planning will supersede unregulated private enterprise and competition." If elected as the government of Canada, the party promised to nationalize banks, insurance companies, public utilities, transportation and communication facilities; and such basic industries as lumbering, mining, and the production of iron

and steel. And the party promised to regulate *all* prices, profits and working conditions. In addition, a CCF government would provide many social services: unemployment insurance, family allowances, old-age pensions, and national standards of medical, hospital and dental care, using profits from nationalized industries to pay for all these benefits.

The Regina convention chose the gentle, quiet-spoken, fifty-nine-year-old James Shaver Woodsworth to lead their party. A former preacher in Winnipeg's immigrant-filled North End, Woodsworth, after his break with the church, had been a dock worker in Vancouver. His lifelong ambition was to bring the farmers and industrial workers together in a mighty reform movement of "Canadian Socialism," and the CCF was his great attempt to replace the free-enterprise system "with its . . . injustice and inhumanity by a social order . . . based upon economic equality."

Woodsworth did not succeed in the attempt, though he did not altogether fail. The CCF was unable to win the support of the trade unions. It had very little popular appeal in the Atlantic provinces and in Quebec. In a country long accustomed to the private-enterprise system, the CCF was considered by most Canadians to be much the same thing as the Canadian Communist Party led by Tim Buck. But Woodsworth and his followers won a few victories. By 1934, the CCF was the official opposition in British Columbia and Saskatchewan and had also won seats in the legislatures of Manitoba, Alberta and Ontario. In the federal election the following year, seven CCFers won seats, including Woodsworth, M. J. Coldwell and T. C. "Tommy" Douglas (both successors to Woodsworth as party leader.)

There was never more than a handful of CCF members in Ottawa at this time, but they became the conscience of Parliament, obliging the

One of the best-known radio personalities in southern Alberta in the 1930s was William "Bible Bill" Aberhart, founder of the Social Credit Party of Alberta.

Scots-born Thomas Clement Douglas, a Baptist minister in Saskatchewan during the 1930s, was attracted to politics by the "practical Christianity" of the Co-operative Commonwealth Federation.

old-line parties — notably the Liberals — to re-think their legislative programs. The CCF never governed Canada, but many of its policies — the revival of the Canadian Wheat Board, unemployment insurance, government-run hospital and medical insurance — were successful because other parties were forced to adopt them. In 1939, for instance, the Liberal government of Mackenzie King introduced a law guaranteeing the right of employees to form and join trade unions, something for which Woodsworth had been pleading for years in the House of Commons.

*

In neighbouring Alberta, a province that was geographically, economically and culturally almost identical to Saskatchewan, there was a new party almost the opposite of the CCF in appeal and aims.

On the night of August 22, 1935, as Canadians listened to their radios, they heard, with amazement and incredulity, that the first Social Credit government in the world had been elected that day in the province of Alberta. Throughout Alberta, of course, everybody was waiting by the radio, whether in family groups, house parties, or political gatherings at party headquarters. Before the tabulation of votes was completed, telephone calls from New York and London, headlines in newspapers, spot news in broadcasts, had confirmed the slogan of Social Crediters, "The Eyes of the World are on Alberta."

To understand why Social Credit appeared and why it triumphed, it is necessary to know something about its leader, William Aberhart.

From an early age, Aberhart combined an exceptional ability to absorb and memorize facts with an equally exceptional ability to teach and preach. He earned his living as a classroom teacher and school administrator, though many who knew him said that religion was the major passion of his life. No sooner had he arrived in Calgary in 1910 than he resumed the Bible teaching he had carried on after school hours in Brantford, Ontario. But it was in his capacity as head of what became the Calgary Prophetic Bible Institute that Aberhart, as one historian has remarked, "stumbled upon the road to glory."

In 1925, one of Aberhart's associates suggested to the owner of Calgary's radio station CFCN ("The Voice of the Prairies") that Aberhart's Sunday afternoon lectures at the Bible Institute should go on the air. They did — and he became a celebrity.

In the early 1930s, CFCN estimated that 350 000 people were listening to his Sunday broadcasts, which were being heard throughout the prairie provinces and also in the western sections of British Columbia. Using simple, homely language and projecting enormous conviction, Aberhart converted tens of thousands to his particular fundamentalist creed. Long before they ever saw the man, thousands of Albertans on farms and in villages and towns became his devoted followers, willing to believe his every statement and to support anything he proposed to do. This was the situation when, late in 1932, his broadcasts began to include economic messages as well as those of future salvation.

Despite a very busy, very successful life, Aberhart realized that the Depression was worsening. It was in the summer of 1932 that Aberhart found his answer to Alberta's money problems. He read and became a total believer in the theory of Social Credit, which had been worked out by a Scottish industrial engineer.

According to Major G. H. Douglas, modern technology produced goods with a greater total value than there was a total of wages and salaries to buy them. Thus, in his phrase, there was always "poverty in the midst of plenty," because people had a limited purchasing power, whereas

Aberhart's Socred government issued prosperity certificates as substitute money. On the back were stamps, which were sold weekly to create a fund for certificate redemption. But banks and businesses refused this "funny money."

THE GOVERNMENT OF THE PROVINCE OF ALBERTA

PROSPERITY CERTIFICATE

DATE OF ISSUE

AUGUST 5, 1936   A   96158

THE PROVINCIAL TREASURER WILL PAY TO THE BEARER THE SUM OF ONE DOLLAR ON THE EXPIRATION OF TWO YEARS FROM DATE OF ISSUE HEREOF UPON PRESENTATION HEREOF PROVIDED THERE ARE THEN ATTACHED TO THE BACK HEREOF ONE HUNDRED AND FOUR ONE CENT CERTIFICATE STAMPS

ONE DOLLAR

William Aberhart
PREMIER

C. Cockroft
PROVINCIAL TREASURER

WESTERN PRINTING & LITHOGRAPHING CO. LTD. CALGARY

In 1935, there was an On-to-Ottawa trek by unemployed men in Vancouver, who hopped freights across western Canada. Here, men clamber aboard an eastbound train in Calgary.

The On-to-Ottawa trek ended in Regina, where the men were met by their leaders, just back from a noisy, abusive meeting with Prime Minister Bennett. On the evening of July 1, police tried to prevent a public meeting — and a riot took place. About a hundred men were injured, and a policeman was killed.

In 1938, to protest cutbacks in relief payments, several hundred unemployed men in Vancouver staged demonstrations at the Art Gallery (seen here), the Post Office and the Hotel Georgia.

the free-enterprise system had an unlimited ability to produce goods. The solution, Douglas maintained, was to increase individual purchasing power by having government issue every citizen with a "social dividend" or cash payment. This simple explanation of complex economic factors was not well developed in detail by Douglas. To Aberhart, however, everything was clear. In one of his favorite comparisons, he told his huge radio audience that credit was just like blood.

As the blood flows out from the heart, it feeds, clothes, and shelters every cell of the body, picks up the impurities of the body, and returns to the heart after purification in the lungs. By analogy, the Social Credit dividends would flow from the state credit house [provincial treasury] to every consumer, on to the retailer, to the wholesaler, and to the producer, and back again to the credit house to start over again. If anything interfered with the bloodstream, it caused disorder and sickness; if anything interfered with the flow of credit, the state was weakened thereby. Interference with its flow of credit had made Alberta a sick province. But the province could be restored to health by the payment of basic dividends of $25 a month to every adult. For 400,000 people such a payment would mean $10,000,000 monthly, but the additional flow of credit would amount to at least $120,000,000, and probably four or five times this sum. Where would all the money come from? Every hour, Aberhart answered, the heart pumps 135 gallons of blood, making 3,240 gallons a day, 97,200 gallons a month, 1,166,400 gallons a year. "Where am I going to get all the blood," he asked . . . "will you tell me that? As a matter of fact, I believe I only have four quarts of blood in me, just about four quarts. Will you tell me how a heart can pump 135 gallons an hour with only four quarts of blood? Well, cannot money circulate the same?"

Between 1932 and 1935, Aberhart made many broadcasts on behalf of Social Credit. Nu-

254

In 1938, in the lobby of the Senate, Prime Minister
Mackenzie King unveiled a commemorative tablet to
those women who led the "Persons Campaign."
Among those present was Nellie McClung (r.).

merous lecture tours were undertaken by several of his associates, notably his star Bible student and friend, Ernest C. Manning (a future premier of Alberta), and Mrs. W. W. (Edith) Rogers. The result was a political revolution in a farming province with a chronic shortage of purchasing power.

Farmers, of course, were not the only ones to appreciate the hope of monetary reform by Social Credit. Merchants in villages and towns had permitted so much credit buying by farm families that they could not pay the bills they owed the wholesalers for goods delivered. Clerks, nurses, salesmen, machinists and teachers were converted by Aberhart's explanation of why there were so many goods, yet people could not provide for their families.

Once in power, the new premier found himself in an awkward position. As premier, he had to govern, and to do that he needed money; so there were no monthly dividends of $25, and poverty continued amidst the clear evidence of plenty. Instead, Aberhart and his cabinet made balancing the budget the immediate priority: spending was reduced; sales and income taxes were increased. He did legislate a Debt Adjustment Act that cancelled all interest on mortgages since 1932 and limited interest rates on mortgages to five per cent, but the act was promptly cancelled by the federal government, which is responsible for interest rates. He also tried to set up credit houses to distribute the dividends that were to be created by the Alberta Social Credit Act, but he again ran afoul of Ottawa, which has control of banking. Aberhart then attempted to distribute "prosperity certificates" and to regulate banking procedures, but was once more overruled by Mackenzie King.

Rightly or wrongly, interference by Ottawa made it impossible to implement Social Credit policies. Rightly or wrongly, Albertans were once more left with the impression that the interests of the East were more important than those of the West. Social Credit remained an ideal, not a reality, and was kept alive only by "Bible Bill" Aberhart's Sunday radio broadcasts.

*

While many Canadians struggled with the Great Depression, dangerous developments were taking place around the world. On the other side of the Pacific Ocean, Japan had begun its planned conquest of Asia by invading China. On the other side of the Atlantic Ocean, Benito Mussolini and Adolf Hitler had established dictatorships in Italy and Germany and begun to prey on weaker nations.

At dawn on 1 September 1939, Hermann Goering's Luftwaffe roared over Poland, bombing road-and-rail centres and air bases. On the ground, panzer divisions, supported by dive bombers and fighters, captured or destroyed Polish army units within seven days. On Sunday, September 3, Britain and France went to war with Nazi Germany. A week later, the Parliament of Canada issued a declaration of war, and the Depression disappeared in the holocaust of World War II.

12 Prosperity and Politics

The war forced Canadians to greatly expand their manufacturing capacity, and set up new industries to produce high-octane gasoline, synthetic rubber, electronic equipment and diesel engines. And workers toiled to produce huge quantities of war equipment: munitions, ships, aircraft and various types of military vehicles. As in World War I, farms and forests were mobilized for war: the production of timber and pulp and paper doubled; agricultural output increased by a third, as farmers found they could sell all the grain, livestock and vegetables they could raise. In fact, the prairies began to become a region of mixed farming, turning to the production of beef, pork, poultry and dairy foods, in addition to such staples as wheat, barley and oats.

As well as organizing and maintaining this wide-ranging war effort, Canada hosted the British Commonwealth Air Training Plan. An agreement made by Britain, Canada, Australia and New Zealand, the Plan produced over 131 000 trained aircrew members. The prairies offered all the land and sky needed for such a massive training operation, and the experience of western Canada's bush pilots was utilized to get the scheme going.

Anson trainers were not the only aircraft in western skies at this time: American combat and transport planes appeared over British Columbia and Alberta on their way to Alaska. In 1942, Japanese forces occupied the Aleutians, the chain of islands off southern Alaska that form a series of stepping stones leading to the heart of the continent. In response, Ottawa and Washington worked out a complex plan called the Canadian Oil Project (Canol), which involved building a series of airfields from Alberta to Alaska, constructing the Alaska Highway from Dawson to Fairbanks, and laying a 960-kilometre-long pipeline from Norman Wells in the

Northwest Territories to a refinery (imported from Texas at horrendous expense) at Whitehorse in the Yukon Territory. From Whitehorse, gasoline and fuel oil would be forwarded to airfields and encampments via the 1920-kilometre-long Alaska Highway.

These were considerable achievements, but there was, unfortunately, one wartime event that Canadians cannot look back on with pride: the treatment of Japanese Canadians.

There has always been racism in Canada — against the native people, Francophones and those of Slavic and Asian origin. But people of Asian ancestry had a particularly hard time because their appearance, language and religion were so radically different from those of the "average" Canadian. They were also disliked, even hated, because they made little attempt to integrate into Canadian society, worked hard, and prospered. Several of these minority groups — Japanese, Chinese, East Indians and the native peoples — were treated as second-class citizens. As late as 1939, none of them had the provincial or federal vote. None could be elected to civic, provincial or federal office. None could serve on juries.

Japanese Canadians, however, suffered an added humiliation during World War II. There were 22 000 of them living in British Columbia: most lived in or near Vancouver, where they were the owner-operators of fishing boats, stores and restaurants; others farmed in the nearby delta of the Fraser River or on the fruitlands of the Okanagan Valley. In the spring of 1941, every resident Japanese or Canadian of Japanese descent was ordered by Ottawa to register with the RCMP. The Mounted Police did not consider this procedure either necessary or justified, but the Liberal government of Mackenzie King thought differently. Thus, when the news of Japan's attack on Pearl Harbor reached Ot-

MEAT 70 VIANDE

MEAT 67 VIANDE

MEAT 66 VIANDE

MEAT 63 VIANDE

MEAT 70 VIANDE

MEAT 67 VIANDE

MEAT 66 VIANDE

MEAT 63 VIANDE

MEAT 69 VIANDE

MEAT 68 VIANDE

MEAT 65 VIANDE

MEAT 64 VIANDE

MEAT 69 VIANDE

MEAT 68 VIANDE

MEAT 65 VIANDE

MEAT 64 VIANDE

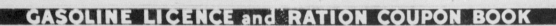

GASOLINE LICENCE and RATION COUPON BOOK

CATEGORY **AA** CATÉGORIE

1945 — 1946

A1058953

CANADA

OIL CONTROLLER FOR CANADA
RÉGISSEUR DES HUILES POUR LE CANADA

For Motor Vehicle Licence Plate No.

96794

Pour la plaque de licence de véhicule automobile No

PERMIS D'ESSENCE et COUPONS DE RATIONS

259

Canadians became accustomed to shortages in World War II. A ration book contained coupons for sugar, meat, tea, coffee and other staples. And without a gasoline ration, the family car stayed put. *See previous page.*

Canadians were encouraged by Ottawa to help win the war at home by saving scrap metal, bones and fat. (The glycerine in fat was an ingredient of high explosives.)

An Anson navigator trainer — which, with the Harvard pilot trainer, formed the basic flying equipment of the Commonwealth Air Training Plan — being serviced by an all-woman ground crew.

To supply gasoline and fuel oil to the Alaska Highway
and airfields constructed alongside it, Canada and the
U.S. laid a pipeline from the NWT over the Mackenzie
Mountains to the Yukon.

In 1941-42 the entire Japanese-Canadian population was herded into prison camps. Families were often broken up, men going to one camp, women and children to another. *See next page.*

tawa, Japanese Canadians were immediately declared enemy aliens; Ottawa ordered the round-up of every individual of Japanese ancestry, on the theory that they were potential spies or saboteurs. It made no difference that many of them had been born in British Columbia and were Canadian citizens.

In wartime, it is not unusual for a democratic government to suspend civil rights, and for fear and suspicion to take the place of reason and logic. This may be why no newspaper protested when Japanese-Canadian males between eighteen and forty-five years of age were separated from their families and sent to work camps in the B.C. interior, Alberta or northern Ontario. This also explains why Parliament did not question the matter when women, children and elderly people were sent to live in British Columbia's ghost towns, shabby relics of the mining boom at the turn of the century. But the most shameful thing of all was the way in which these people lost their possessions. Early in 1942, Ottawa established an Office of the Custodian of Enemy Alien Property and gave it authority to "liquidate, sell, or otherwise dispose of" Japanese-Canadian property. Thus, if homes, businesses, farms, cars, fishing boats and other possessions had not been sold privately for whatever their owners could get, they were sold publicly for the highest price — and the highest price offered was rarely the fairest price.

It is to the great credit of these "enemy aliens" that they endured indignity and injustice with patience and fortitude, the more so since not one of them proved to be, as Ottawa (and Victoria) feared, a threat to national security.

Nothing ever happened. There was never a bridge burned, blown up, a railway switch broken causing a derailment, a highway dynamited, an irrigation or power dam blown up. None of these terrible things.

None once. Not one single instance.

You know why? Because they were loyal. The Japanese people were loyal.

*

Like much of the rest of Canada, the West that heard the news of VE Day and VJ Day in the spring and summer of 1945 was, in many ways, the same small-town society of 1939. Most of its residents still earned their living from farm or forest, mine or fishery. There were stores on Main Street, but no suburban shopping centres for the simple reason that there were few suburbs. There were apartment blocks, but no high-rises; roads, but no highways. Railways were the major means of transportation, and air travel was still an adventurous novelty. Nonetheless, the Canada to which a million servicemen and servicewomen returned in 1945 was not what it had been in 1939.

The hunger and despair of the Great Depression were now memories: the busy years of wartime production and the growth of manufacturing had created a new level of prosperity. The average national wage was $32 a week, almost $10 higher than that in 1939. And the postwar slump that people had feared did not materialize. Wartime industries were successfully changed over to peacetime goods and continued to expand. There was also the reassuring hope that hunger and despair would not return, because the federal government had begun to turn Canada into today's welfare state. In 1940, after many a reminder from the CCF party, unemployment insurance had been introduced by Mackenzie King's Liberal government. In 1944, Parliament passed the Family Allowances Act, which provided a monthly "baby bonus" for every child under age sixteen in the family.

That same year, the CCF in Saskatchewan ,

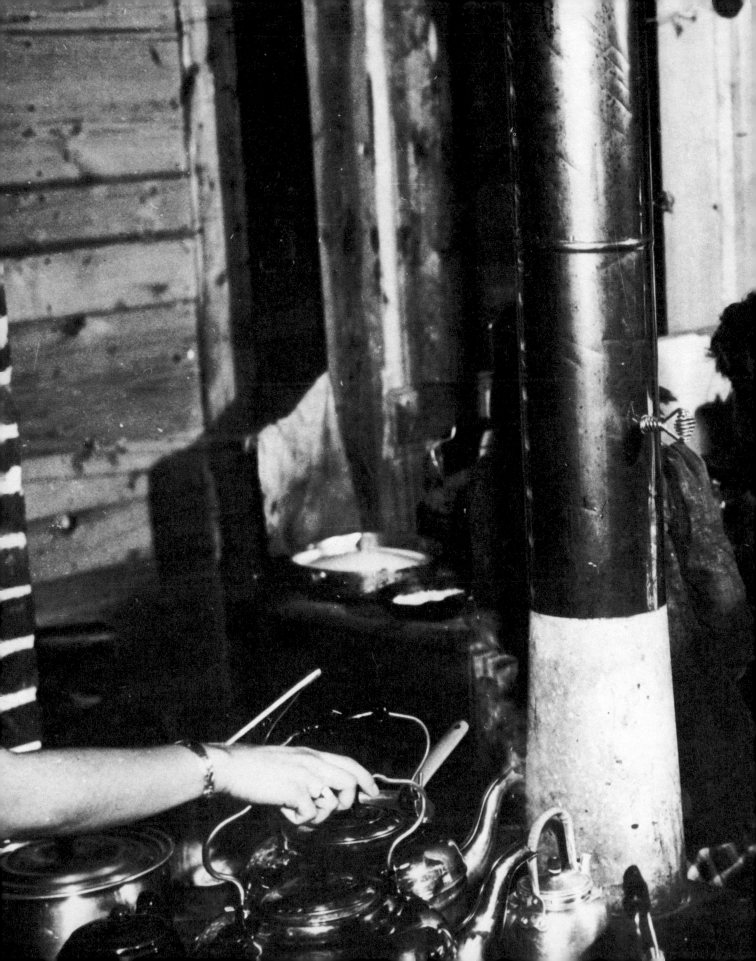

267

For years, Turner Valley wells were tapping only the natural gas from the cap of a billion-barrel reservoir of crude. In 1936-37, oilmen drilled right into the reservoir – and the rush for black gold was on. *See page 266*.

Canada's first major petroleum field was discovered in Turner Valley, Alberta, in 1913-14. This turned nearby Calgary into the nation's oil-promotion capital. *See page 267*.

led by Tommy Douglas, won power at the polls. This, the first socialist government in North America, managed to implement further CCF ideals: provincially-operated automobile insurance, transportation and ambulance services; and the first hospital and medical government insurance schemes in Canada.

Many returning veterans – Indian and Metis as well as those of British or European ancestry – used their war-service gratuities to pay for further education. Enrolment at universities and colleges doubled, and the most popular choice of study was engineering. It was a timely choice. A new age of resource development was beginning in the four western provinces.

*

On the outskirts of Edmonton, alongside the highway linking that city and Calgary, is an oil derrick bearing the sign "Edmonton: Oil Capital of Canada." Calgarians would argue that claim, but not with the fact that this steel tower is an historic object – the derrick that brought in Imperial Oil's Leduc No. 1 in 1947. Imperial crews had to drill 133 consecutive dry holes before hitting pay dirt with this, the 134th. The discovery of a major geological reef a little south of Edmonton gave Albertans their first positive proof of petroleum wealth. And it came at a time when Canadian homes were being heated with costly coal imported from the United States, and when there were financial limitations on any significant expansion of the nation's hydro-electric production.

Immortalized in the literature of oil as Leduc No. 1, this discovery made the Canadian West a prime hunting ground for teams of geologists and seismologists. From a spending rate of something like one million dollars a month in 1946, oil investment zoomed to one million dollars a day by the next decade. Spending sky-

rocketed to three million dollars a day in the 1960s. Leduc triggered explorations that have resulted in the discovery of hundreds of oil wells and natural gas deposits in western Canada.

An army of workers poured into Alberta to help develop this new resource: thousands of kilometres of pipelines had to be laid, scores of processing plants and refineries had to be built and operated. To meet these construction needs, steel plants were built. These and dozens of spin-off industries drew workers by the thousand, and only twenty-five years after Leduc, the population of Alberta had doubled. The province had a broader economic base; in addition to farming, it now had – thanks to petroleum-derived wealth – construction, manufacturing and a significant forest industry.

All four western provinces have become producers of oil; all, except Manitoba, produce natural gas. Nowadays, pipelines crisscross the face of western Canada and angle off east, south and west to supply Americans and Canadians with energy. But, of the four, Alberta has been called the "Texas of Canada" with good reason. Its production has been astronomical: billions of barrels of oil, trillions of cubic metres of natural gas, and, more recently, millions of tonnes of coal. Together, they amount to something like eighty per cent of all Canada's fossil-fuel reserves discovered to date.

Saskatchewan, with forty per cent of Canada's farmland, had long produced sixty per cent of its wheat and little else of significance. However, the search for oil and gas revealed deposits of potash laid down by long-gone seas. A crude form of salt, potash, when refined, is an essential plant food and is also used in certain manufacturing processes. Below the fields of grain in the Unity-Vera-Patience Lake area of Saskatchewan lies the largest deposit of potash in the world, and like petroleum it has proven to

The Fitzsimmons sands-processing plant near Fort McMurray, Alberta, in 1942. R. B. Fitzsimmons, a Maritimer, was the first entrepreneur to produce crude oil from tar sands on a commercial basis.

Natural gas, once a bothersome by-product of oil, became a money-making export in the 1950s. Here, a crew near the Banff Springs Hotel lays pipe to British Columbia.

Crew at the first oil well in Virden, Manitoba.

be a rich bonus for a province so long dependent on the uncertainties of world wheat markets. Capital investment in potash has been heavy, and today the "Wheat Province" is, after the Soviet Union, the world's leading producer of potash-derived fertilizer. Potash will, in time, prove to be far more valuable to Saskatchewan than its oil and gas — with the qualification that potash has already shown itself to be subject to the same boom-and-bust cycle as wheat.

Mineralogists also struck it rich in northern Saskatchewan. The mining camp of Goldfields on the north shore of Lake Athabasca had become a ghost town during World War II; in 1950, it was revived as an exploration centre when enormous finds were made nearby of pitchblende ore, the source of uranium and atomic energy. Gunnar Mines began construction of a processing mill, and in 1952 the provincial government laid out Uranium City, complete with airstrip. As for the province's resources of wood, these have become so important to the economy that the Saskatchewan Timber Board regulates the cut and sale of forest products. Indeed, Saskatchewan was the first province to protect its forests from fire loss by flying in smoke-jumpers prior to the arrival of heavy-duty firefighting equipment.

Manitoba's oldest and newest settlements — based on resources — are in the northern half of the province. Just over three hundred years ago, the HBC opened for business on the shores of Hudson Bay. Today, grain instead of pelts is being shipped out via that great inland sea. An hour to the southwest by plane, construction companies built, in the 1950s, the town of Thompson amid the rock and timber of the Shield for the employees of the world's first industrial plant to mine, smelt and refine nickel at the same location. Farther south and west, on the Manitoba-Saskatchewan border, the copper-and-zinc re-

fining complex at Flin Flon was expanded to receive the ore output of several new mines. (At one time, digging and blasting at Flin Flon resulted in ore being taken out of both Manitoba and Saskatchewan soil, so both provinces collected royalties on the ore being extracted.) Two hundred and forty kilometres to the north, rich copper and nickel claims were staked in the Lynn Lake district, and a railway built to take ores to Flin Flon. As in Alberta and Saskatchewan, growth in the lumbering and pulp-and-paper industries encouraged the founding of new towns. At The Pas, for example, an immense complex for the processing of forest products was funded by Canadian and Swiss capital.

In British Columbia, trees are half its treasury: forest industries account for fifty per cent of all dollars earned in the province. After 1945, there was a twofold improvement in the harvesting of wood. Lumbering ceased to be a largely coastal operation; with expanded rail and road communications, forest firms sent their crews into the untouched reserves of the interior. And, instead of just being exported, timber was also processed into such more profitable forms as plywood, veneers and wood pulp. Papermaking became as major an industry as the smelting of metals. But a significant postwar development in B.C. was the exploitation of a different natural resource: water.

In the process of increasing hydroelectric capacity, there were some astonishing feats of engineering in the province. For instance, in the 1950s, the east-flowing Nechako River (a tributary of the Fraser) was made to flow westward. On the upper reaches of the river, the giant McKinnie Dam created a 160-kilometre-long lake that backed up and spilled Nechako water into a 16-kilometre long tunnel blasted through one of the Coast Mountains. Before entering the Kemano River, the water dropped 780 metres

In 1959, at Kelowna, B.C., Premier Bennett fires an incendiary arrow at a bargeload of provincial bonds to dramatize what he claimed was the elimination of a large government deficit. *See next page.*

---

into an underground powerhouse (also dynamited out of the mountain's interior) to generate additional electricity for the huge aluminum smelter at the town of Kitimat, eighty kilometres farther west on Pacific tidewater.

*

The discovery and exploitation of the West's new resource wealth heightened the traditional tensions between the four western provinces and the federal government. Westerners had been unhappy enough to establish new political parties to support their particular regional interests. In Manitoba, first the United Farmers of Manitoba, then the Progressive party, then coalition governments held power from 1922 to 1958. The CCF became the elected government in Saskatchewan in 1944 and won election after election until 1964. Alberta, the home base of Social Credit in Canada, was ruled by that party for thirty six years, from 1935 to 1971. And British Columbia had a coalition government from 1941 to 1952, followed by the Socreds under W. A. C. Bennett from 1952 to 1972.

These western parties, however, never had any success on the federal level. Nor were the two established national parties – the Liberals and Conservatives – popular in the West, or prepared to listen to its grievances. Denied a voice in federal deliberations, western politicians turned in frustration to creating powerful provincial governments.

British Columbians, for example, in the words of a litterateur and historian resident in the province,

see themselves as divided from the rest of Canada by geography . . . by personal interests and even by class interests, and this has always made them a politically volatile people, not to be tamed by the mass Canadian parties whose organizations are based on the Ontario-Quebec axis. Instead they are

liable to give their loyalties rather capriciously to populist local leaders – like John Oliver and Duff Patullo, like the Bennetts and Dave Barrett – with whom they can make some personal identification . . . if Trudeau's apparent arrogance has often angered British Columbians, significantly few of them took any exception to their own flamboyant premier W. A. C. Bennett's habit of declaring "I'm plugged into God."

*

W. A. C. Bennett (1907-1979) had flamboyance – and chutzpah – to spare. He behaved like the leader of a quasi-state – even to the extent of changing his official title from premier to prime minister.

Like the ebullient "R. B." Bennett, William Andrew Cecil Bennett was born and bred in New Brunswick. Also like his federal namesake, Bennett was of Loyalist stock, religious, and a self-made millionaire, in his case by selling hardware to people in the Okanagan. In fact, he made money in chainstore merchandising during the worst of the Depression.

By 1952, Bennett had served several years in the B.C. provincial legislature, nominally as a member of an uneasy coalition government of Liberals and Conservatives, though the dullness of deliberations in Victoria had motivated him twice to try for election to Parliament. He finally walked away from the coalition to sit as an independent. In the June election of 1952, the provincial Social Credit party – which now included Bennett, who calculated that the party was a likely winner – won the right to form a government. A month later, he was elected party leader. Those Liberals and Conservatives who held the balance of power preferred the Socreds to the CCFers, so Bennett became premier on 1 August 1952. "Cec" to his friends and "Wacky" to his enemies, he retained the premiership until

Constructing the W. A. C. Bennett Dam in 1965. Engineers diverted the raging waters of the Peace River (background), which had forced even the hardbitten Alexander Mackenzie to make a long portage.

---

30 August 1972, when he was beaten at the polls by former social worker Dave Barrett of the New Democratic Party (who was, in turn, defeated in 1975 by Bennett's son, William).

"Wacky's" numerous foes could no more accuse him of giving the province twenty years of populist programs than could critics of Ernest Manning's Social Credit government in neighbouring Alberta. In the case of each man, the exploitation of natural resources converted the socioeconomic philosophy of the Socred movement into that of a party devoted to prosperity based on co-operation with big business.

If anything, Bennett was a reincarnation of an earlier B.C. premier, Richard McBride (1903-1915), whose devotion to provincial growth by any and all means was akin to religious fervour. Just as McBride had provided the political-legal environment that allowed the corporate exploitation of mines — and miners — in the Kootenay region of the southern interior, so Bennett allowed the American-dominated forest industry and pulp-and-paper industry to work the softwood stands of the northern interior — often at the expense of small, independent Canadian logging companies. The premier also rescinded legislation protecting the prairie and parkland of the Peace River country and gave the right of unrestricted development to the largely U.S.-owned oil-and-gas industry.

Bennett wooed support for this raw-growth policy not just in the urban centres, but from residents of remote towns, ranchers, farmers and miners. With his small-town background as a retailer, he knew well how to appeal to a prime need of country people: transportation routes. So his Socreds became, as one historian puts it, "the new Romans, who moved mountains of rock and gravel in a grand splurge of road-building." But the roads did break down the isolated regionality that had long hampered British Colum-

bia's economy. And where roads and bridges could not buy votes, Bennett subtly substituted home-owner grants for the normal increase in monies given annually by Victoria to municipalities.

A major item of Bennett policy was the simultaneous hydroelectric development of the Peace and Columbia rivers. The Peace scheme was a relatively simple project, and Bennett believed it would attract into the northern interior American firms whose operations required vast amounts of hydroelectric power. The second scheme, however, brought Bennett up against the federal government, because the mighty Columbia is an international waterway.

An International Joint Commission (IJC) had been studying the Columbia's watershed since 1944. The Canadian section of the IJC, chaired by the fiercely patriotic General "Andy" McNaughton, favoured building storage dams north of the 49th parallel, both to control the river's habit of flooding its U.S. course and to conserve water to drive Canadian generators. But this plan only partially suited the Americans, who badly needed power dams on their side of the border to provide electricity for the states of Washington and Oregon. And the plan didn't suit Bennett at all.

The onetime merchandiser was a tough bargainer. Without a federal cash grant, Bennett would not yield to Ottawa on the Columbia project: he was willing to spend provincial money on the Peace project, but certainly not on the Columbia. Let the Americans build dams on their side of the border, he argued, and pay B.C. for a proportion of the power they generated by using B.C. waters. These American payments would help to pay for Canadian dams on the river. The fact that the McNaughton plan would avoid giving the U.S. a long-term lease on Columbia water and would supply reasonably cheap, Canadian-generated electricity was cleverly obscured.

Despite opposition from Ottawa, Bennett continued to hold out for his way of doing things. The only problem, he insisted, was that Ottawa was standing by the letter of an archaic law (passed in Laurier's time) that gave the federal cabinet authority to license annual exports of power. Bennett's speechifying blurred and distorted the truth, the technicalities and finances of which were complicated. The contest was about the cost of kilowatts, but the premier turned it into a war of kilowords in which he outtalked his critics and convinced most of his bemused fellow British Columbians that he was their economic champion. Bennett even ignored diplomatic protocol when he arranged, directly with Washington, D.C., a meeting with President Kennedy to discuss Columbia power.

In 1963, the election of Lester Pearson, whose Liberal government was committed to a firm policy of power exports, smoothed the way for a Bennett-style treaty. The terms were just as the premier wanted them: money enough, in terms of downstream power derived by the U.S. and flood-control measures provided by Canada, to build dams and generators in the province on the upper Columbia. Bennett's victory, however, weakened national sovereignty. By treaty, the whole upper watershed of the Columbia was placed under international, not Canadian, control. Thus, any future scheme to divert the waters of the Kootenay River into the Columbia, or Columbia waters into the Saskatchewan River, will be contingent upon American consultation and agreement. Dependence on Washington was the price of independence from Ottawa.

Bennett's actions were an indication of the growing power of provincial governments in the West; their new energy-based prosperity gave them confidence in their traditional role as opponents of the federal government.

*

In Ottawa, postwar politics were dominated by the Liberals, with the exception of a period of Tory administration when, for a third time, a western politician was prime minister.

Unlike his predecessors Meighen and Bennett, the new Tory leader grew up in the West, on homesteads in Saskatchewan. So he knew all about crops of grain that were either shoulder-high and seed-heavy, or stunted and shrunken. He knew, as W. P. Webb remarked in his book, *The Great Plains*, that if a homesteader survived in the prairie west "far from markets, burned by drought, beaten by hail, withered by hot winds, frozen by blizzards, eaten out by grasshoppers, exploited by capitalists and cozened by politicians," then he survived because of his own and his family's efforts.

John Diefenbaker worked out his credo of Canadianism in the course of his many failures to win election to political office. The federal government is the paramount power, but has a commitment to assist poorer provinces and underprivileged groups. Loyalty to the traditions of parliamentary government, and to the British connection and its symbols. A policy of, to use his words, "unhyphenated Canadianism": respect for different cultures, yes, but the assimilation of ethnic groups into the practicality of an English-speaking "One Canada." Last, but far from least, a desire to prove to his fellow Canadians that the future of Canada was nationalism, not sectionalism of the Quebec variety — or the western variety.

It was in the western wheatfields that his Tories garnered their greatest electoral gains.

Prairie farmers were fed up with the government's inability to sell their wheat on international markets (which happened to be glutted with grain) and furious with Ottawa's unwillingness to compensate them for their losses, as the U.S. government was doing for its farmers. And while other factors were at work, a notable one was the Liberal party's lack of interest in the needs and well-being of its provincial brethren (as later with Trudeau and his entourage). Indeed, during Louis St. Laurent's nine-year tenure as prime minister, the Liberal governments of British Columbia, New Brunswick and Nova Scotia were ousted, while the Liberal parties of Saskatchewan, Alberta, Quebec and Ontario became accustomed to defeat at the polls. Thus, come the federal election of 1957, there were few grassroots resources available to St. Laurent and his overconfident followers.

The initial triumph of John Diefenbaker in 1957 disguised the fact that his tragedy had already begun. As was the case a year later, when, with his thrilling "Vision of the North," he won the greatest electoral victory since Confederation – 207 seats. And, thereafter, by some impressive legislative achievements, including: the establishment of the Board of Broadcast Governors (the forerunner of the Canadian Radio and Television Commission) and the National Energy Board; a Canadian Bill of Rights; oil exploration and mineral exploitation in the Northwest Territories; the construction of the Liberal's long-promised, long-delayed South Saskatchewan Dam; massive wheat sales to a new customer – China; a foreign-trade surplus in manufactured goods; and crop insurance and farm-credit legislation. All these successes, however, were offset by his gradual alienation of his cabinet, his caucus and the party itself, notably by his mishandling of financial and foreign-policy matters.

In 1963, defeated in the House by a motion of nonconfidence, beaten in a spring election in which his campaign oratory – always pungent – had been marred by an anti-Americanism that cost him the resignations of several cabinet members, John Diefenbaker ceased to be prime minister. Four years later, he was removed from the party leadership, but characteristically continued to do battle in his more-familiar Commons' role of crusty critic.

Discredited though he was in the urbanized parts of the nation, Diefenbaker was always accorded a special respect in rural Canada, particularly in the West. One measure of his appeal and authority is that, between 1957 and 1965 and through five elections, his party commanded a majority of western seats. He was always the farmer's friend. Above all, he was the man who made it to the top, but never lost touch with his humble origins; in an age of television and jet travel, he still took the time and trouble to campaign by train from one whistle-stop community to the next.

*

Western prosperity continued to depend on resource exports, but the base had widened from fish, lumber and wheat to include oil, natural gas and potash. Moreover, the West had finally become industrialized as a result of World War II and the development of these newly discovered resources. There were now smelters, refineries, processing plants, mills and a multitude of related industries. With increasing industrialization – and its thousands of jobs – came a shift in the population from rural areas to urban centres.

Patterns of immigration accentuated this shift from country to city, for the 2.5 million "New Canadians" who arrived between 1946 and 1966 did not come in search of land. They

This 1962 photograph suggests a noisy argument between Prime Minister Diefenbaker (l.) and Liberal leader Pearson. Actually, it's an accidental double exposure of film used at two different political rallies.

settled in cities, where they could use their training in managerial, professional, commercial and industrial skills.

In the 1970s, fifty per cent of all Manitobans were living in the heavily industrial metropolitan centre of Greater Winnipeg. Half the population of Alberta resided in Calgary and Edmonton. Not only did Vancouver contain fifty per cent of British Columbia's population, but another twenty-five per cent had crowded themselves into the Lower Mainland and Victoria. Even in the great grain country of Saskatchewan, two of every three people were urban dwellers. The mechanization of farming had made the old quarter-section farm unprofitable, and the average prairie farm was about 600 acres (240 ha) in size — and becoming larger as agribusiness groups bought and consolidated individual land holdings. As farmers moved to jobs in the cities, the tiny rural service communities around elevators and railway tank towns began to feel the slow erosion of disfavour and decay.

In the opinion of one Westerner, however, agriculture *is* prairie Canada. And it is also her opinion that the last chapter of that story is now being written on the pages of history.

Between 1966 and 1971, Saskatchewan lost 30,000 people, and its rural population decreased by more than 50,000. Alberta is losing 500 rural people a year, Manitoba 3000. Most of them move to cities: the young go east, the old go west. Almost all of them are farmers. Agriculture is no longer the economic backbone of the prairies. In Manitoba and Alberta, farming accounts for less than 20 percent of gross productivity; in Saskatchewan, it's less than half: urban people outnumber rural people in all three provinces. The retreat from the land has been in progress for 30 years. . . . Most of those who are left are old, and within the next generation they will die.

The West is young. Many of the original settlers are still alive; their own lives have spanned the birth and death of an agricultural civilization. For all Westerners, even city people, the farmer is the touchstone, our fertility symbol, the core of our mythology. He is the grass roots, the salt of the earth, the moral fibre of the nation: he is The People. His gradual disappearance shakes our sense of identity and makes us question the validity of our history. Those of us who remain in the West feel a small chill, as if the farmer's flight from the land has blighted our own hopes and brought on us a sense of attenuation and decay . . . the farmer is the guardian of the western dream; without him, the West is just the East.

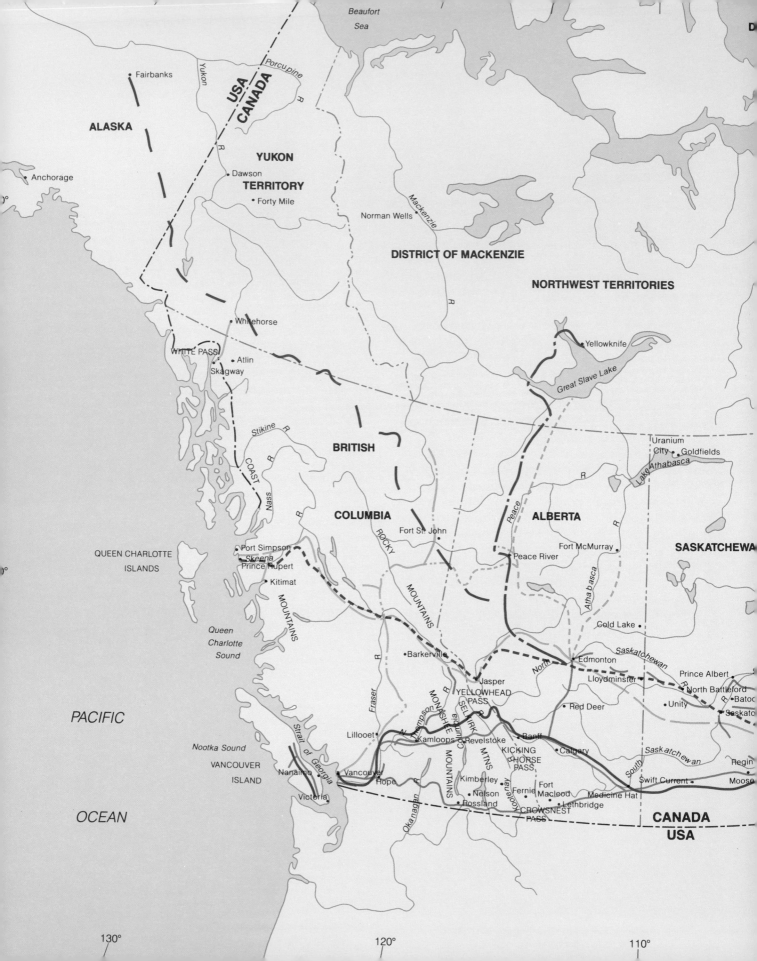

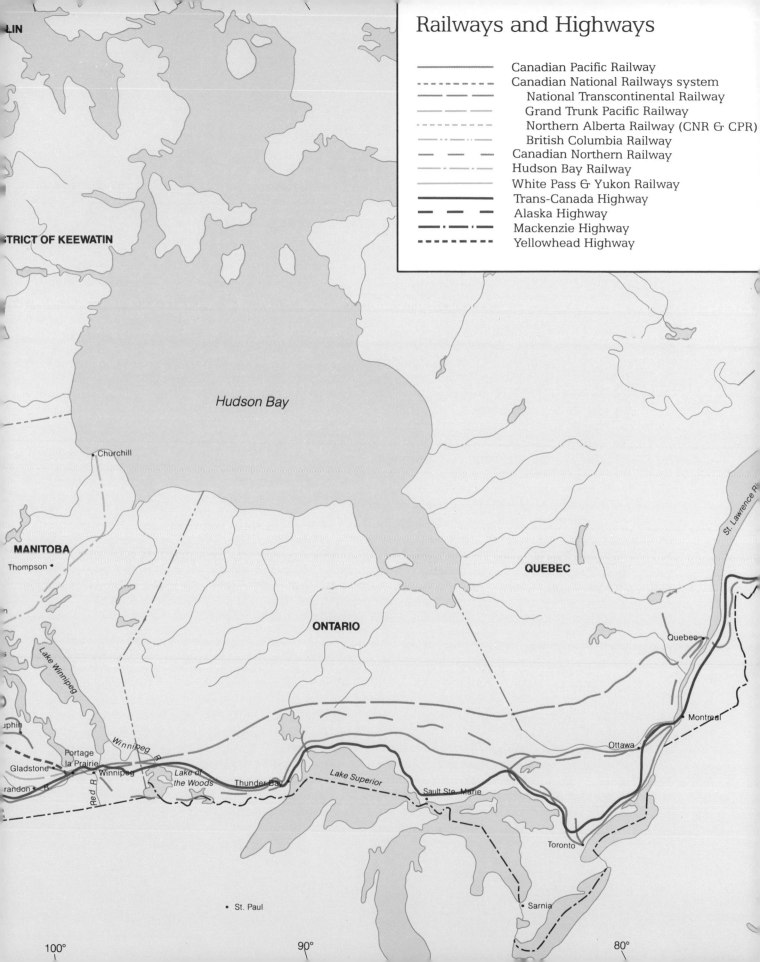

Railways and Highways

————	Canadian Pacific Railway
- - - - -	Canadian National Railways system
—‐—‐—	National Transcontinental Railway
— — —	Grand Trunk Pacific Railway
··············	Northern Alberta Railway (CNR & CPR)
—··—··—	British Columbia Railway
— — —	Canadian Northern Railway
————	Hudson Bay Railway
————	White Pass & Yukon Railway
▬▬▬▬	Trans-Canada Highway
▬ ▬ ▬	Alaska Highway
▬·▬·▬·	Mackenzie Highway
▬ ▬ ▬ ▬	Yellowhead Highway

LIN

STRICT OF KEEWATIN

Hudson Bay

Churchill

MANITOBA

Thompson •

QUEBEC

St. Lawrence R

ONTARIO

Quebec

Lake Winnipeg

Montreal

uphin

Winnipeg R

Ottawa

Portage
la Prairie

Winnipeg

Lake of
the Woods

Thunder Bay

Lake Superior

Sault Ste. Marie

Gladstone

Red R

randon

Toronto

• St. Paul

Sarnia

100°   90°   80°

13 Power and Alienation

In July 1970, when Manitoba celebrated the hundredth anniversary of its entry into Confederation, it had a million residents compared to the 25 000 reported in the census of 1871. Exactly twelve months later, another centenary took place in British Columbia, where the former Gold Colony of a few thousands was now boasting a population of two million. And when Saskatchewan and Alberta held their seventy-fifth birthday parties in 1980, these provinces were home to a further 2.5 million people.

There was much for which to give thanks during all these festivities. The three prairie provinces contain approximately seventy-five per cent of the nation's farmland and contribute about fifty per cent of Canada's agricultural exports. Grain was still the basic crop, and new strains produced by plant scientists were maturing more quickly and yielding more heavily. Dairying, poultry-raising and livestock were well established staples. New products — honey, and vegetable oils from rapeseed and sunflower seeds — were being successfully marketed. As for the Pacific province, it was producing just over half of Canada's multiplicity of forest products and, when there was a good fishing season, accounted for at least thirty per cent of all freshwater and saltwater fish caught in Canada. Its mineral output was just over half the value of all national production. And, of course, from the four western provinces come virtually all the nation's oil and natural gas.

Despite all this abundance of natural wealth, Westerners were — as they had long been — discontented with Confederation. And for the same old continuing reasons: the tariff, transportation policies and freight rates, agricultural policies and access to political power. One new and important issue particularly raised passions — the share-out of oil and gas revenues.

*

A basic western grievance was explained, simply and clearly, by a member of Parliament from Winnipeg, James Richardson, in a speech in his home town.

The problem is this. Western Canada is a producer of great natural wealth and we sell our products on world markets at world market prices. We do not sell very much of our production in Toronto and Montreal. Our nickel, our potash, our forest products, our oil and gas, and, of course, our wheat are sold to buyers all around the world. But when we buy the manufactured products that we need — appliances of all kinds, textiles, radios, television sets, and even carpets for the floors of our houses, we cannot buy these products at world prices. . . . These manufactured goods are increased in price by a tariff . . . which is designed to protect the manufacturing plants, most of which are located in Eastern Canada.

If Western Canada were able to determine its own tariff policy, our standard of living would go up because we would still be obtaining the same prices which we obtain now for the goods we sell. But we would be able to buy in exchange the manufactured products which we need at a lower price.

Or, as Alberta Premier Harry Strom once put it, "We see the logic of protecting infant industries, but some of the infants are over eighty years of age and we are tired of paying their pensions." And who are the pensioners of the tariff? The persons it most protects: the factory owner and factory worker, businessman and banker in central Canada.

An equally sore point is that rail freight rates discriminate against western industries. Western Canada depends upon rail transport, for, unlike central Canada, it has no vast inland waterway like the St. Lawrence Seaway and no dense network of highways to offer keen competition to railways.

Ever since the issue of the first CPR freight-rate schedules in 1883, there has been discrimination against the West. Even today, there is a similar situation known, officially, as "fair discrimination": subject to the approval of the federal Board of Transport Commissioners, railways set low rates in areas where alternative forms of transportation offer competition, but, in areas where there is no effective competition, set rates at much higher levels. The Crowsnest Pass Agreement of 1897 did lower freight rates — but only for grain shipments. The fact that these rates did *not* apply to industrial raw materials and finished products was a strong irritant.

Western Canada . . . is no longer the exclusive domain of the grain farmer. As technology and mechanization reduce the numbers of people needed to tend to the grain fields, there are more and more demands that western raw materials be processed in Western Canada, and that more new primary and secondary industries locate in the region. Unfortunately the discriminatory rate structure is a major obstacle to such economic diversification.

It is almost impossible for many western businesses and industries to compete with eastern rivals if the freight rates for everything they bring into the region and everything they take out are significantly higher than the comparable rates paid by their competitors.

*

Federal agricultural policy has been a major western worry ever since fur traders were replaced by farmers. Agriculture has been a mainstay of the prairie economy for decades and even today is exceeded in output by mineral and industrial production only in Alberta. Grain is the main product, though livestock and poultry make up forty per cent of total western farm receipts.

Wheat sales in the years following World War II repeated the same old historic pattern of boom and bust. Prices were excellent until the late 1950s, when agriculture in Europe recovered and a world glut of grain developed, slowing the demand for Canadian grain. Wheat backed up all along the line from terminal elevators at a port to farm buildings — or simply lay in piles on the ground, where it was fed to livestock, or rotted. In the 1960s and 1970s, there were booms when the USSR and China became major customers. But other wheat-producing nations often undersold Canada because their governments subsidized the production of grain with payments to farmers of so much per export bushel. Ottawa refused to do the same thing for Canadian farmers. In other words, when there was a wheat price war, the prairie farmer lost every time. He still loses today, because there is still no federal subsidy on export wheat sales.

In the 1970s, the prairie farmer was also paying at least three times as much for his machinery as his father had in the 1940s. The urban housewife may or may not have been annoyed at paying one hundred per cent more for bread than thirty years earlier, but the farmer was angry that he paid higher costs for machinery, gasoline, electricity, fertilizer and interest on bank loans but could not get comparably higher prices for his wheat. His farm might be worth $100,000 but his annual income was often less than $5,000. He was caught in a cost-price squeeze. To help him keep the farm in the family, he wanted — but could not get — a two-price system for his wheat. He wanted a guaranteed price, higher than the export one, for the millions of bushels of wheat sold each year in Canada. This would be paid for by adding perhaps a couple of cents to the price of a loaf of bread.

Another thing the farmer wanted was better rail transportation and bulk-handling systems.

Grain elevators in Saskatchewan.

Threshing wheat in Manitoba.

Rural branch lines built decades ago have not been well maintained, with the result that many of them cannot handle the heavier, faster rolling stock now being used. More rolling stock for grain is needed, but the railways have flatly refused to maintain, let alone increase, their grain-carrying capacity unless they receive an adequate return for grain haulage. And they have a legitimate grievance: the actual cost of grain shipment has far outdistanced the statutory freight rate established by the Crowsnest Pass Agreement. However, this is but one of many inequities that plague western rail transportation. For instance, systems built to haul crops east and manufactured goods west are now hauling nearly half the prairie grain west to the major export port of Vancouver. Both it and the other major grain export port of Churchill need updating and expansion of their facilities, if Canada is to continue to compete in world markets.

*

The future of oil is another worry. A prime one. Of all the various resource developments in western Canada, the most profitable has been the exploitation of oil and gas. It is also the most contentious resource development, since the monies generated by these resources are the subject of blunt speaking, publicly and privately, among federal and provincial governments.

Leduc No. 1 and other gushers did not convert Alberta into a land of petrodollars overnight. In the late 1940s and early 1950s, the major American oil companies, the largest producers of Alberta crude, were quite content to service the modest market needs of western Canada — but otherwise sat on the petroleum potential of their exclusive leases. They made their money by importing dirt-cheap crude from the Middle East or Venezuela to their refineries in eastern Canada, piping the then much more expensive western crude to other refineries in Sarnia, Ontario, then selling the many by-products from each source — notably gasoline and home heating oil — at the same markup. In the late 1950s, Canadian oil producers agitated for Ottawa's protection against the foreign inflow. The ultimate response of the Diefenbaker government was a national oil policy that gave Alberta access to the Ontario market by extending the pipeline from Sarnia to Toronto. Further frustration, however, was just a little way down the road. Although diplomatic nudgings in Washington by the Liberal government of Lester B. Pearson produced a remarkable rise in oil exports to the midwestern and western states, Alberta still had enormous oil reserves — yet no access to markets in Quebec and the Maritime provinces.

Pearson was succeeded early in 1968 as party leader and prime minister by Pierre Elliott Trudeau. To many Canadians, the charismatic, centralist-minded minister of justice seemed the man to lead the nation (particularly a refractory Quebec) into its second century of Confederation. In June 1968, Trudeau fought and won his first federal election on the major issues of national unity and a more equitable regional distribution of Canada's wealth.

A year later, the Independent Petroleum Association of Canada (IPAC) warned the new administration about the Organization of Petroleum Exporting Countries. Calgary oilman Carl Nickle recalled:

We correctly forecast . . . though we couldn't, naturally, pinpoint the exact year in which it would happen . . . that prices would be raised as the OPEC nations saw fit. . . . And it had now, as we saw it, become vitally important that Canada extend the oil

Pierre Elliott Trudeau campaigning outside City Hall,
Edmonton, in May 1968.

The moment of victory. On the night of 31 August 1971, a sweaty, rumpled Alberta Premier-elect Peter Lougheed is congratulated by his wife, Pat, and a party worker.

pipeline on to Montreal – not to help western Canada but to ensure security of supply in the crisis that lay ahead in the 1970s.

However, the IPAC delegates were told, in effect, to go peddle their oil somewhere else.

Until the 1970s, the higher price of western oil in relation to that of other nations had handicapped sales but, as world prices began to rise rapidly, the domestic demand for Canadian oil grew. So did the possibility of immense profits. The division of these profits soon brought the federal and western provincial governments into conflict. Alberta, with the most oil reserves and the most to lose, was at the forefront of the confrontation, led by a determined Peter Lougheed.

*

The story of the Calgary branch of the Lougheed family begins with James Alexander Lougheed, a Toronto-trained lawyer who followed the westward-reaching CPR in 1883 and hung out his shingle in the tent town called Calgary. His shrewd speculations in local real estate became the basis of the family fortune, and his later public career was capped by an appointment to the Senate and a knighthood. This family political tradition continues with his grandson, Peter, whose early adult years included several stints in the Edmonton Eskimo backfield, student politics at the University of Alberta, and further law and business studies at Harvard.

In the fall of 1964, after ten years of practising law, Peter Lougheed became deeply concerned that Alberta needed a long-term development plan to avoid again becoming an economic backwoods when its energy resources were depleted. So he determined to win the leadership of the provincial Conservative party, then that of the province itself. The first task took four months to organize, the second seven years

– though he had figured on a ten-year struggle to defeat the longtime Socred government of Ernest Manning and his successor Harry Strom.

Two months after he became premier, Lougheed told the National Press Club in Ottawa that he insisted on being present at Canada-U.S. energy discussions: "If Alberta poker chips are involved at the poker table, we will be at that table!" The reaction of the Trudeau government then, and at later formal energy conferences with the premiers, was coolly negative. This partly explains the western war of words with "the Feds," the occasional negotiations to reach a compromise – and increasing alienation of the West.

*

In October 1972, the federal Liberals ended up at the polls only two seats ahead of the Conservatives. A year later, the minority Trudeau government, as payment for continued NDP support in the Commons, announced a new oil policy. Canada would become energy self-sufficient by 1980. The main measures sounded impressive: an extension of the Alberta-Toronto pipeline to Montreal (which actually came to pass); official approval of a Mackenzie Valley pipeline to piggy-back Mackenzie Delta gas – when found in commercial quantities – on Alaskan supplies; the creation of a publicly-owned petroleum company (Petro-Canada, a name said to have been picked by Trudeau himself); and an increase in domestic prices to help subsidize the cost of imported crude, which OPEC had announced would rise from $3.00 to $11.00 a barrel in January 1974.

An increase from $3.80 to $6.50 a barrel was agreed upon by Alberta and Ottawa. Discussions around the bargaining table produced much provincial-federal wrangling, but also a steady series of mutually-determined price increases: the wellhead price of a barrel of Canadian crude rose, by stages, from $6.50 in 1974 to $17.78 in 1981 (when OPEC's price was $40.00).

From 1972 to 1980, the West was largely a Tory stronghold, a result of the West's growing disgust with the Liberals, linked to the growing confrontational attitude of Trudeau. So would a Conservative government have been more sympathetic to the energy concerns of the four western provinces? The brief period in power of Prime Minister Clark does not suggest that such a circumstance makes a significant difference.

*

Joe Clark of High River, Alberta, was a campaign organizer for Peter Lougheed in Alberta and Davie Fulton in British Columbia, and staff assistant to Robert Stanfield, Diefenbaker's successor as party leader. In 1976, Clark was the Tory member of Parliament for the sprawling, ranching-mining constituency of Rocky Mountain. Young, bilingual, and with the advantage of being from an anti-Trudeau West, he sought his party's leadership in February that year. He overcame the other ten candidates to win on the fourth ballot. Three and a half years later the Clark Conservatives gained power, mainly by recapturing the urban support that John Diefenbaker had lost in the early 1960s.

In contrast to his Liberal predecessor in office, Clark's caucus included fifty-seven western members of Parliament, twenty-one from Alberta alone. But his actions did not elicit much approval from fellow Westerners. The appointment to cabinet office of the two MPs elected in Quebec brought grumbles of "the return of French power." There were complaints that not enough Albertans had been given portfolios. This dissent became much-publicized protest when energy-revenue sharing was discussed with the four western premiers. As in earlier years, the federal argument was that the still-rising price of imported oil necessitated a substantial tax revenue from domestic oil in order to cushion eastern Canadians from the effects of skyrocketing fuel costs. Thus, the share-out of petroleum profits should be changed to give the federal treasury twenty-five per cent. Prime Minister Clark wanted the producing provinces to contribute to an "energy bank" that would finance new energy projects and, also, to accept a much heavier federal tax on gasoline. The goal, he said, was energy self-sufficiency by 1990. But no Clark proposal or revised petroleum proposal was totally acceptable. Either the price offered was too low, or the revenue sharing was considered too punitive for a non-renewable resource, or the proposals infringed on what were viewed as provincial property rights. The only item that *did* appeal happened to be in the Tory budget of December 1979 — regular increases in wellhead prices to bring Canadian oil up to eighty-five per cent of the rapidly increasing world price — but that budget was rendered stillborn by the Liberal return to the front benches two months later.

*

Late in 1980 came the Trudeau government's announcement of the National Energy Program (NEP), which recreated the battle lines between Alberta and the federal government, and also infuriated British Columbia and Saskatchewan.

According to the NEP, the nation will be self-sufficient in oil by 1990 and there will be a fifty per cent Canadian-owned energy industry — thanks to the NEP's front runner, Petro-Canada. In the matter of fair distribution, the NEP promised Canadians subsidized prices for oil and gas, a redistribution of revenues away from pe-

In July 1977, Opposition Leader Joe Clark and his wife, Maureen McTeer, were among the notables attending the fiftieth-birthday celebration of Barrhead, Alberta.

A lowering-in crew embedding a section of natural gas pipeline in Alberta.

troleum-producing provinces and firms to Ottawa through taxation measures, and some regional redistribution of federal oil revenues via various programs.

Oil-industry spokesmen in western Canada claimed that, under NEP, the nation is headed for a drastic domestic oil shortfall by 1990. (As a blueprint for energy security, the NEP pays surprisingly scant attention to *the* real energy problem: that Canadians are among the highest per capita consumers of energy in the world.) Despite the present twenty per cent shortfall between oil production and consumption in Canada, the NEP assumes not a dramatic increase in domestic oil production, but nationwide substitution of natural gas – of which there is a plenitude – for oil. It also assumes that the steady decline in the supply of conventional crude from western Canada can be offset in the late 1980s by expansion of the Suncor and Syncrude nonconventional facilities to extract oil from the Athabasca tar sands, the establishment of a third extraction plant there (the now-dead Alsands project), and the success of so far markedly unsuccessful attempts to produce petroleum from the huge, heavy-oil deposits at Cold Lake, Alberta.

However, the biggest flaw in the NEP is its unilateralism: its provisions were worked out without consulting the governments of Manitoba, Saskatchewan, Alberta and British Columbia. Nothing could have been better calculated to provide deadly ammunition to the advocates of western separatism – notably in Alberta – than an arrogant fiat from Ottawa as to how the profits of the nation's energy wealth should be divided up. To them, and to many other Westerners, the "Feds" simply wanted to grab a greater piece of the energy-revenue pie. In immediate reaction, British Columbia refused to pay the NEP's new tax on natural gas and gas-derived liquids; an outraged Premier Lougheed had Alberta cut back oil production, forcing Ottawa to import more high-priced foreign crude; and Saskatchewan protested to the Supreme Court the illegality of the NEP's gas levy.

Unfortunately, the unilateral nature of the grab obscured reasons why Ottawa may well be entitled to an increased share of oil and gas royalties. In the past, federal authorities gave the energy sector billions of dollars in the form tax write-offs or tax deferrals; yet, as soon as a particular energy source was discovered and developed, the provinces assumed that the tax revenues therefrom belonged to them. Further, Ottawa makes equalization payments to Canada's "have-not" provinces in order to provide some common level of public services. But soaring energy revenues in the western provinces have obliged Ottawa to make larger equalization expenditures. By 1980 Ottawa had an operating deficit of $14 billion, whereas Alberta had surplus funds of $10 billion. The Alberta Heritage Savings Trust Fund alone, set up by Peter Lougheed to ensure his province's economic future, had over $8 billion.

Westerners, however, can also claim an expenditure similar to Ottawa's equalization payments. They, too, have been giving petrodollars away to the rest of Canada. For each cent that the price of Canadian oil is below the world price, Alberta and Saskatchewan forego millions of dollars. Thus Alberta, in particular, has contributed heavily to the maintenance of Confederation.

Of course, a basic western resentment is any federal tax of any kind on oil or gas, which are nonrenewable resources. Westerners ask why there is no federal tax on the export of Quebec's hydroelectricity (a renewable resource). And if Ontario and Quebec can receive world prices for such resources as nickel and asbestos, why can't

In Athabasca, Great Canadian Oil Sands uses a monstrous digging machine to claw up 4500 tonnes of tar sands an hour and load them onto a conveyor belt leading to a processing plant.

Saskatchewan and Alberta receive world prices for oil? What's more, in western minds the NEP revenue-sharing in oil and gas is a rigged game. Historically, the average was a 45:45:10 allocation to industry, the producing provinces and Ottawa. The NEP indicates an initial 33:43:24 arrangement which, with rising energy taxes during the 1980s, could well change to something like 32:40:28.

The 115-page National Energy Policy is a watershed in Canadian history. The document's bland, bureaucratic prose did not fool those it most directly affected. American oilmen knew they had been relegated to the status of undesirables. Canadian oilmen realized they were now automatic partners of Petro-Canada. Western politicians, editorialists and businessmen interpreted the NEP as a willful power grab at rich resources and a contemptuous flouting of provincial ownership rights. Oil became the rallying cry. A diminishing resource was being given away at bargain-basement prices, and the wealth would be gone as suddenly as it had been found.

*

In the years since Confederation, the government of Canada has signed eleven treaties with the Indians of the West. Thereafter, they became a forgotten and neglected people with a steadily declining population because of poverty, disease, despair and drink. Protests and petitions brought about a gradual improvement in services (health care, education, housing). By the late 1950s, their population rate was on the rise, along with a reawakened pride that led to the formation of vocal, politically aware organizations determined to win back their long-denied rights.

Indians argue that the treaties ceding half of Canada were in some cases not fully explained —

In 1970, Alberta's Social Credit Premier Harry Strom, Indian spokesman Harold Cardinal, and federal Minister of Indian Affairs Jean Chretien meet to discuss the Trudeau government's proposal to repeal the Indian Act.

even misrepresented — to those who signed them. They also insist that treaty terms have not been kept and that the spirit of the treaties has not been honoured. And they point accusingly to the loss of Indian reserve lands (sold off without approval or for low prices, or illegally expropriated), as well as the mismanagement of band funds by the federal government. But the most important element of these claims is land, for it is essential to their traditional way of life. They also want a voice in land use, which affects hunting and fishing, and they want a share in the riches derived from exploitation of the land's resources. Disputes concerning land are complicated by overlapping jurisdictions: Ottawa is responsible for treaty terms and settling claims, but lands and resources are the responsibility of the provinces, which are reluctant to fulfil provisions agreed to by the federal government. In addition, Ottawa is responsible for status Indians and Inuit, but the provinces are responsible for non-status Indians, including Metis.

In 1969, after a number of ill-fated attempts to deal with the Indian Act and Indian claims, Ottawa produced a White Paper on Indian Policy. It proposed to do away with the special status of Indians and discontinue the Indian Affairs Branch, downplaying the significance of treaties, and denying claims to aboriginal rights. However, the federal government would provide interim economic funds, return reserve lands to Indian control, and set up an advisory Indian claims commission. Reaction from native people was vehemently negative, and they rebutted this policy with their own position papers. Four years later, the government retreated, announcing that it would recognize the loss of use and occupancy in areas not covered by treaty and would negotiate a settlement.

Some native people have never signed treaties ceding their lands to the government, including the Dene and Inuit, whose aboriginal territories cover large areas of British Columbia, the Yukon and the Northwest Territories. The proposal to build a pipeline down the Mackenzie Valley fired their fears about damage to the environment and consequently their way of life. Their cause drew support from other concerned Canadians and was widely publicized. The federal government set up the Mackenzie Valley Pipeline Inquiry, popularly known as the Berger Inquiry after the man who headed it, Mr. Justice Thomas Berger of the British Columbia Supreme Court. In twenty months of hearings, about a thousand people gave heartfelt testimony: they spoke sadly about what white men had already done to the north, tried to convey their feelings and ties to the land, and stated their determination to save it for their children, for the future. In his report, Berger says that these people told him, time and time again, that they want to determine their place in, not assimilation into, Canadian society. They want to *begin* with a settlement of their land claims. "In the past," Berger observes, "special status has meant Indian reserves. Now the native people wish to substitute self-determination for enforced dependency."

*

For all the people of western Canada, events since Confederation have proved to be a burden as well as a blessing. Manitoba came into being only after Louis Riel and his Metis forced Ottawa to grant it provincial status, a bilingual administration and a separate school system. Alberta and Saskatchewan gained provincial status with much less difficulty but, like Manitoba, were denied ownership of their public lands and natural resources until 1930. In the 1920s, when wheat growers began their complaints (and they are still complaining), they attempted to make themselves heard in Parliament by supporting one or other of the old-line parties – and failed. They formed their own political parties – and were still unsuccessful, because the prairie provinces could elect only a handful of members to Parliament. These members were not numerous or powerful enough to influence decisions in the cabinet and debates in the Commons. There is much truth in the observation that:

The power of Quebec votes and the necessity of the federal government to pay as much heed to Quebec as it does to Ontario reveals the existence of one region – Central Canada – with common characteristics. It is industrialized, populous, part of the St. Lawrence heartland, the holder of an absolute majority of seats in the House of Commons . . . making it possible for a government to sit at Ottawa without one Western or Maritime representative. . . . Central Canada is where the votes are and where elections are won and lost; this was true at Confederation, and it remains true today.

Ask any Westerner for an opinion on the matter, and the answer is instantaneous: "Federal elections are decided before the polls close in Manitoba!"

The only time that the West might have become a decisive power bloc on Parliament Hill was during the boom years of Laurier's administration, when the population growth rate of western Canada exceeded that of eastern Canada. From the fifteen MPs of 1891, the West's representation was expanded to twenty-seven by 1904, fifty-six by 1917, and sixty-eight by 1925. The census of 1931 caused a redistribution of seats, and the West was given seventy-four. Had this growth rate continued, the West would ultimately have had more power in Parliament than Ontario and Quebec combined. But the years of depression, drought and dust reversed that trend. The West's overall growth rate fell well behind the national average until the 1960s – in spite of significant growth in British Columbia. Even in 1980, after considerable prosperity and a return to rapid population growth, the political power of the West at Ottawa only approximated that of 1931: Manitoba, 14 members; Saskatchewan, 14 members; Alberta, 21 members; British Columbia, 28 members. A total of 77 western members in a 282-member House of Commons.

The Liberal party, which has been in power in Ottawa for sixty-seven of the past eighty-seven years, has little support in the West; in recent years, in fact, the majority of western representatives in the Commons have usually been in opposition to the governing Liberals. Following the 1979 federal election the Liberals won only three seats west of Ontario; this was further reduced to two seats in 1980. Clearly, the West strongly distrusted Trudeau's absorption with Quebec, with language policy and with constitutional change. And the Liberal party record in provincial politics since 1968 has been dismal. With the exception of Premier Ross Thatcher's Liberal administration (1968-1971) in Saskatchewan, provincial governments have been Social Credit, as in Alberta and British Columbia; NDP, as in Manitoba, Saskatchewan and British Columbia; or Progressive Conservative, as in Manitoba and Alberta.

Westerners have good reason to feel left out of the federal governing process. And this has led to feelings of frustration and alienation since, without power, they cannot bring about change.

In the fall of 1980, when Trudeau and his Liberals imposed the National Energy Program, it triggered anger enough to boost the appeal of what the media called western separatism. (The term is inaccurate: the act of opting out of a federation is secession.)

Of the various quasi-political groups opposed to Trudeau-ism, two emerged as popular exponents of independence. One, now known as the Western Canada Concept (WCC), was first formed in British Columbia in 1975 by Doug Christie, an ex-Manitoban practising law in Victoria. In his speeches to "Free the West!" he said he would organize a referendum on independence and somehow form a new western nation, complete with monarchy and a two-chamber, elected parliament — but he would do away with provincial governments. All western resources would be sold at world prices in order to finance the creation of an economy supported by a huge, secondary manufacturing industry operating on the free-enterprise principle.

The second party was the Western Canada Federation (West-Fed) organized by Edmontonian Elmer Knutson. The millionaire businessman and his friends incorporated their party in May 1980. West-Fed proposed that the western provinces legally federate under a constitution formulated by an elected constituent assembly, ratified by voters and provincial legislatures alike, and relayed to the Queen for her approval. The party also acquired a much-publicized respectability when Carl Nickle, a former Conservative MP, prominent oilman and publisher of the *Daily Oil Bulletin* confessed his conversion from long-time federalism to western independence.

Secession is the aim of a tiny, if noisy, minority. The WCC and West-fed are fringe movements that know what they are against — the all-too-familiar catalogue of eastern sins that begins with freight rates — yet have no clear-cut, plausible plan as to how to achieve a new nation.

*

The inhabitants of Manitoba, Saskatchewan, Alberta and British Columbia are, however, Canadians first and Westerners second. They are not seeking to opt out of a nation their forebears helped to create and a Canada that they themselves are helping to maintain. "But," as Premier Alan Blakoney of Saskatchewan once observed, "there's no doubt that most Westerners are concerned that the essential bargain of Confederation has not been kept by Ottawa."

Westerners can accept the fact that every Canadian pays a price in tariffs and taxes for being Canadian. They can also accept the complication of distinctly regional realities. This means living with the knowledge, for example, that the West is under-industrialized because of distance to markets, and its lack of raw materials, labour pool and transportation. Or the knowledge that the sale of much of the West's products — wheat, oil, minerals, lumber, fish — is heavily dependent upon distant and unstable markets around the world. What Westerners do *not* accept is that their primary concerns — tariffs, freight rates and transportation systems, international and interprovincial trade, all the concerns of what could be called a frontier society — should be surpassed by centralist (meaning Quebec and Ontario) needs. It is this sense of powerlessness and frustration, a feeling that the West simply does not count in national policy-making, a resentment for having carried the burden of Confederation for so long, that keeps western alienation alive.

*

An English academic once wrote that there is "only one safe rule for the historian: that he should recognize in the development of human destinies, the play of the contingent and the unforeseen." This observation applies even to the interval between the completion of the manuscript of this book and its publication. In light of the many failures to repatriate the constitution, who could have predicted the celebratory visit of Her Majesty in April, 1981? Who could have foretold the disintegration of Western megaprojects that were to aid economies both provincial and national? And, to mention but one international event affecting Canada, the dissolution of OPEC?

Significantly, these events repeated the confrontation and compromise, the "bust" of boom and bust, and the resulting frustration that have long been the experience of western Canadians. Despite the emergence of the prairie west as a granary and a major petroleum producer, despite the transformation of the transmontane west from a fur fiefdom to an economy based on mills and mines, the problems of a hinterland remain. Prominent among these are the uncertainties of selling natural resources on fluctuating world markets, and the desire for increased participation in policy-making at the federal level. The ever-recurring story of the frontier versus centralized control.

There are those who say that the power base of the nation is shifting inexorably westward and that this will, ultimately, resolve the conflicts between the four provinces, and Ottawa. I hope, then, that the bitterness brewed over many decades will be tempered by time. It would be a tribute to each man and woman who ever lived in the West and, in some way, known or unknown, helped to make it Canadian.

Notes

Text Notes

Chapter 2 Trappers and Traders

"They neither grow . . ." George P. Hammond and Agapito Rey, eds., *Journal of Diego Pérez de Luxán* (Los Angeles: Quivira Society, 1929).

"A knife blade . . ." Bernard DeVoto, *The Course of Empire* (Boston: Houghton Mifflin, 1952). Copyright 1952 by Bernard DeVoto. Copyright © renewed 1980 by Avis DeVoto. Reprinted by permission of Houghton Mifflin Company.

"it was far . . ." Lawrence J. Burpee, ed., "York Factory to the Blackfeet Country: The Journal of Anthony Hendry, 1754-55," *Transactions of the Royal Society of Canada*, Section II (1907).

"The story of . . ." W. Stewart Wallace, ed., *Documents Relating to the North West Company* (Toronto: The Champlain Society, 1934). Used by permission of the society.

Chapter 3 West of the Mountains

"not, on any . . ." Alexander Mackenzie, *Voyages from Montreal, on the River St. Laurence, through the Continent of North America, to the Frozen and Pacific Oceans; in the Years 1789 and 1793* (London, 1801).

"there was a . . ." W. Kaye Lamb, ed., *The Letters and Journals of Simon Fraser, 1806-1808* (Toronto: Macmillan of Canada, 1960). Used by permission of the author.

"which to me . . ." Richard Glover, ed., *David Thompson's Narrative, 1784-1812* (Toronto: The Champlain Society, 1962). Used by permission of the society.

Chapter 4 A Battleground for Furs

"the Columbia is . . ." Mackenzie, *Voyages from Montreal.*

"to get them . . ." DeVoto, *The Course of Empire.*

"The Highland clan . . ." Margaret Laurence, *Heart of a Stranger* (Toronto: McClelland & Stewart, 1976). Used by permission of the publishers.

"From over the . . ." John Perry Pritchett, *The Red River Valley, 1811-1849* (1942; reprint, New York: Russell and Russell, 1970).

"had come to . . ." Ibid.

"The two parties . . ." Margaret Arnett Macleod and W. L. Morton, *Cuthbert Grant of Grantown: Warden of the Plains of Red River* (Toronto: McClelland & Stewart, 1963). Used by permission of the publishers.

"It seems unlikely . . ." John Morgan Gray, *Lord Selkirk of Red River* (Toronto: Macmillan of Canada, 1964). Used by permission of Macmillan of Canada, a division of Gage Publishing Ltd.

Chapter 5 "The Father of British Columbia"

"A stout . . ." Glyndwr Williams, ed., *Hudson's Bay Miscellany 1670-1870* (Winnipeg: Hudson's Bay Record Society, 1975). Pages 104-5. Used by permission of the society.

"without headquarters . . ." Margaret A. Ormsby, *British Columbia: A History* (Toronto: Macmillan of Canada, 1958). Used by permission of Macmillan of Canada, a division of Gage Publishing Ltd.

"in the colony . . ." Ibid.

"Boats, canoes . . ." Derek Pethick, *James Douglas: Servant of Two Empires* (Vancouver: Mitchell Press, 1969). Used by permission of the author and publisher.

"The Hudson's Bay . . ." Ibid.

"He shared with . . ." Ormsby, *British Columbia.*

Chapter 6 The First Prairie Province

"The British . . ." Douglas Hill, *The Opening of the Canadian West* (London: William Heinemann, 1967).

"The freemen . . ." Pritchett, *The Red River Valley.*

"Sir, The National Committee . . ." J.-P.-A. Benoit, *Vie*

de Mgr. Taché: archevêque de St. Boniface (Montreal, 1904).

Chapter 7 "From Sea to Sea"

"turn your . . ." Canada, *Sessional Papers*, 1871, no. 20.

"at Fort Edmonton . . ." Report on the North-Western Provinces and Territories, 10 December 1872, C.O. 42/715, Public Record Office, London, England.

"Patrols were . . ." Roderick C. Macleod, "The Problem of Law and Order in the Canadian West, 1870-1905" in *The Prairie West to 1905: A Canadian Sourcebook*, ed. Lewis G. Thomas (Toronto: Oxford University Press, 1975). Used by permission, copyright © Oxford University Press, Canadian Branch.

"The reports . . ." Ibid.

"In recommending . . ." House of Commons. Debates, 1886, p. 225 (letter read by Edward Blake).

Chapter 8 "The Last, Best West"

"While the first . . ." Hill, *The Opening of the Canadian West*.

"It was so . . ." Barry Broadfoot, *The Pioneer Years 1895-1914: Memories of Settlers Who Opened the West* (Toronto: Doubleday Canada, 1976). Used by permission of the publisher.

"The *Abyssinia* . . ." Alan Morley, *Vancouver: From Milltown to Metropolis* (Vancouver: Mitchell Press, 1961). Used by permission of the publisher.

"Sometimes, visitors . . ." Ormsby, *British Columbia*.

Chapter 10 War and Peace

"In 1917 . . ." J. F. C. Wright, *Saskatchewan: The History of a Province* (Toronto: McClelland & Stewart, 1955). Used by permission of the publishers.

"On her first . . ." Linda Rasmussen, Lorna Rasmussen, Candace Savage, Anne Wheeler, eds., *A Harvest Yet to Reap: A History of Prairie Women* (Toronto: The Women's Press, 1976). Page 208.

Used by permission of The Women's Press, copyright © 1976 by The Canadian Women's Educational Press.

"One day the . . ." Bruce Hutchison, *The Unknown Country: Canada and Her People* (Toronto: Longmans, Green, 1949). Used by permission of the author.

"The farmers . . ." Margaret McWilliams, *Manitoba Milestones* (Toronto: J. M. Dent & Sons, 1928).

"Doc Smith . . ." Frank H. Ellis, *Canada's Flying Heritage* (Toronto: University of Toronto Press, 1961). Page 229.

Chapter 11 Poverty and Politics

"There came . . ." Barry Broadfoot, *Ten Lost Years 1929-1939: Memories of Canadians Who Survived the Depression* (Toronto: Doubleday Canada, 1973). Used by permission of the publisher.

"The Palliser . . ." Ibid.

"contributions came . . ." James H. Gray, *The Winter Years: The Depression on the Prairies* (Toronto: Macmillan of Canada, 1966). Used by permission of Macmillan of Canada, a division of Gage Publishing Ltd.

"On the night . . ." John A. Irving, *The Social Credit Movement in Alberta* (Toronto: University of Toronto Press, 1959). Page 3.

"As the blood . . ." Ibid. Page 113.

Chapter 12 Prosperity and Politics

"Nothing ever . . ." Barry Broadfoot, *Years of Sorrow, Years of Shame: The Japanese Canadians in World War II* (Toronto: Doubleday Canada, 1977). Used by permission of the publisher.

"see themselves . . ." George Woodstock, *The Canadians* (Toronto: Fitzhenry & Whiteside, 1979). Used by permission of the publisher.

"Between 1966 and 1971 . . ." Heather Robertson, *Grass Roots* (Toronto: James Lorimer, 1973). Used by permission of the publisher.

Chapter 13   Power and Alienation

"Western Canada is . . ." David Jay Bercuson, ed., *Canada and the Burden of Unity* (Toronto: Macmillan of Canada, 1977). Used by permission of David Jay Bercuson.

"We correctly forecast . . ." Phillip Smith, *The Treasure-Seekers: The Men Who Built Home Oil* (Toronto: Macmillan of Canada, 1978). Used by permission of Macmillan of Canada, a division of Gage Publishing Ltd.

"The power of . . ." Bercuson, *Canada and the Burden of Unity*.

Illustration Notes

We gratefully acknowledge the courtesy of various institutions and companies in granting permission to reproduce photographs, paintings, drawing, maps and documents from their collections. Every effort has been made to identify and credit all sources used in this book; any further information received will be acknowledged in subsequent editions.

Illustrations are listed by page number. Principal sources are credited under the following abbreviations:

GM   Glenbow Museum
PAA   Provincial Archives of Alberta
PABC   Provincial Archives of British Columbia
PAC   Public Archives of Canada
PAM   Provincial Archives of Manitoba
SA   Saskatchewan Archives

Endpaper: Ox-drawn wagons of the North American Boundary Commission cross Dead Horse Creek while mapping the Saskatchewan border, 1873. Courtesy Public Archives of Canada, PA-74645.

Frontispiece: Courtesy Canadian Pacific Corporate Archives, 8454.

/xiii GM, 62.9.29 /2 PAC, C-5181 /5 PABC, 16481 /6-7 Geological Survey of Canada, 255 /9 PABC, 81182 /10 GM, 64.19 /11 GM, 65.40.2 /14 GM, 62.90.2 /15 National Museum of Man, National Museums of Canada, 77013 /17 GM NA-1810-1 /18-19 GM, 60.45.11 /21 PAC, B-773 /22 Confederation Life Collection /27 National Historic Parks and Sites Branch, Parks Canada /28 GM, NA-1406-39 /29 GM, 60.71.8 /35 PABC, CM A-176 /36-37 National Historic Parks and Sites Branch, Parks Canada /38 PABC, 53503 /39 PABC, 12440 /41 PABC, pdp 285 /42 PABC, pdp 2252 /44 National Gallery of Canada, Canadian War Memorials Collection, 8000 /46 PAC, C-8711 /47 PABC, pdp 100 /50-51 Archives of Ontario, A-001 /52 GM, 60.76.6 /60 PAC, C-1346 /63 GM, 60.71.7 /67 Hudson's Bay Company /68-69 PAC, C-8714 /71 GM, 55.31.3 /72-73 PAC, C-1918 /75 PAM, John Kerr Collection, 5 /77 PAC, C-167 /78-79 *Castorologica* by H. T. Martin (Montreal, 1892) /80-81 PAC, C-1934 /84 GM, NA-841-164 /86-87 GM, 60.71.11 /89 PABC, 2652 /90 PABC, pdp 2143 /92 PABC, 9326 /94-95 PABC, pdp 2894 /99 PABC, 2323 /100 PABC, 10110 /101 PABC, 39082 /103 Confederation Life Collection /105 PABC, 25799 /106 City of Vancouver Archives, P-170 /108 PAC, C-4164 /112 GM, NA-1406 21 /113 GM, NA-1406 6 /116 GM, 61.103.2 /118-19 GM, 55.18.6 /122-23 PAC, C-2773 /124-25 GM, NA-20-8 /126-27 Hudson's Bay Company /130 31 PAC, C-2775 /132 Geological Survey of Canada, 594 /134 GM, 75.10.9 /135 GM /136-37 PABC, 24439 /138 PAC, C-15037 /139 RCMP Museum, Regina /142 Canadian Pacific Corporate Archives, 9461 /143 PAC, C-9078 /147 PABC, 75081 /148-49 PAA, E. Brown Collection, B-6014 /152 PAM, Bannatyne Collection, 97 /155 Geological Survey of Canada, 614 /157 GM, NA-1063-1 /158 59 GM, NA-363-36 /160 Metropolitan Toronto Library, T-14824 /163 GM, NA-264-1 /164 PAA, E. Brown Collection, B-705 /166 PAC, PA-19823 /167 GM, NA-474-2 /168-69 GM, NA-2365-34 /171 Travel Manitoba, 18076 /172 SA, R-A 2310 /173 Vancouver City Archives /175 Canadian Pacific Corporate Archives, A-6405 /176 PAC, C-1229 /177 Geological Survey of Canada, 37 /179 PAC, C-4490 /181 PABC, 6314 /183 PAC, RG76/243/161973 /184 GM, NA-3304-3 /186 PAA, E. Brown Collection, B-1917 /187 GM, NA-1566-2 /190-91 PAC, PA-29941 /192 GM, NA-406-3 /193 GM, NA-1029-27 /195 SA, R-A 787 /198-99 SA, R-B 1964(2) /200 PAC, C-14118 /201 PAA, E. Brown Collection, B-6661 /202 GM, 59.35.1 /204 Vancouver Public Library /206 GM, NA-984-2 /207 Vancouver Public Library, 2023 /208-9 SA, R A 4552 /211 GM, NA-2168-3 /212 City of Trail Archives /213 PAM, Foote Collection, 981 /215 National Aeronautical Collection, S-74-2258 /216 GM, NA-692-21 /217 PAA, H. Pollard Collection, P-592 /219 PAM, Foote Collection, 1670 /220 PAM, Foote Collection, 1696 /224 GM, NA-2003-103 /227 GM, NA-2180-6 /228 City of Edmonton Archives /230 PABC, 82610 /231 GM, NA-1448-18 /232-33 PAC, PA-11645 /235 PAM, Foote Collection, 288 /237 PABC, 40005 /240-41 GM, ND-3-6343 /243 SA, Saskatchewan Wheat Pool Collection, R-A 15.077(1) /244 PAC, C-6548 /247 SA, R-B 5801(2) /248 GM, NA-2771-2 /249 SA, R-A 7915 /251 GM, NA-1170-4 /252 SA, R-B 3485(1) /253 SA, R-B 171(1) /254-55 Vancouver Public Library, 1309 /256 PAC, C-54523 /259 SA, R-B 2478(1) and (3) /260 PAC, C-29458 /261 City of Edmonton Archives /262 PABC, 48535 /264-65 PAC, C-24452 /266 PAA, H. Pollard Collection, P-1262 /267 PAA, H. Pollard Collection, P-1120 /269 GM, NA-3394-57 /270 GM, NA-1446-16 /271 GM, NA-1282-3 /274-75 Vancouver Public Library, 45223 /276 PABC, 80225 /280 Copyright © Toronto Star Syndicate /286 Saskatchewan Tourism & Renewable Resources, 71-632-05 /287 Travel Manitoba, 43274 /289 PAA, Edmonton Journal Collection, J 208/2 /290 PAA, Edmonton Journal Collection, J 702/22 /293 PAA, Edmonton Journal Collection, J 3457 /295 Kenting Limited /296-97 PAA, Edmonton Journal Collection, J 1190/14 /298 PAA, Edmonton Journal Collection, J 547.

Index

Wilderness of Fortune was designed in Vancouver
by Robert Bringhurst and Barbara Hodgson,
and was manufactured by D. W. Friesen & Sons Ltd.
at Altona, Manitoba. There the type was set,
the colour separations and duotones made
and the sheets printed and bound.

Most printers in North America during the
nineteenth century favoured heavy, slab-serifed
types suited for quick work on poor paper.
The heavier of these faces came to be known
in the trade as Egyptians, while the somewhat
lighter, less angular forms of the same vintage
have come to be called Ionics or Clarendons.
With these Victorian workhorse letterforms as
inspiration, André Gürtler and a group of his
senior students at Basel in the mid-1960s
set out to create a more refined but still
unpretentious face for the setting and printing
of text by contemporary means. The result is
the face used in this book, which Gürtler
and his students christened Egyptian 505.